# Latin American Perspectives on Globalization

# Latin American Perspectives on Globalization

## Ethics, Politics, and Alternative Visions

Edited by Mario Sáenz

ROWMAN & LITTLEFIELD PUBLISHERS, INC.
*Lanham • Boulder • New York • Oxford*

ROWMAN & LITTLEFIELD PUBLISHERS, INC.

Published in the United States of America
by Rowman & Littlefield Publishers, Inc.
A Member of the Rowman & Littlefield Publishing Group
4720 Boston Way, Lanham, Maryland 20706
www.rowmanlittlefield.com

PO Box 317
Oxford
OX2 9RU, UK

British Library Cataloguing in Publication Information Available

**Library of Congress Cataloging-in-Publication Data**

Latin American perspectives on globalization : ethics, politics, and alternative visions /
edited by Mario Sáenz.
  p. cm.
Includes bibliographical references and index.
ISBN 0-7425-0776-9 (cloth : alk. paper)—ISBN 0-7425-0777-7 (pbk. : alk. paper)
  1. Globalization. 2. Latin America—Foreign relations. 3. Latin America—Politics and
government—1980– I. Sáenz, Mario, 1956–

JZ1318 .L38 2002
327'.098—dc21                                                            2002001221

∞™ The paper used in this publication meets the minimum requirements of American
National Standard for Information Sciences—Permanence of Paper for Printed Library
Materials, ANSI/NISO Z39.48-1992.

# Contents

# Foreword

### Linda Martín Alcoff

Cortés has no country, he's a chilling thunderbolt, a cold heart clad in armor.

—Pablo Neruda

The contemporary current of discourse in the North is a repetitive rumination over a newfound sense of dislocation, disorientation, and decenteredness. Finance capital has drifted offshore, "prime" labor markets are easily accessible and exploitable elsewhere, and, despite the fall of its major political competitor in the world—the Soviet Union—the United States finds that it cannot easily bend the United Nations or other international bodies to its will, nor can it unilaterally direct political action in world events. Terrorist threats from abroad have rocked the foundation of the firmament, effectively targeting the weaknesses of a network society built on travel, mail, and quick commercial delivery systems. No sooner does the U.S. government attempt to spin the news in its favor than its citizens seek out news sources on the Internet from abroad, which often provide different information and quite different points of view.

Globalization has, without a doubt, changed the world. But from the point of view of the globalized South, the change has been incremental rather than qualitative. In the South, the "integrity" of national borders has almost never existed, and threats from abroad can rarely be thwarted, even to the extent of having democratically elected popular governments overturned in coups d'état engineered by foreign agencies. These problems have been continuous in the New World since it was globalized in 1492, as transatlantic trade in precious goods, human flesh, and colonizing opportunities spread throughout the Americas and brought with it a genocide of native peoples that is simply unparalleled anywhere in the world at any time in history.

For five hundred years Latin America has been the most global of continents, the product of a race mixing that has produced not only a cultural heterogeneity but a racial and ethnic heterogeneity never seen before. Despite the "melting pot" rhetoric in the United States, the fact of the matter is that throughout Latin America and the Caribbean, a true melting pot of peoples, cultures, and races was created unlike anything north of the border. The liberal, secular, modernist-based vision of transcending one's narrow cultural roots in favor of cosmopolitan assimilation succeeded best in the premodernist, Catholic, Iberian-influenced countries, while the proponents of secularism and modernism to the North were too busy to notice. Richard Rodriguez points out that, still today, "Mexico City is modern in ways that 'multiracial,' ethnically 'diverse' New York is not yet. Mexico City is centuries more modern than racially 'pure,' provincial Tokyo. . . . Mexico is the capital of modernity, for in the sixteenth century, . . . Mexico initiated the task of the twenty-first century—the renewal of the old, the known world, through miscegenation. Mexico carries the idea of a round world to its biological conclusion."[1] So much for the clash of civilizations.

Although Rodriguez wishes to secure the honorific title of "modern" for the cultures of the South, it has actually been the displacement of "modernist" narratives by globalization narratives that has opened up the possibility of rearranging the political, theoretical, and epistemological formations that rendered Latin America a mere "periphery." The narrative of modernity, still virulent today, has represented a single road for political, moral, cultural, and economic progress, imagining it as emanating from France and England, growing mature in North America, and then slowly spreading out to the backward areas of the world. Anglo-European societies were and still are seen as the vanguard of modernism, with the rest straggling unevenly behind. Today this metanarrative is being challenged both from within and from without, both empirically and ideologically. And as the truths of U.S. foreign policy become public, there is a loud publicized drop from the vanguard to the rearguard, causing understandable dislocation and resistance.

Liberals try to recoup gracefully by pluralizing the narrative of modernity, from a narrative about a single modernity for all to a narrative of potential modernities that can take various forms. But this easy pluralism conceals the interlocking, interdependent nature of societies today and the integrated histories from which they have arisen. In one sense, we have all been forcibly dragged together on the same road, but on a journey that for many has been a Trail of Tears rather than a March of Progress. Modernist values such as the cult of the individual were made possible in no small part by a sanctioned transformation of whole societies of individuals into the objects of commerce, a practice that continues through the export processing zones that appropriate the most vulnerable labor power while taking its profits offshore.

Thus, the narrative of modernity may not be recoverable for the project of social justice or for the attempt merely to imagine new possibilities and new futures. Postmodernism and antimodernism as cultural and philosophical trends continue to center modernism as their organizing idea; it is no wonder that these critical narratives continue to place colonialism at the periphery of their thought, if it even appears at all. Ironically, the continents that made modernity possible, both economically through the wealth that Europe gained and imagistically in providing an external vantage point from which Europe could imagine itself as "Europe," were effectively eclipsed in the story of "human" history that Europe then wrote. "Subaltern" agency, though it conforms to the modernist value of autonomy, has been rendered invisible, especially in its causal contributions toward the intellectual, political, and cultural developments of the center.

Today these subaltern representations are providing new articulations of our time that provide not only correctives to the past partial and distorted accounts but concepts and political values better suited to current realities for both the global North and South. One will find many such examples in this volume. Instead of the unilinear progressive narrative of modernism, the idea of a temporal simultaneity is invoked in which it becomes possible to see multiple forms of life coexisting in the same city, from the premodern, to the modern, to the postmodern, without politically ranking these or assuming that all will follow the same path. Mestizaje, creolization, and syncretism are valorized over border control, based on understanding the confrontation of difference and a creative reciprocal assimilation as what, in truth, these have always been: an enrichment, rather than a dilution. There has emerged a new form of revolutionary discourse, not surprisingly originating from the Lacandon jungle in Chiapas, dominated by indigenous communities, in which revolution requires no temporalized march of progress or takeovers of state power but instead aims at local control and the material conditions for human dignity. And perhaps most important, models of transcultural and intercultural relations are replacing center/periphery or world-systems approaches, thus removing the need for a central reference point and focusing attention on the more constructive questions of building toward dialogic relationships based on equality and epistemic cooperation rather than subsumption to a universalized paradigm.

These new narratives and discourses of historical representation and political analysis, applicable both to the past and to the future, are too rarely included in globalization studies emanating from former colonial powers (or present day neocolonial powers). Political struggle is still too often theorized in the terms of categories developed out of European historical experience, and the highest possible values for humankind are still taken entirely from Anglo-European cultures. What if the majority of the world's peoples reject individualism and free markets? Would the value of democracy alone be sufficient to trump the stubborn will of the North to impose these values, nonetheless, for "our own good"?

This volume of essays will provide readers with a wonderful array of globalization analyses on and from the perspective of Latin America and the Caribbean. But as I have tried to establish, the importance of their critical arguments and suggestions for alternatives ranges far beyond a single region and offers a significant contribution toward the revision of a concrete plan for the world's future. Today we are in a crisis of nihilism where the old projects are quickly losing ground without being replaced by workable new ones. The project of modernity has been shown up as a form of cultural imperialism, and whether it is reformable is very much up for debate. The project of development through free trade has been empirically challenged as the gap between the rich and poor grows in countries (such as Mexico) where free trade agreements have been the strongest. The project of national autonomy has been revealed as pure illusion as structural adjustment programs imposed by world financial institutions elicit social crises around the world that local governments are almost powerless to solve. And even the project of liberation through nationalism has come under severe criticism in Third World countries themselves by feminists and ethnic minorities who were not liberated by nationalist movements—and whose freedom to politically participate was even in some cases curtailed via excuses that made recourse to the nationalist project.

The old global binaries as understood by the left in industrialized countries have also given way out of necessity, not merely because of the fall of the socialist bloc countries but also because of the way in which the northern left itself assumed total agency on the part of the First World and zero agency on the part of the Third World in regard to various local struggles over corruption, tyranny, and so forth. Thus, the globalization narratives fashioned by the northern left have been challenged by charges of Eurocentrism and by sharp critiques of nationalism. Even binaries of "East" and "West" have been shown inadequate in theorizing the formidable threat of fundamentalism that has mushroomed across the globe, from the United States to Israel to Guyana to Algeria to Afghanistan and to India, in nearly every major religion. Meanwhile, the right has rallied around Samuel Huntington's secular fundamentalism that calls for a retrieval of basic "Western" traditions as the only solution to the attacks the West is experiencing. Edward Said has pointed out that Huntington's error lies in the assumption that civilizations are "shut-down, sealed off entities that have been purged of myriad currents and countercurrents that animate human history, and that over centuries have made it possible for that history not only to contain wars of religion and imperial conquest but also to be one of exchange, cross-fertilization and sharing."[2] Thus, Said would have us leave behind a "West versus the rest" paradigm, which merely reformulates the Cold War discourse for a global but decentralized moral language that repudiates brutality whether it comes in a political, religious, or an economic form.

But to move toward such a utopian ideal, we need a new analytical language. It will not do to merely extend the liberatory concepts of Anglo-European societies, as if liberation comes in one size fits all. We need an analysis of the possibility of diversity within universality, of political power even without hope of complete autonomy, of global ethics that can critique enforced homogenization, and of transnational justice. Rigoberta Menchú's recent articulation of a global progressive agenda—what she calls a "Code of Ethics for a Millennium of Peace"—explains the interdependence of these goals:

There will be no Peace if there is no Justice.
There will be no Justice if there is no Equity.
There will be no Equity if there is no Progress.
There will be no Progress if there is no Democracy.
There will be no Democracy if there is no respect for the Identity and Dignity of the Peoples and Cultures of the World.

How different this utopia reads from the modernist vision of a uniform future, in which secularism and rationalism ensure progress and democracy. Might our shared hopes hinge on, not the transcendence of identity and culture, but their protection? In a world where cultures could creatively interpret and adapt their traditions in a climate of equality and peace, without cultural and economic imperialism overdetermining every choice and proscribing otherwise viable options and creative interpretations, the Zapatista vision of a world in which many worlds can flourish could perhaps become closer to a real possibility. But in any case, utopias need not be actualizable to be important and useful; they also provide the measuring tools by which we can identify present inadequacies and engage in social critique, as well as charting a direction toward which we should aim our efforts. In this rich collection of essays, readers will find the foundation for what may hopefully become a new enlightenment, this time emerging not from the hubris of colonial adventure but the wise humility born of a quincentenary of difficult survival.

## NOTES

1. Richard Rodriguez, *Days of Obligation* (New York: Penguin, 1992), 24–25.
2. Edward Said, "The Clash of Ignorance," *The Nation* (22 October 2001): 12.

# Introduction:
# Periphery at the Core

*Mario Sáenz*

Capital from its inception tends toward being a world power, or really *the* world power.[1]

## I

Globalization has come to mean historically either the tendency of capital toward being a world power (as in world-systems theory) or capital's accomplishment of hegemonic world power in human transactions and relations. The latter ideal is realizable, according to Manuel Castells, only with the collapse of time into the instantaneousness of "real time" or "timeless time" and the transformation of nations, states, and other "places" into the "nodes" that smooth the flow of capital in virtual space.[2]

Beginning with the conquest of the Americas, capital has always sought to expand within the spaces of its core, semiperipheral, and peripheral regions; it always did so by means of a parasitical relationship with a peripheral and productive global "other" that has successively assumed the forms of conquered, subordinate, and excluded.[3] Whether globalization refers only to this last relationship of exclusion or to all three, we can distinguish among them in terms of the shape the relation has taken between the rich and the poor regions of the world as "historical structures."[4] Furthermore, if Ankie Hoogvelt is correct, the latest phase of capitalism is expressed macroeconomically, not as an expansion of capital into new spaces but as a "thickening" of the flow of capital within established spaces.[5] What for Hardt and Negri expresses the transformation of capital into *the* world

1

power is for Hoogvelt the *end* of the "expansive" phase of capital and the *beginning* of a *"deepening but not widening, capitalist integration."*[6] This last phase, a period of systematic exclusion of large sectors of humanity from the global system of capitalism, is defined by Hoogvelt as globalization, and it is thus distinguished from previous phases of capitalist global expansion.

Early modern conquest established mercantile colonialism (1500–1800), which accompanied the birth of the modern nation-state in the West, itself made possible by plunder and slavery. Mercantile colonialism was followed by imperialism, which established an international division of labor favorable to the imperial powers (1800–1991).[7] And imperialism, in turn, is mutating into a new sociohistorical structure—Hardt and Negri's "Empire"—which augurs for some the end of the global organization of nation-states and for others the reconstitution of the nation-state as the military-political apparatus for the free flow of global capital, particularly finance capital. In both cases, it is certainly characterized by a post-Fordist informational economy, the neoliberal state (in some cases unwilling and in others unable to define itself in terms of the social welfare programs that formed the political complement to the Fordist mode of production),[8] a global consumer culture, but also and most dramatically by systematic exclusion from the global system.

Exclusion and containment, says Hoogvelt, become fundamental for the preservation of the current world order. Progressively, sectors of the world population become areas of exclusion. Today about 50 percent of the world is excluded from participation in the global market. In fact, the market share of global trade of 83 percent of the world's population (1997 figures) amounts to 18.3 percent only, down from 25.9 percent in 1950 (when the non-core countries' share of the world's population was 81.2 percent).[9] This segment of the population (4.8 billion) also includes the 1.2 billion who live in extreme poverty, as well as the poorest continents, such as Africa, which has seen its share of world trade drop from 5.7 percent in 1950 to 1.7 percent in 1995, and Latin America, the trade share of which has dropped from 10 percent to 4.8 percent for that same period.[10] There are growing pockets of exclusion in all regions of the world, just as the high-tech economy has entered select regions of the so-called Third World, making the terminology of first, second, and third or fourth "worlds" somewhat anachronistic. In any case, the excluded and marginalized are for now left out of the global economy.

Performing neither a productive function, nor presenting a potential consumer market in the present stage of high-tech, information-driven capitalism, there is, for the moment, neither theory, world-view nor moral injunction, let alone a programme of action to include them in universal progress.[11]

Globalization has thus entailed not only the rule of finance capital, in part because of the ease with which it can move instantaneously in virtual information space, but also the growth of an outer region of marginalization. We could thus define globalization by both the ultrafinancialization of the global economy and the paradoxical growth of a world outside the globe.

However, before physical time collapses and space is regarded as an obstacle to the power of capital at the levels of the economy, the political system, and culture, the world has to be appropriated and transformed into the image of capital. Spaces of extraction of raw material, effluences of excess population from the core countries, and territorial expansion of imperial nation-states were created beginning with mercantilism and culminating with the wars of national liberation four and a half centuries later.

Extraction, effluence, and expansion represent the materiality of the nation-state. This political form legitimated the materiality of the exploitation of the peripheral other; it also established the conditions for knowing that other as first a savage,[12] then a barbarian,[13] and finally uncivilized.[14]

The republican and then the republican-democratic form of government are the forms most closely associated with the West's self-image of its right to expansion. To this self-image we now turn.

# II

When Immanuel Kant called for the formation of a league of nations for regulating peaceful international relations, he recognized the difficulty of organizing such an association.[15] He said that it required a prior reformation of the nation-state along the lines of a republican form of government. Left unsaid, for it was accepted as the mere means of historical reason, was a reference to the cluster of forms of domination of those excluded from the class of "civilized" states that were forming or were already formed under the skin of that supranational coordination of homogeneous republican states. Also, the class composition of the civil society of the core states was glossed over in the description of the formal structure of legal and political relations.

Most apparent to some of Kant's continental critics were the forms of social, political, and economic domination over the masses that were developed in the creation of the bourgeois individual that would become the consumer of politics in the capitalist nation-states of the center. Michel Foucault would thus speak of the disciplinary techniques implicit in the new human sciences: Economics, medical psychiatry, modern education, and penology, all sought to understand the objects of their knowledge—the human—while aiding in its production as a modern subject. But it is important to realize that this subjectivity is not simply and purely a dominated subjectivity. It contains juxtaposed within itself its own "conspiracy" in the domination (as well as its own possibilities to resist as a "multitude").[16] At the intra-European level, Foucault would speak of the increase in the power of the body in terms of its utility and the decrease of its power vis-à-vis the political docility imposed on it.[17]

However, it is important to examine the juxtaposition in terms of the otherness that it creates at the national level. The integration of the nation under the aegis of the state meant also, as Hegel asserted in his *Philosophy of Right,* the creation of colonies and the exportation of excess population to the colonies, that is, the creation of colonial forms of domination through conquest.[18]

In this way, Hegel completes the Kantian project, for Hegel elucidates what is already implicit in Kant's "Idea for a Universal History" and in "Perpetual Peace": Republican pacification in Europe requires the expulsion of excess alterity from Europe, as well as rigid control at the margins. Enrique Dussel would later speak about the negation of alterity that began with the conquest of America as the beginning of modernity and its myth.[19]

Indeed, the other is negated and invented in that very conquest.[20] Paradigmatic subjectivities are created in the Americas: the Christian and the savage, the European and the cannibal, and the capitalist and the barbarian. These will excite the imagination of European modernity. Shakespeare's literary figures of Prospero and its allied spirit (Ariel), and the savage Caliban who threatens Prospero's feminine creation (Miranda) were already analyzed by Fernández Retamar in his *Calibán: Apuntes de la cultura de nuestra América*, in which he contrasts Sarmiento and Martí as two different forms that the Latin American Ariel can take beyond Rodó's cultural contrasts.[21] Certainly, Prospero and Caliban are literary creations,[22] subjectivities that arise from the European imaginary in the context of its formation of an imperialist and globalist identity, as it domesticates the demons of its own ethnic tensions and conflicts. We find this doubling of subjectivity nicely folded and unfolded in a story by Garcilaso de la Vega, "El Inca" (1539–1616), a contemporary of Shakespeare (1564–1616), in the whimsical story of the shipwrecked Christian/Spaniard in *The Royal Commentaries of the Incas.*[23] In this story, the Christian Spaniard becomes the hairy man of the woods only to be revealed later as the civilized Christian he has been all along: the civilized soul in the uncivilized body, a future image of the dependent mind of Sarmiento and the modern degradation of the oppressed as the embodiment of danger.[24]

In practice, the doubling of subjectivity appears in violent form in, for instance, the Spanish rules for confession designed to conquer the Nahuatl-speaking peoples.[25] Foucault had spoken about how the new forms of discipline created the modern subject. He also speaks about how the disciplinary techniques were used in the monastic cell before they were used to weaken the power of the body vis-à-vis the political body of the state. But their extension took place first in the Americas so that, to use Foucault's suggestive remark, "the soul is the prison of the body" in the central valley of Mexico in the 1500s, long before the rise of the human sciences. Garcilaso's whimsical story of the shipwrecked Spaniard assuming the outer form of the hairy European savage is also a story about a body that needs to be contained and eventually civilized.[26]

Whether modernity is born in the conquests of the 1500s with the creation of a world-system and the first periphery on a global scale (Wallerstein, Dussel) or only inside Europe culminating in the late 1700s (Foucault, Habermas),[27] the first process of global expansion is characterized in practice and later in theory by the production of a dichotomized subjectivity: a Eurocentered subjectivity that finds its center in the nascent bourgeois ideology of property rights and its ripple effect of "altered" proto-subjectivities—the indigenous, the African, the hands of manufactories and factories, the mental patient, and the criminal. In the history of philosophy, the latter forms of subjectivity are born from the Cartesian body. But this Cartesian body has already been brought under control by the conquest. In Dussel's suggestive remarks, the *ego conquiro* prepared the ground for the *ego cogito*.[28]

Today's wave of globalization expresses, I think, a similar phenomenon. The fear of the other and the demand for the recolonization of all forms of alterity are again coming to the surface in the imperial nationalisms of so-called Middle America, but also of other Western middle classes. At a deeper level, we witness a reproduction of the concentration of multinational capital to which Marx and Engels referred in *The Communist Manifesto*.[29] It also reproduces a global proletariat without the statist-capitalist ties that characterized much of the twentieth century; however, this global proletariat goes beyond the industrial working class to which Marx and Engels referred, and it includes, as Hardt and Negri stress, a heterogeneous "multitude" under the domination of capital: "All those whose labor is directly or indirectly exploited by and subjected to capitalist norms of production and reproduction."[30]

The return to some of the international social relations of the nineteenth century described by Marx is striking, nonetheless, all the more so since the centrality of the industrial machine in the imaginary of social relations of the nineteenth century has been replaced by postindustrial capital and the communications industry. This is due in part to the dominance that these new forms of capital have acquired at the levels of production and circulation. Also, the transformation of the state into a direct agent of the transnational big bourgeoisie suggests a recolonization of the world, although this recolonization is not, of course, simply using labor to extract raw materials, but rather producing consumer goods from Nike shoes to electronics in the factories of the "postcolonial world."

Today with the transformation of state-power mechanisms into instruments for transnational finance capital, exploitation, oppression, and exclusion are intensified and, perhaps, radically altered. The transformation of labor processes into, often, high-tech sweatshop operations, the loss of state power in dependent nation-states by even the traditional bourgeoisie for the benefit of the transnational bourgeoisie and its representatives (whether the latter be defined in terms of "empire" or "imperialist states"), the use of direct military force or international mechanisms of transnational legitimacy—to wit, the U.S. and English militaries, but also the World Bank, the International Monetary Fund, and the UN Security Council—and, finally, an exclusion predicated on the colossal oversupply of the labor power just mentioned relative to the demands of transnational capital, all conspire to make a mere cultural analysis of difference into a tool of the empires in the interests of the empire and for the ideological stability of class relations within the empires. But that is easier said than done.

The statist-welfarist model of capitalism is in crisis in large part because of the changes that this new wave of globalization is forcing on the nation-state. This does not entail a disappearance of the nation-state; instead, a change in the nature of the classes that the nation-state represents requires the reproduction of the nation-state as the agent of global finance capital. The gains that workers had made in many countries in terms of social security and welfare are being contested again; in some cases, they are being lost in the wave of privatizations, that is, the transformation of state capital earmarked for the welfare apparatus back into the private capital of large corporations or for funding the military and the police.

Antonio Negri and Michael Hardt suggest that the new political subject arising in and through globalization is "Empire." By Empire, they do not mean the imperialist reflection in rich nation-states of transnational capital. Instead, they refer to an entity that seeks to be a limitless ruling subject, with a self-image of timelessness, as it dedicates itself to the achievement of a universal peace and extends its rule to the totality of the social order, seeking to create, in fact, its own world of domination.[31] Negri and Hardt avail themselves of Foucault's concept of biopower when referring to the project of complete rule over all facets of life and, thus, of Foucault's discussion of the transition in the exercise of power from "disciplinary society" to the "society of total control." Only in the latter, there is a projected totalization of power: "It becomes entirely biopolitical," say our two authors; "the whole social body is comprised by power's machine and developed in its virtuality."[32]

This projected totalization of power that Hardt and Negri attribute to the latest phase of globalization is somewhat similar to Francis Fukuyama's conception of the end of history, in which posthistorical society is characterized by the harmonious coexistence of "megalothymia" and "isothymia" in the world-historical victorious order: the so-called liberal-democratic order in which the struggle for recognition of both master and slave are themselves recognized in, respectively, the capitalist will to accumulate and the ordinary citizen's will to be recognized as a member of an egalitarian community.[33] Of course, the synthesis of Hegel and Nietzsche that undergirds Fukuyama's dream is different from the nightmare described by Hardt and Negri; for their conceptions of the human, the good life, and the dialectics of life are fundamentally different. However, the same ahistoricity and total victory of capitalism are *apparently* described in both: Posthistorically or in terms of the processes of globalization, capitalism is the only game in town. Resistance is either futility mired in history (Fukuyama) or an interruption/irruption of the difference and its resistances that the global machine itself creates (Hardt and Negri). Of course, if the global machine absorbs everything so that nothing is outside of it, then there is no history.

This becomes an important difference between *The End of History* and *Empire*; for in the former posthistoricity is neoliberal reality actualized; while in the latter it is ideological self-image, a false consciousness that admits only of binary oppositions, and thus, today, of the end of all significant opposition to capital. There is, however, the life of the "multitude" beyond the binary self-image of capital, according to Hardt and Negri:

> In our terms, the end of history that Fukuyama refers to is the end of the crisis at the center of modernity, the coherent and defining conflict that was the foundation and raison d'etre for modern sovereignty. History has ended precisely and only to the extent that it is conceived in Hegelian terms—as the movement of a dialectic of contradictions, a play of absolute negations and subsumption. The binaries that defined modern conflict have become blurred. The Other that might delimit a modern sovereign Self has become fractured and indistinct, and there is no longer an outside that can bound the place of sovereignty. The outside is what gave the crisis coherence. Today, it is increasingly difficult for the ideologues of the United States to name a single, unified enemy; rather there seem to be minor and elusive enemies everywhere. The end of the crisis of modernity has given rise to a proliferation of minor and indefinite crises, or, as we prefer, to an omni-crisis.[34]

In terms of the "logic" of globalization, the "flood of capital"[35] seeks to drown the various manifestations of particularity (Negri and Hardt's "singularities")[36] of the oppressed by reducing everything, from articles of clothing to poetry, to the status of spectacular commodities, that is, to the media's appearance as the only thing behind the appearance.[37] This negation of particularity not only produces the false consciousness of homogenization, but it also produces extreme dehumanization and pauperism among those marginalized by the system (about one-fifth of the world lives today in extreme poverty). It reduces the poor to the status of sweatshop laborers or permanently unemployed at the margins of capital. The revolt of the oppressed against globalization is simultaneously the affirmation of their own humanity and a condemnation of global capitalism even if the struggles are only local or perhaps in part because the struggles are local: they are revolts against globalism and capitalist globalization.

Hardt and Negri see in today's struggles against globalist ideology and capitalist globalization a radical reconstitution of the nature of subversive struggle. These movements are, they argue, so localized in terms of language that they are incommunicable and thus unable to generate a cycle of struggles. They propose the simile of the undulating snake on the surface of Empire to replace the simile of Marx's subversive mole:

> Marx tried to understand the continuity of the cycle of proletarian struggles that were emerging in nineteenth-century Europe in terms of a mole and its subterranean struggles. Marx's mole would surface in times of open class conflict and then retreat underground again—not to hibernate passively but to burrow its tunnels, moving along with the times, pushing forward with history so that when the time was right (1830, 1848, 1870), it would spring to the surface again. . . . Well, we suspect that Marx's

old mole has died. . . . Empire presents a superficial world, the virtual center of
which can be accessed immediately from any point across the surface . . . this new
phase is defined by the fact that these struggles do not link horizontally, but each one
leaps vertically, directly to the virtual center of Empire.[38]

I suspect that the mole is still alive in the ground under our feet, the material
foundation of our virtuality,[39] but that it has yet to learn to speak the languages of
the postcolonial world. A multilingual and pluricultural mole will discover the
commonality of interests among the empire's "multitudes." This commonality is
not simply attained through a rejection of capitalist globalization, for implicit in
that negation, there is the affirmation of the dignity of human life.

The rejection of a system that if carried to its logical conclusion would annihi-
late human life, even if only in terms of production and consumption, is leading
to the realization that the human life of the excluded is worth preserving and defending: Afghans, Palestinians, Colombians, Iranians, Cubans, no less than the
French, the English, or "United Statians," have a right to live in dignity. Slowly,
these relations of solidarity are forming across borders, at the same time the Empire seeks to transform its crises into ethnic tensions so that it can intervene militarily.

The struggles against capitalist globalization are now many and yet incipient
in terms of their power: the Zapatista indigenous movement in Chiapas (Mexico),
the antiglobalization protests in Seattle and Milan, the riots in Indonesia, the en-
vironmentalist actions in Brazil, the indigenous mobilizations in Ecuador against
repression, the Bolivarian movement in Venezuela, the anti-NAFTA and anti-
FTAA mobilizations, Christian liberation theology as well as antiimperialist Islam, the labor rights struggles against multinational oil corporations in Nigeria,
the strikes in Argentina against a bankrupt government and its neoliberal economy, and so forth.

It is true that these struggles do not yet threaten capitalist globalization in a
systematic way. But it is also true that a significant number of people in the more
privileged areas of the postcolonial world no longer accept the illusions of neoliberal globalization.

Global neoliberalism (i.e., globalism) has reached an ideological dead end. The
instability that the global world-system has created is the only constant left in
the new world order. Hence, we stand in need of a theory and a set of practices for
undermining the world-system in a determinate direction toward radical political and
economic democracy, toward, that is, the elimination of that difference asserted by
Aristotle and authenticated as the ideal of the bourgeois intellectual by Nietzsche.
But this latter is an ideal that is defended only in the "bastions of democracy,"
namely, among the middle classes of the United States, who unjustly accept the murder of *other* innocents, while justly decrying the murder of their own (thus asserting
the impossible contradiction that one can be simultaneously just and unjust about the
same things, with the same concepts, under the same circumstances), solely for

the sake of preserving their relative privileges in a world of increasing want and misery. It is not an ideal defended by the rest of the world.

I also suspect that motivating the struggles against globalization is a desire to put an end to exclusion. But exclusion is the systematic and ideological purpose of the beneficiaries of Empire.

This is the point where Fukuyama's theory of the end of history collapses against a multiplicity of still weak possibilities created by what he calls "democratic liberalism" (although he has come to recognize that it is possible to be a liberal without being democratic). If the system that neoliberalism has won for itself is posthistorical, so are the possibilities that it generates in spite of itself and that it seeks to suppress. Of course, neither democratic liberalism nor the contradictions it generates are posthistorical in Fukuyama's sense, for they challenge the global system itself. These possibilities are still immature, the links are weak, and the theories of radical transformation that may redirect human history in an egalitarian direction are just being formulated. But we can sense their direction in the *mestizaje from below* expressed in the acceptance of differences among the oppressed and the common goal of affirming human life and its rights by destroying the empire and its profits.[40]

Mestizaje from below rejects what is. It points beyond itself in history. Its meaning rests precisely on an affirmation of diversity that asserts the inequality to be overcome. Exclusion, oppression, and exploitation are the marks of that inequality: exploitation in the sense of the use of labor power to satisfy the demands of variable capital for the sake of the profits of the bourgeoisie; oppression in the sense of, to use bell hooks's terms, an "absence of choices"; exclusion in the sense of a marginalization from resources; and decision making for the good life.

Is there a universal subject therefore reasserted by a reformulation of class analysis at the global level? Is mestizaje from below merely recalling alternative "grand narratives" to Fukuyama's so-called democratic liberalism? But the postmodern dissent against modernity[41] has become exhausted in the face of its positivist acceptance of the capitalist conditions for there being "difference,"[42] namely, inequality. The affirmation of an agonistic dissensus must give way to a consensus among the victims of globalization and global capital. For, if we examine the state of political life in the contemporary state, we see a weakening of those institutions of civic life that are necessary for effective republican or parliamentary democracy. In the United States, for instance, the big bourgeoisie rules with little semblance of democratic participation by the population. In the poor countries, state mechanisms that are necessary for the transnational bourgeoisie—from the military to financial institutions—have been strengthened, while those that legitimated the rise of the bourgeois nation-state in the West in the late eighteenth century and in the postcolonial world afterwards have been weakened. Castro-Gómez thus refers to the loss of the central role of the nation-state, which defined its character in the modern age.[43] An increasingly large number of the population is left to find its identity in its repressed culture and in the exploited workplace.

A principal figure of liberating identity (or rather of liberation from identity) in postmodern thought had been the nomad that moved along different identities of the periphery, without having a home to which to return: an anti-Odysseus. This may seem appropriate, if the alternative is a return to a position of class, ethnic, and gender privilege.[44] I tend to see myself, and by implication, the position of all people coming from the privileged sites of the empire to the postcolonial world more along the lines of the narrator protagonist in Alejo Carpentier's *Los pasos perdidos*: the "Greek" Yañez said it best when he told the narrator as the latter searched for his Rosario at the edges of the Venezuelan forests: "She is no Penelope."[45] That is, this is neither your home nor does she belong to you, for she belongs to no one. Should that be the position of the archetype of the margins? Methodologically, is this the *methodos* of postdevelopment studies? What if, on their way to the other (in their plurality as others in the post-Hegelian version of opposition), we find no one that mirrors our repressed hopes and desires? What if we find an other willing to assert his or her identity, desires, and hopes that belong to other histories, more deeply immersed in life? Will we then say Yea! to that life, or will we simply go back to our imperial fortresses because those are not *our* steps?

### III

Any process of liberation (whether women's liberation, a liberation of *etnias*, class, gay and lesbian liberation, and so forth) should have all of the following elements: (1) awareness of inequality; (2) an ethical consciousness of the injustice of that inequality; (3) a theory of the social and ideological conditions that produce that inequality, as well as the possibilities of overcoming it; (4) a practical program related to the specific dynamics of a society, thus laying the conditions for the struggles that may lead to liberation; (5) a popular despair with the system and its gods; and (6) a new hope that arises out of the struggle itself.[46] Obviously, a theory of globalization with an interest in human emancipation must address the process of liberation.

Justice is inequality, Nietzsche said and meant,[47] or it is an affirmation of poverty as difference, as some strands of postmodern thought seem to express. Nietzsche's affirmation of life was limited to affirming the life of the self at the expense of the life of the other (even if the smallness of the Nietzschean other will come/has come for all eternity to foul the air of the Nietzschean heights). Those formulations of the relation between inequality and just desserts are often at the heart of contemporary justifications of inequality and its dramatic increase; it is also often followed by the statement that everyone touched by the magic wand of neoliberalism has now the opportunity to reach the top.

The material or concrete negation of equality has been accomplished politically by the so-called neoliberal state,[48] that is, by the abandonment of the Keynesian welfare state; economically by the so-called free market, that is, by the free flow of capital through the flexibility of production, thus moving beyond Fordism; and culturally by consumerism.

To the extent that a social system is responsible for this negation, the ethical problem is structural and not simply personal.[49] The injustice of the situation is exacerbated by the *formal* acceptance of human rights while those rights are denied *in concreto*, when it is technically possible for all in the contemporary world to have housing, food, leisure, and dignified work conditions.

One of the most significant responses against this concrete negation of the humanity of the other is found in Leopoldo Zea's reformulation of the question of being as a questioning of the right of being human that was used by what Zea called the first wave of globalization to justify the conquest five centuries ago and subsequent colonialism. The process of liberation begins with the awareness of the injustice of this inequality or asymmetrical position established both discursively and nondiscursively by the conqueror, in the name of the conqueror, and for the sake of the conqueror.

Now that we are undergoing a complete and thorough process of globalization (which, as I said above, entails exclusion), it becomes central to the theory and practices of Latin American thought to reformulate the question of liberation within the context of the new historical process. The essays in this volume represent significant and varied attempts to do that.

Castro-Gómez in his chapter "No Longer Broad but Still Alien Is the World: The End of Modernity and the Transformation of Culture in the Times of Globalization" shows how the central instance of the modern world, the state, loses that centrality and with it the identities and conceptions of culture built on it. Instead, new forms of organization of identity develop, which accompany the new international economic formations, for better or for worse. To the modern formation of identity around the nation-state, there corresponded nomothetic and idiographic ways of knowing; for Castro-Gómez these ways of knowing functioned during modernity as taxonomies expressing in their classificatory function the *telos* of modernity, namely, absolute control over social and natural processes. The collapse of the modern leads to crisis in the human sciences. Thus, idiographic discourses that legitimated the function of the nation-state as a central instance of order by bringing together nation, culture, and people in a type of organic unity can no longer do so under conditions of deterritorialization of culture and people and the creation of international economic mechanisms that bypass the mediative function of the nation-state. It is this crisis in the sciences and not the postcolonial deterritorialization under conditions of globalization that, argues Castro-Gómez, requires a rethinking of epistemological disciplinary borders. The function of cultural studies is precisely to rethink the social and human sciences *without* foundations and the subject-object schema: to think of scientific discourses as contingent reflections on the contingency in which they/we are caught.

Cervantes, Gil, Regalado, and Zardoya present an alternative view of the modern state in their essay "Transnationalization, the State, and Political Power." They argue that new forms of democratization use democratic formalism for disguising the strong antidemocratic and antipopular character of the new types of transnational political organization. In fact, the new theories of governance, which apparently rely on legitimacy and efficiency, while seeking to construct a new political order through various international organizations, respond best to the interests of transnational capital, particularly large financial monopolistic capital, as they seek to increase their profits not only at the expense of workers worldwide but also at the expense of middle classes and national bourgeoisies of Third World countries. In reality, then, the new international economic and political organizations are antipopular representatives of imperialist transnational capital. But this does not spell the end of the nation-state, according to Cervantes et al. Instead, it represents the reorganization of the nation-state, in the imperialist and the neocolonial regions of the world, to more efficiently represent the interests of the big transnational bourgeoisie and to legitimate this transformation as a step forward in the democratization of nations.

Eduardo Mendieta's chapter "The Ethics of Globalization and the Globalization of Ethics" maps out various types of globalization theory. Mendieta's typology moves from theories of globalization that regard it simply as an intensification of European modernity to those that reflect on reflections of globalization itself. Such second-order reflection helps Mendieta prepare the ground for a phenomenology of globalization that describes it as a process of extraordinary demographic expansion and urbanization, the institutionalization of continuous change in the means of production, the permeation of social life by technology and science, and the compression of vital space and time with the consequent quotidianization and deontologization of alterity. That presents a fundamental ethical problem: how to think alterity based on a planetary ethics that neither banalizes nor homogenizes the other.

While some of our authors (e.g., Castro-Gómez, Raúl Fornet-Betancourt, and Leopoldo Zea) express a measured optimism about the possibility of overcoming abstract universalism in the encounter with difference, Jorge J. E. Gracia ("Globalization, Philosophy, and Latin America") analyzes current trends in relation to philosophy and Latin American philosophy in particular, and Debra Castillo ("Going Home: Tununa Mercado's *En estado de memoria*") presents the contrast between the universal and the particular as one in which it is unfortunately possible to erase all difference. Gracia sees current processes of globalization as a mixed blessing: on the one hand, they increase homogeneity and the power of the already powerful; on the other hand, they undermine local abuses by diminishing the power of nations. In terms of Latin American philosophy, however, Gracia sees the technological possibilities of globalization with some ambivalence: They make it possible for Latin American philosophers to be up-to-date in terms of the latest developments in North American and European philosophy, but neither European nor North American philosophers have moved beyond their provincialism to regard the Latin American philosopher as someone more than a poor relation. Nonetheless, the communication avenues opened up by globalization may make Latin American philosophers realize that they can do as well as their counterparts

in the rich countries; however, they will need to resist, says Gracia, the temptation to belong to hegemonic philosophical families.

Debra Castillo sets globalization in relation to a "particularized" narrative consciousness, in her analysis of Tununa Mercado's *In a State of Memory*. Castillo
argues that this juxtaposition is present in Mercado's contrast between a "memory Argentina," which grows and develops during years of exile, and a "lived Argentina," which arises with the return of the narrator to her native home. But this
lived Argentina is no longer home. There are certain similarities here to Alejo
Carpentier's *The Lost Steps*:[50] Both narrators are cosmopolitan bourgeois intellectuals unable to enter into a dialogue with a concrete other (in Carpentier, moving to the edge of civilization and expecting that Rosario would be a Penelope
waiting for the narrator's return from exile; in Mercado, a dialogue with a homeless man that never moves beyond a mere contrast of lives). In Castillo's reading
of Mercado's *In a State of Memory*, issues of gender and privilege come to the
forefront of the frustrating dialogue between the exiled woman and the homeless
man. But the attempt to bring together the cosmopolitan experience, on the one
hand, and the concrete everydayness of those left behind, on the other, may in fact
erase all differences and destroy not only their separateness but also the very reason of/for the encounter.

In Latin America, there have been attempts to philosophize authentically, with
full awareness of our circumstance and context. On the one side is Leopoldo Zea
and on the other is Walter D. Mignolo, who have both been notable figures in this
attempt. While Zea developed a historicism that sought to show how Latin American identity was a genuine philosophical problem, Mignolo has done so through a
critique of identity and an affirmation of the otherness of being covered up and
marginalized by imperial identities. Thus, Mignolo has contrasted the "monotopic"
hermeneutics that has limited the conditions of dialogue in the sites of the core,
with the "pluritopic" hermeneutics that is necessary for understanding both core
and periphery, the democratic nation-state and its colonialist projection, globalization and particularity. In this book, Mignolo's chapter ("Globalization and the Borders of Latinity") makes the very conception of a Latin American identity problematic as he traces its roots to competing conceptions of imperial identity. Latinity
versus Anglicity may provide different options for the Western intellectual, but
they clearly leave out the African and the Afro-American, the indigenous, and what
could indeed be called a mestizaje from below. Such mestizaje reveals its roots in
conquest and the nihilistic will to power of the conqueror, a will disguised by the
false consciousness of a merely apparent multiculturalism. Thus, Mignolo proposes the renaming/rethinking of the continent and its identity.

Leopoldo Zea in "Humanity and Globalization" proposes an alternative vision
of globalization that neither accepts an imperial restructuring of the world in
terms of international economic organizations that respond to the interests of the
center nor rejects the phenomenon of globalization as merely an imperial imposition of the center over the postcolonial periphery. Zea proposes as one of the

possibilities of today's processes of globalization—which is only the latest chapter in a process that began with the conquest of America—the creation of a world order in which it is possible to "compete while sharing" to ensure that no one is left behind. Also, that the concretely different ways of being human are not reducible to the postracism of the end of history thesis, which regards the West as the goal and *sine qua non* of human civilization today and in the future or its latest reincarnation—for example, Fukuyama's technoscientific call for the overcoming of the human.

In "A Global Democratic Order: A Normative Proposal," María Pía Lara-Zavala sees globalization processes as promising an end to wholesale violations of human rights. Lara-Zavala argues that mass violations of human rights have taken place only in undemocratic countries (e.g., the Holocaust during the Nazi period in Germany). The introduction of democratic processes is therefore necessary for the protection of human rights. Globalization processes at the political and juridical levels do in fact introduce, argues Lara-Zavala, the real possibility of democracy in formerly undemocratic nation-states. The right to have rights, as Hannah Arendt says, is a Western democratic phenomenon in which the human is constructed morally as the bearer of rights. While the nation-state was the principal protector of human rights in the past, an obvious limitation has been, Lara-Zavala argues, that the nation-state may be undemocratic. Thus, we can see how for Lara-Zavala the internationalization of political life and the legal apparatus, with the creation of a global subject, represent the best possibility for the protection and enhancement of human rights.

In contrast to Lara-Zavala's positive characterization of global forces of democratization for the protection of human rights, other chapters in this book see globalization as either a more ambivalent process or as creating other forms of disempowerment. María Mercedes Jaramillo ("Latin American Feminism and the New Challenges of Globalization") sees globalization processes within the context of the social, economic, and political gains made by women during the twentieth century. Jaramillo says that women's movements have been at the forefront of the democratization of society; however, with the depolitization of the public sphere, some ground has been lost. Furthermore, neoliberal policies widen the gap between the rich and the poor, exacerbating the process of the feminization of poverty.

Ofelia Schutte makes the latter point very forcefully in her chapter "Feminism and Globalization Processes in Latin America." Neoliberal globalization has increased the gap between rich and poor. The consequences on poor women have been most severe, particularly as a significant amount of their work is unpaid care work. Furthermore, neoliberal globalization has tended toward favoring transnational market flows and multinational corporations at considerable expense to social programs. Parallel to this, the state has moved toward a "pluralism" that incorporates the other, but only in terms of the privileged North's representations of it. There are, however, ways of fighting neoliberal globalization through progressive political action, and these have been found and used by women's organizations. The decentering of women's social and political activism, says Schutte, has led to a widening of the sphere of the struggle by many women's organizations from traditionally defined gender issues to wider political and social issues. At the same time, the grassroots organizations that have been formed have done so independently of the church, a well-established political party, or any other "masculine entity." Schutte concludes by stressing the importance of maintaining a critical ethical position toward a neoliberal globalization that, directed toward the maximization of profits, is often blind to the ideals of equality and social justice.

The collapse of really existing socialism, however, has not only sped up the process of neoliberal globalization, but has also thrown into crisis one of the most important theories developed in the twentieth century—Latin American Liberation Theology. Iván Petrella argues in his chapter "Latin American Liberation Theology, Globalization, and Historical Projects: From Critique to Construction" that liberation theology's response can be analyzed in terms of attempts to reassert and revise some of the central concepts of the movement and a critique of contemporary forms of idolatry. The reassertion of the core ideas of liberation theology—namely, liberation, the preferential option for the poor, and the reign of God—has been done at the expense of the sociopolitical mediation between theological reflection and social praxis, argues Petrella. But that has left the theory empty and open to an appropriation and co-optation of those central ideas by the right. The central categories must thus be revised, but often it has been done by overemphasizing the importance of civil society, giving up on the state, and replacing political and economic analysis of globalization with community conversion. That critical analysis is essential. The critique of idolatry, undertaken by liberation theology in the face of neoliberal globalization, is one of the ways in which it has met the challenge. In this way, liberation theology seeks to recover the transformative content of liberation theology by showing how its preferential option for the poor, the meaning of liberation, and the reign of God cannot be appropriated by the market and its laws, since these generate contradictions that produce death were they to be universalized, and transform the market into an idol. Petrella thinks, however, that the attempt by this variant of liberation theology to ground itself in life is too abstract, while at the same time it has not produced an alternative to the market. A historical project is needed to construct concrete alternatives that would thus give specificity and content to liberation theology's terms. It would mediate between the ideal and the practical tasks of today, while being irreducible to either. That project, present in early liberation theology, is now missing; hence, it has been easy for neoliberalism to appropriate and co-opt the discursive practices of liberation theology, by simply making them—emptied of any content critical of neoliberalism—the goals of a monolithically conceived capitalism. Petrella's historical project rejects such absolutization of capitalism, the market, and globalization, for that would make social change impossible. He proposes "revolutionary reform," rather than a dichotomous reform or revolution, for the sake of a "democratized market economy." Castro-Gómez's move beyond and against imperial discourses—in the essay with which we begin this book's collection—receives concrete formulation as an intercultural philosophy of liberation in the last essay of this book, Raúl Fornet-Betancourt's "An Alternative to Globalization: Theses for the Development of an Intercultural Philosophy." Fornet-Betancourt presents "intercultural philosophy" as a discursive alternative to the monocultural structures of traditional philosophies, for rather than beginning from the assumption that *qua* philosophy it has no cultural limitations, it begins "from below": aware of the cultural limitations inherent in the doing of philosophy, intercultural philosophy grounds itself on relations of solidarity with the philosophical endeavors of other cultures. It is at the places of these encounters that a concrete universality arises. Thus, at the practical level, intercultural philosophy promotes a "plurivisional mundialization" of thinking and being in the world, by contrast to the imperial imposition of neoliberal globalization.

Fornet-Betancourt integrates in a coherent way the meaning of liberation to which I referred at the beginning of this section, for he offers a concrete and fruitful proposal for a discursive practice that is able to listen to all the voices for human life in a community. An intercultural philosophy is thus open to the articulation of differences.

"Because I want diversity, I open up my senses," says Zemon Masarov. Truly, only in community and difference is hope kept alive and the joy of life expressed:

> The First Father of the Guaranís rose in darkness lit by reflections from his own heart and created flames and thin mist. He created love and had nobody to give it to. He created language and had no one to listen to him.
>
> Then he recommended to the gods that they should construct the world and take charge of fire, mist, rain, and wind. And he turned over to them the music and words of the sacred hymn so that they would give life to women and to men.
>
> So love became communion, language took on life, and the First Father redeemed his solitude. Now he accompanies men and women who sing as they go:
> *We are walking this earth,*
> *We are walking this shining earth.*[51]

## NOTES

1. Michael Hardt and Antonio Negri, *Empire* (Cambridge, Mass.: Harvard University Press, 2000), 225.

2. Manuel Castells, *The Information Age: Economy, Society and Culture,* vol. I: *The Rise of the Network Society* (Oxford: Blackwell, 1996), 471–72.

3. Following Castells, Ankie Hoogvelt has neatly contrasted the politics of identity that arises from "subordinate development" and that one which follows from "exclusion" in Ankie Hoogvelt, *Globalization and the Postcolonial World: The New Political Economy of Development*, 2d ed. (Baltimore: Johns Hopkins, 2001), 199: "Islamic resurgence is best understood as a politics of identity in response to exclusion, rather than (as was the case during the heyday of Arab nationalism) as a response to subordinate incorporation." In the case of Latin America, Latin American dependency theory, the first generation of the liberation theology, and Marxist and populist movements of the mid-twentieth century would correspond to a critique of "subordinate development" or to Augusto Salazar Bondy's destruction of the notion of *underdevelopment*, "*under* these powers" [Augusto Salazar Bondy, "The Meaning and Problem of Hispanic American Thought," in *Latin American Philosophy in the Twentieth Century: Man, Values, and the Search for Philosophical Identity*, ed. Jorge J. E. Gracia (Buffalo, N.Y.: Prometheus Books, 1986), 241]. Hoogvelt contrasts the antidevelopmentalism of Islamic fundamentalism with the postdevelopmentalism of postcolonial and postdevelopment studies in Latin America in Hoogvelt, *Globalization and the Postcolonial World*, 254–56.

4. This concept is fundamental to Ankie Hoogvelt's reconstruction of the history of capitalism. She borrows it from Robert Cox, "Social Forces, States and World Orders: Beyond International Relations Theory," *Millennium: Journal of International Studies* 10, no. 2 (1981): 126–55.

5. At a time when popular versions of globalization—Thomas Friedman's *The Lexus and the Olive Tree* (New York: Anchor Books, 2000) for instance—praise globalization as the best thing this side of heaven, Hoogvelt argues convincingly against globalism by showing that globalization is best characterized by exclusion and not by the simplistic juxtaposition of tradition and high tech. Thus, Hoogvelt shows how the share of developing economies in world trade has increased by only 3.6 percent from 1953 to 1996 (from 25.5 percent to 29.1 percent, although the trend appears to be cyclical with a low of 17.2 percent in 1970 and another of 22.7 percent in 1990). Most significantly, however, is that the 1996 number *includes* the four "Asian Tigers" (Hong Kong, Korea, Taiwan, and Singapore), which, although representing only 1.5 percent of the population of the developing world, account for over 33 percent of the developing world's share of world trade! In fact, then, adds Hoogvelt, "all the gains, and more, may be attributed" to those four economies. Hoogvelt then introduces the reader to another significant set of numbers (from UNCTAD's *Trade and Development Report 1998*, 183, table 47): In 1995, the global share of market participation by developing economies amounted to only 18.3 percent (excluding the 10.8 percent global share of the four Asian Tigers). But that is down from the 1950 share of 25.9 percent (excluding the 3.0 percent global share of the aforementioned four economies and less than the 1970 low for the whole period (16.1 percent excluding the 2.7 percent of the four Asian Tigers in the UNCTAD numbers or 17.2 percent including the four Asian Tigers in the UN 1982's *Yearbook of International Trade Statistics*, xx–xxvii, table A). Thus, what accounts for the moderate increase in the developing world's increase in the share of world trade and what has served as the material foundation for globalist propaganda has been the explosive growth of the economies of four countries with a total population of 71 million people, or 1.5 percent of the total population of the developing world: Hong Kong, South Korea, Taiwan, and Singapore increased their combined share of global trade from 2.2 percent in 1960 to 10.8 percent in 1995. Finally, adds Hoogvelt, while those four countries together with Japan and the other countries of the core (the rich

countries) represented only 17 percent of the population of the world in 1997, that number is in fact lower than the 18.7 percent core countries' share of the world's population in 1900 and 18.8 percent share in 1950 (excluding Japan and the Asian Tigers). In other words, while the population of the postcolonial or Third World has increased, its participation in the global economy has decreased. Statistically, then, exclusion is the most significant feature of globalization (Hoogvelt, *Globalization and the Postcolonial World*, 72–76).

6. Hoogvelt, *Globalization and the Postcolonial World*, 121.

7. I borrow Hoogvelt's periodization of the history of capitalism's historical structures: mercantilism (1500–1800), the colonial phase (1800–1950), the neocolonial period (1950–1970), and either postimperialism (according to David Becker) or second neocolonial period (following Samir Amin). See Hoogvelt, *Globalization and the Postcolonial World*, 17, 43.

8. I do not mean to imply by this that government becomes smaller or less intrusive. On the contrary, when we look at two model neoliberal economies in the Americas, Chile in the south and the United States to the north, we see extraordinary increases in politico-military intervention: In Chile neoliberalism was built on the basis of the neofascist state by the pro-U.S. military state during the 1970s. In the United States, corporate welfare is rampant; it is today accompanied by proto-fascist extrajudicial intervention by the state, such as military tribunals and indefinite detention for noncitizens, searches without warrants or without communication with their victims (citizen or not), suspension of the right of *habeas corpus* for noncitizens suspected of terrorism together with the suspension without a court order of attorney-client privilege of confidentiality in their conversations; all of these seem to point out toward the constitution of a quasifascist state in preparation for future international crises in the postcolonial world. The Orwellian defense of civil liberties by attacking them reveals a George Bush, Jr., administration out of control. It is still possible, although it appears unlikely now because of the terror scare, to roll back those policies through the formation of a left-libertarian right coalition against "big government." Beyond the threat of Al-Qaeda-sponsored terrorism, however, it seems reasonable to assert that big capital needs big government to remove political and human obstacles to its free flow; it is something like "collateral damage" at the "home front."

9. See note 5.

10. Hoogvelt, *Globalization and the Postcolonial World*, 73.

11. Hoogvelt, *Globalization and the Postcolonial World*, 259.

12. "The men of the mainland of the Indies eat human flesh, and are more sodomite than any other generation. There is no justice among them; they go about naked; they cannot love nor do they have any shame; they are like asses, foolish, crazy, insensate; they do not care to kill or be killed; they are not truthful, unless it is to their advantage; they are inconstant; they have no idea about counsel; they are most ungrateful and friends of novelties; they pride themselves of being drunkards. . . . [T]hey are bestial in their vices; the young show no courtesy towards the old, nor do children towards parents . . ., they are treasonous, cruel and vengeful, and never forgive; inimical to religion, lazy, thieves, liars, of low judgment and diffident; they neither keep faith nor order; husbands are unfaithful to their women and women to their husbands; they are witches, soothsayers, [and] necromancers; they are as cowardly as hares, as dirty as pigs; they eat lice, spiders, [and] raw worms, whenever they find them; they have neither art nor the ways of men; when they forget the things of the faith that they learned, they say those things are meant for Castile [Spain] and not for them, and that

they do not want to change customs or men" [Tomás Ortiz, cited in Francisco López de Gómara, *Historia general de las Indias*, 2 vols. (Madrid: Espasa-Calpe, 1932), I:242].

13. "The Caucasian race, which is the main type of immigration [to Argentina], increases the numbers of white peoples; and they come with the traditions of European governments: This is an element that will help in the uplifting of the moral and political character of the indigenous, prehistoric races, which drain from us the energy that comes from civilized and free traditions" [Domingo Faustino Sarmiento (1811–1888), *Conflicto y armonía de las razas en América*, in Domingo Faustino Sarmiento, *El pensamiento vivo de Sarmiento*, ed. Ricardo Rojas, 2d ed. (Buenos Aires: Editorial Losasada, 1944), 208). Along a similar vein, Theodore Roosevelt said in 1905: "Race purity must be maintained" [cited in Angela Davis, *Women, Race & Class* (New York: Vintage Books, 1983), 209].

14. "Limiting or restricting the entry of beautiful products from the outside so that inferior domestic products may be kept at a high value is similar to setting up obstacles to the entry of beautiful foreign women so that ugly native women will marry better; or it is similar to not allowing blond white men into the country because mulattoes, who make up the stock of the nation, would then be rejected because of their inferiority by women" [Juan Bautista Alberdi (1810–1884), *El crimen de la Guerra* (Buenos Aires: Rodolfo Alonso Editor, 1975), 71].

15. Immanuel Kant, "Idea for a Universal History from a Cosmopolitan Point of View," in Immanuel Kant, *On History*, ed. and trans. Lewis White Beck (Indianapolis: Bobbs-Merrill Educational Publishing, 1963), 18–21.

16. See Hardt and Negri, *Empire*, 13, on their distinction, and Hobbes's, between "people" and "multitude."

17. Michel Foucault, *Discipline and Punish: The Birth of the Prison*, trans. Alan Sheridan (New York: Vintage Books, 1979), 138.

18. Georg Wilhelm Friedrich Hegel, *The Philosophy of Right*, trans. T. M. Knox (Oxford: Oxford University Press, 1967), 151–52 (par. 248) and 278 (add. to par. 248).

19. Enrique Dussel, *El encubrimiento del Indio: 1492. Hacia el origen del mito de la modernidad*, 2d ed. (Mexico City: Editorial Cambio XXI, 1994), 19 ff., 52.

20. Edmundo O'Gorman, *The Invention of America* (Bloomington, Ind.: Indiana University Press, 1961).

21. Roberto Fernández Retamar, *Calibán. Apuntes sobre la cultura de Nuestra América* (Buenos Aires: Editorial La Pléyade, 1973), 16 ff.

22. Gayatri Spivak, *A Critique of Postcolonial Reason: Toward a History of the Vanishing Present* (Cambridge, Mass.: Harvard University Press, 1999), 117–18.

23. Garcilaso de la Vega, El Inca, *Royal Commentaries of the Incas and General History of Peru*, trans. Harold V. Livermore (Austin, Tex.: University of Texas Press, 1966), 27–30 ("The Description of Peru").

24. Domingo Faustino Sarmiento, *Life in the Argentine Republic in the Days of the Tyrants; or, Civilization and Barbarism*, trans. Mary Mann (New York: Haffner Publishing Company, 1868), 54: The Argentine Revolution of 1810 was, on the one hand, a war of "the modern European spirit" against Spain; on the other hand, it was a war of the "barbarians" against that spirit "for the purpose of freeing themselves from all civil restraint . . . and unleashing their hatred against civilization."

25. See the Rules for Confession designed by the Spaniards for Mesoamerican peoples during the Sixteenth Century, for instance, Fray Alonso de Molina, *Confesionario mayor en lengua mexicana y castellana* (1569; Mexico: Unam, 1984).

26. Foucault, *Discipline and Punish: The Birth of the Prison*, 30: "The soul is the effect and instrument of a political anatomy; the soul is the prison of the body."

27. Enrique Dussel, *El encubrimiento del Indio: 1492. Hacia el origen del mito de la modernidad*, 45: "For the intra-European definition of modernity, [the] New Age begins with the Renaissance, the Reformation, and culminates in the *Aufklärung*. Whether Latin America, Africa or Asia exist has no significance for the philosopher from Frankfurt [namely, Habermas]. He proposes an exclusively 'intra-European' definition of modernity; that is why, it is self-centered, eurocentric, where the European 'particularity' is identified with world 'universality.'"

28. Dussel, *El encubrimiento del Indio: 1492. Hacia el origen del mito de la modernidad*, 66.

29. Karl Marx and Frederick Engels, *The Communist Manifesto* (New York: International Publishers, 1948), 12, 14–15.

30. Hardt and Negri, *Empire*, 52.

31. Hardt and Negri, *Empire*, xiv–xv.

32. Hardt and Negri, *Empire*, 24.

33. Francis Fukuyama, *The End of History and the Last Man* (New York: Avon Books, The Hearst Corporation, 1993), 182, 313–21.

34. Hardt and Negri, *Empire*, 189.

35. "And I worried about the immigration: Americans diffusing like a gas along the concentration gradient into India." Shreyas Roy, "Flooding Season," in Shreyas Roy, *Quantum Love and the Screaming Electron: A Misinterpretation of Science for Poetry* (Le Moyne College's Integral Honors Projects, Falcone Library, Le Moyne College, Syracuse, N.Y., 2001).

36. Hardt and Negri, *Empire*, 103, 395.

37. Guy Debord, *The Society of the Spectacle*, trans. Donald Nicholson-Smith (New York: Zone Books, 1994). Thus, while for Kant, the noumenal was behind the phenomenal, and for Schopenhauer there was the will as one lifted the veil of appearances, the spectacular capitalist society seeks to reduce what is to what appears.

38. Hardt and Negri, *Empire*, 57–58.

39. Over four decades ago, in reference to the view of a scientist that space travel will free us from the Earth, Hannah Arendt asked: "Should the emancipation and secularization of the modern age, which began with a turning away, not necessarily from God, but from a god who was the father of men in heaven, end with an even more fateful repudiation of an Earth who was the Mother of all living creatures under the sky?" Hannah Arendt, *The Human Condition* (Chicago: University of Chicago Press, 1958), 1–2.

40. Fidel Castro's speech in Teheran, Iran, in which he points to the commonalities between the overthrow of the Shah and the struggle to overthrow "the imperialist king" is a good example of the rich possibilities for revolutionary practices that combine diverse cosmovisions into the revolutionary humanism that is needed to globalize in full consciousness the struggle against capitalism.

41. Jean-Francois Lyotard, *The Postmodern Condition: A Report on Knowledge*, trans. Geoff Bennington and Brian Massumi (Minneapolis, Minn.: University of Minnesota Press, 1979).

42. Zygmunt Bauman, "Postmodernity, or Living with Ambivalence," in *A Postmodern Reader*, ed. Joseph Natoli and Linda Hutcheon (Albany, N.Y.: State University of New York Press, 1993), 9–24.

43. See Santiago Castro-Gómez, "No Longer Broad but Still Alien Is the World: The End of Modernity and the Transformation of Culture in the Times of Globalization" (this volume).

44. Patricia Jagentowicz Mills, "Memory and Myth: Women's Time Reconceived," in *Taking Our Time: Feminist Perspectives on Temporality,* ed. Frieda Johles Forman and Caoran Sowton (Oxford: Pergamon Press, 1989), 61–74, 67–68.

45. Alejo Carpentier, *The Lost Steps,* trans. Harriet de Onís (New York: The Noonday Press, 1989), 276.

46. See Sandra Lee Bartky, "Toward a Phenomenology of Feminist Consciousness," in *Philosophy and Women,* ed. Sharon Bishop and Marjorie Weinzweig (Belmont, Calif.: Wadsworth, 1979), 252–58, for the use of the notion of intolerable contradiction as well as the notion of the recognition of the fact of inequality. I am indebted to her discussion in that essay exposing inequality and making me aware of the intolerability of that condition in my presentation of the fourfold elements of a process of liberation. Regarding the new hope as a true historical transcendence, one can find that idea in Mariátegui's unsystematic discussion of the myth of socialism in Perú. It is my view that Mariátegui was not simply proposing a *Deus ex machina,* but rather a truly historical transcendence. As the reader will observe, I believe that such transcendence is still possible in the Third World by taking seriously the vision of liberation that comes out of the "cultures of the oppressed." Finally, I am indebted to Professor Nancy Ring of the Department of Religious Studies at Le Moyne College for the inclusion of a sixth element of the liberation process, namely, the element of hope.

47. Friedrich Nietzsche, *Thus Spoke Zarathustra,* Walter Kaufmann, trans. (London: Penguin Books, 1978), 101: "I do not wish to be mixed up and confused with these preachers of equality. For, to *me* justice speaks thus: 'Men are not equal'. Nor shall they become equal! What should my love of the overman be if I spoke otherwise!"

48. Mario Vargas Llosa denied that there is such a thing as "neoliberalism." For him there is only "liberalism"—free elections and free markets. Vargas Llosa is trying to save liberalism from what he considers to be antiliberal bias. But there are historical and analytical reasons to distinguish between liberalism and neoliberalism. Although neoliberalism may construct a *self-image* of itself as liberalism redeemed, neoliberalism is characterized socially by an exclusion and marginalization of large sectors of the world's population from production. This permanently unemployable surplus labor calls attention to what Ankie Hoogvelt called a "'thikening' network of human social and economic interaction" and "time/space compression" [Ankie Hoogvelt, *Globalization and the Post-colonial World,* 3, 121].

49. It is difficult to understand the importance of structural conditions in the United States. Because of the heavy dosage of individualist ideology that United Statians swallow throughout their lives, coupled with the economic power of a large middle class, social cretinism regarding the role of social conditions in one's life's chances is widespread.

50. Carpentier, *The Lost Steps.*

51. Eduardo Galeano, ed., *Memory of Fire: Genesis,* vol. I, trans. Cedric Belfrage (New York: Pantheon Books, 1985), 11.

# I

## THE NEW CONDITIONS OF INEQUALITY

# 1

# No Longer Broad but Still Alien Is the World: The End of Modernity and the Transformation of Culture in the Times of Globalization

*Santiago Castro-Gómez*
*(Translated by Mario Sáenz)*

One of the most important achievements of cultural studies has been, without a doubt, the demystification of the modern idea of "national culture," which we understand as the expression of an idiosyncrasy born and anchored in specific territorialities. The rupture consists mainly in showing that modernity taxonomizes culture; that is, it produces culture as something telluric and organic, a "national" form of being-in-the-world. Culture is conceived by modernity as a specialized function of social reproduction to be studied by specialists, reorganized by official institutions of various types, linked essentially to the avatars of the market, and, finally, offered to the public as a "product" or else as a public service to which all citizens have a right.[1] In short, cultural studies show that the idea of a national culture is produced and reproduced by mechanisms of control and selection that give origin to violent exclusions and create new forms of professionalization and division of labor.

Even so, one of the criticisms made against the project of cultural studies is its gradual abandonment of what it promised to be at the beginning, to wit, a kind of nomadic social theory, capable of opening spaces of understanding *between* the disciplines, breaking in that way with the technical languages and indices of modern social science. The critics of cultural studies point out that these studies are becoming a new explanatory macronarrative of society, reviving the enlightenment epic of teleological knowledge, and ending up institutionalizing themselves as a new "discipline" at the interior of the productive apparatuses of knowledge.[2] There is thus the suspicion that the project of cultural studies follows a restructuring of academic politics in accordance with the new necessities of the market in the times of "late capitalism." According to these critics, the vision that cultural studies proj-

ects about culture would be nothing else than a "postmodern" version with a conservative bent, which contemplates with resignation the globalization of North
American mass culture and the imperial interests of the United States south of its
borders.[3]

I would like to show in what follows that, even though cultural studies are still
anchored in some way in the epistemologies defined by modernity, this is not because of a global *reorganization* of the economy and politics under the sign of
neocolonialism. On the contrary, it is due to the conceptual challenges that a situation of global *disorganization* presents to contemporary social theory. Such disorganization responds in the last instance to the crisis of the project of modernity
itself and to the politics of knowledge and power linked directly to that project.
My strategy will consist, then, of interrogating the meaning of modernity as a
"project," trying to show the common genesis of two elements that are mutually
complementary—the nation-state and idiographic discourses about culture. I will
then show that what today we call "globalization" cannot be understood as a new
colonial project directed by some type of national or multinational agent; it is, instead, the chaotic and unpredictable result of the *dissolution* of the normative
framework in which the two aforementioned elements have played a taxonomic
role. I will end with a reflection on the role that the social sciences in general, and
cultural studies in particular, will play with the intensification of the crisis of
foundations.

## THE FEAR OF EXPOSURE: MODERNITY AS A "PROJECT"

What do we mean when we speak of "the project of modernity"? In the first place
and in general terms, we are referring to the Faustian attempt of subjecting the
whole of life to man's absolute control under the firm guidance of knowledge.
The sociological genesis of this project must be found toward the end of the so-
called Middle Ages, when a series of events were unchained that provoked great
social, political, and cultural instability in Europe: the Crusades, the Black Death,
the birth of the burghers, the moral crisis of the Papacy, and the configuration of
monarchic powers opposed to the authority of the Church. At the level of *thought,*
this social instability is reflected in the theological nominalism of Scotus and
Ockham. The German philosopher Hans Blumenberg shows that the modern attempt to restore order and *harmonia mundi* arises precisely as a response to the
idea of God's absolute sovereignty, that is, the nominalist belief in an inscrutable
and indispensable deity.[4] God does not rule over the world on the basis of laws
that are understandable to humans (for instance, rational and eternal laws), but
rather on the basis of His own will. This implies an unbearable *depotentiation* of
reality and human life. Man and world were seen as puppets at the mercy of an
unknowable divine will (*Deus absconditus*); man's life and fate seemed to be at
the mercy of the sheerest contingency. The world was reduced to the pure *Fak-*

*tum* of a sovereign will that could not be measured by using the standards of human reason. In Blumemberg's view, the result of this theological absolutism is a feeling of abandonment and "ontological solitude."[5] In a world that resists being trapped in rational categories, man appears subject to the arbitrariness of pain, suffering, and misery.

Faced with this situation of chaos and irrationality, modernity will try eliminating the feeling of ontological insecurity by restoring the knowability of the world. According to Blumemberg, modernity [*Neuzeit*] represents itself as a secure shelter against all contingencies. For this, it was necessary to elevate man to the rank of ordering principle of all things. It is no longer God's inscrutable will that decides the events of individual and social life; instead, it is man himself who, making use of reason, is able to decipher the laws inherent to nature in order to put them at his service. This rehabilitation of man [*Selbstbehauptung*] goes hand in hand with the idea of dominion over nature through science and technology, the true prophet of which was Bacon. In fact, nature is portrayed by Bacon as the great adversary of man, as the enemy that has to be defeated to domesticate contingency and establish *Regnum hominis* over the earth.[6] The best tactic for winning this war is to know the inner nature of the enemy and probe its most intimate secrets so that afterward it may be subjugated with its own weapons to the human will. The role of science and its practical application, or technique, are to be used precisely to penetrate nature's most hidden and remote secrets with the purpose of compelling it to obey human imperatives. In short, Bacon realizes that science and power coincide: knowledge is power; power is knowledge. Ontological insecurity will be eliminated only to the degree that there is an increase in the power and scope of the mechanisms of control over the magical or mysterious forces of nature, and over all that we cannot understand. Max Weber calls this increase in power and control through knowledge the "disenchantment of the world."

## KNOWLEDGE AND GOVERNABILITY

I want to show now that when we speak of modernity as a project, we are also mainly referring to a *central instance* [*instancia central*] that warrants and coordinates ontological security. That central instance is the nation-state, which guarantees the "rational organization" of human life. By rational organization, I mean in this context the regimentation by the directive action of the state of those processes of disenchantment and demystification of the world, to which Weber and Blumemberg refer. The nation-state understands itself as the sphere in which all opposing interests can arrive at a synthesis; that is, it sees itself as the locus capable of formulating collective goals valid for all its members. This requires the strict application of "rational criteria" that would allow the state to channel the desires, interests, and emotions of its citizens toward goals it has

defined for itself. This means that the modern state not only acquires a monopoly on violence, but also that it uses it for domesticating the minds and bodies
of its citizens, making all of them feel that they are part of one and the same
collectivity, of only one nation. I agree, then, with Gellner's classic thesis; for
him, nation and national identity are nothing other than taxonomic inventions
by the modern state.[7]

I am now interested in examining the role played by *knowledge* in the process
of invention of the nation. Giddens shows that a central characteristic of modernity is the regular utilization of knowledge about the circumstances of social life,
insofar as knowledge is a constitutive element in the organization and transformation of social life. This means that knowledge is not merely an adjunct added
to the framework of organization as defined by the nation-state, but it is constitutive of them instead. Without the collaboration of science, and particularly of
the social and cultural sciences, the modern state would not find itself with the
capability of exercising control over people's lives, defining medium- and short-
range collective goals, and assigning to its citizens a cultural identity. A large
quantity of scientific information on the mode of functioning of reality was required not only for the restructuring of the economy according to the new exi-
gencies of international capitalism but also for the redefinition of political legitimacy and even for the identification of the character and the values peculiar to
each nation. Only on the basis of this information was it possible to organize and
carry out governmental programs.

In this way, two ways of knowing [*saberes*] are born, which Immanuel Wallerstein calls *nomothetic* and *idiographic*.[8] Nomothetic disciplines [*saberes*], such as
economics, sociology, and political science [*politología*], specialize in discover-
ing the laws that rule the realm of human action. By contrast, in idiographic disciplines [*saberes*], such as history, anthropology, and ethnology, what is investi-
gated is not human life insofar as it is governed by invariable laws, but rather
human life as the *result* of very long historical processes. Despite these differences, both nomothetic and idiographic ways of knowing assumed a normative
pretension over their object of reflection, in the sense that they saw themselves to
be dissociated from the economic, social, political, historical, and cultural conditions of their own production. Imagining themselves to be inhabitants of an anti-
septic world of logical statements, both types of knowledge functioned as taxonomies of the social being.

However, these taxonomies did not limit themselves to the elaboration of a
system of rules called "science," but instead they had practical consequences insofar as they were able to legitimate particular regulative state policies.[9] The
practical matrix that would give rise to the emergence of nomothetic and idiographic ways of knowing is the necessity to "adjust" the lives of men to the productive apparatus. All state policies and institutions (namely, the school, the constitution, the law, hospitals, prisons, etc.) will be defined by the "civilization"
imperative, that is, by the necessity to discipline the passions and direct them toward the benefit of the collectivity through work. Thus, all the citizens were be-

ing linked to the process of production through the subjection of their time and bodies to a series of social norms, which were defined and legitimized by knowledge. Nomothetic and idiographic ways of knowledge instruct us on the laws that govern the economy, society, political life, and history. The state, on the other hand, defines its governmental policies on the basis of a normativity legitimized by science.

## THE INVENTION OF "CULTURE" AS AN OBJECT OF KNOWLEDGE

I want to focus now on idiographic knowledge and, specifically, on the taxonomic function that "culture"—one of the objects of knowledge generated by this type of knowing—fulfills. Culture is a *modern* idea that must be understood in relation to the emergence of a series of ways of knowing that postulate "Man," "History," and "Society" as objects of knowledge; that is, we must understand them in relation to the birth of what Heidegger calls "the metaphysics of subjectivity." From this point of view, neither the ancient societies of Greece and Rome nor the feudal societies of medieval Europe had the epistemological capacity (or necessity) to think about something like culture. The Greek concept of *paideia* or the Latin *colere* do not refer to customs, values, or beliefs shared by a nation; least of all do they refer to the results of a historical evolutionary process. These concepts have rather an ethical-individual connotation, since they refer fundamentally to the type of education received by the intellectual elites. Thus, for example, when Seneca and Cicero speak of *cultura animi,* they are referring to the individual practice of virtue, to the work required to control the body's passions by means of the cultivation of the sciences and the arts. Those terms refer then to "caring for the self," which Foucault calls the "technologies of the self." Thus, when Werner Jaeger, for instance, identifies the concept of *paideia* with the "national spirit" of classical Greece, which is expressed organically in the customs, religion, art, and philosophy of a people, he is extrapolating toward antiquity, a concept articulated by a modern episteme. The same happens when we speak of a "Muisca culture" or a "Mayan culture," to mention only two examples. For only from a fundamentally *modern* set of stratagems [*dispositivos*] of knowledge–power is it possible to invent the Greeks, the Mayas, and ourselves, Latin Americans, as cultures.

I will illustrate what I have just said with a brief examination of Herder's and Hegel's philosophies of history. We should note, with Koselleck, that these authors' reflections on culture lead to a kind of "Copernican Revolution." In fact, they begin working with a *type* of discourse in which the concepts of people and culture become directly linked to the concept of "nation."[10] The nation becomes for them the maximum political expression of the culture of a people. As a matter of fact, both Herder and Hegel take up the literal sense of the Latin word *natio* and refer to it not only as the natural "birth" [*nacimiento*] of a people, but they also use it as a normative criterion that organizes determinate persons according to geographic, religious, ethnic, moral, or linguistic categories.

Now it is necessary to make clear that the identification Herder and Hegel make between nation and culture has a double political presupposition. On the one hand, and as I have pointed out before, the new political organization of Europe in the eighteenth century required a constitution of centralized powers capable of assuming rational control over a specific territory, promoting the mobility of goods and labor, as well as driving forward the exploitation of natural resources and the distribution of wealth. Thus, the state arises as an entity that carries out territorial, economic, and political functions. It defines a concrete geographic space over which it exercises economic-military sovereignty and within the parameters of which citizens—that is, those persons legitimately subject to the state's government and protection—must live. The state also defines a series of political rights and duties for its citizens; furthermore, it creates mechanisms that tend to give legitimacy to rights and duties. But that is not all; in order to be able to exercise sovereignty, the state needs to function with the idea that the members of the nation are united by only one culture, that is, a set of shared beliefs, values, and traditions.

On the other hand, the constitution of the European states rested in large measure on Europe's domination over its overseas colonies. In fact, the positing of culture as an object of knowledge would not have been possible without the large quantity of information about the existence of "the others," which had begun to circulate in Europe in the sixteenth century. One only has to look at books that were key to the birth of idiographic discourses on culture, such as *The Spirit of the Laws* by Montesquieu or *Discourse on the Origin and Foundation of Inequality Among Men* by Rousseau, to notice this phenomenon. In these texts, the normative criteria for the configuration of European states are obtained from the "backlighting" set up by the habits and customs of barbarians. The European nations had to possess a culture, but this one had to be clearly distinguished from the habits that characterized the people subject to colonial domination. In Hegel, this hierarchization of culture will reach extremes such as the "fixing" of African and Latin American peoples in the still unconscious sphere of nature; that is, they were placed at a point in the phenomenological scale much inferior to the realm of "Spirit," the maximum expression of which would be, of course, the central European nations.

With all this I mean the following: The discourse that establishes the identity of nation with culture fulfills a clear taxonomic function, for it sets limits between individuals, groups, or peoples on the basis of a normative scale defined by the state's colonial power. Humanity is subdivided into peoples with greater or lesser degrees of culture, cultural development, civilization, and spirit. In some cases, one could reach the conclusion that those peoples classified in the lower part of the scale cannot even be considered as human.

We see then that the idiographic concept of culture, especially as it was developed during the eighteenth and nineteenth centuries, expresses, on the one hand,

Europe's feeling of superiority toward the peoples subordinated to its colonial power and, on the other hand, the necessity to normalize [*normativizar*] the life of those same European citizens subject to the government of the state, in accordance with the new necessities of capital. The citizen had to be identified with state policies by showing that this was nothing other than the "organic" expression of the "general will" of the people.

It is not surprising, then, that in Herder's narrative, nations are represented as organic entities, that is, as natural products like trees and plants.[11] The state is telluric as the plant: It is born from the earth and, because of that, it keeps an intimate link with the geography in which the people have been born and grow up. A state is not invented, Herder tells us, but rather, "inherited." When the state unfastens itself culturally from the people, when the state is not *national-popular*, as it happens with cosmopolitan states, it becomes a machine: an entity without life and telluric roots, which must then support itself exclusively by means of absolutism and military tyranny.[12] According to Herder, a good ruler is not the one who tries to transform his or her people into something other than what they are; instead, the good ruler is the one who is able to adjust political institutions to the culture of the people.[13]

In accordance with Herder's cartography, peoples are constituted by an "individual soul" that manifests itself fundamentally in the maternal language. The development of the maternal language is, therefore, the basic presupposition of nationality.[14] Thus, for example, Greece could not have been what it was if it had not expressed its most profound feelings through the Greek language. Greece was great because it was able to create a *national mythology,* namely, a set of representations of life and the world that faithfully reflected the character of the Greek people, the geography in which their life unfolded, and the type of social relations that constituted them.

The poets, who were the true articulators of the maternal language, played a fundamental role in this. Homer was to Greece what Shakespeare was to England, Goethe and Schiller to Germany, and Cervantes to Spain: All of them were true "fathers of nationhood." As the maximum expression of the genius of the language, literature thus transforms itself in the purest expression of the national character.

But it is perhaps in Hegel that one may better appreciate the organic identification of state, nation, and culture. For Hegel, the process of growth of universal reason is not just impelled by the actions of historical individuals. Instead, *Volksgeist,* the national spirit of a people, is the unity of the concrete development of the Spirit in time and the true motive force of universal history.[15] Insofar as it is a "moment" of the universal Spirit *(Weltgeist),* the spirit of a people appears as an organic unity, as it was in Herder and Montesquieu. Art, religion, customs, language, the economy, and political institutions—all these expressions are dialectically interconnected and constitute a homogeneous unity. None of these levels functions independently or fulfills particular ends, since all of them are coordinated harmoniously with the one reason that governs the whole. And the ultimate end *(telos)* to which that reason tends is nothing other than self-knowledge. That is why the culture of a people is, in Hegel's view, the mode of consciousness that a people has of the Spirit; culture is, in other words, the Spirit's representation of itself through a people.[16] This consciousness is different in each historical people and constitutes the very foundation of identity. In the same way that each people expresses organically a different moment of the same universal Spirit, every individual participates entirely in the national culture to which he or she belongs and cannot transcend the identity that corresponds to him or her as part of a people.

Nevertheless, the highest expression of the spirit of the people is, for Hegel, the state, the true carrier of the national *ethos* and identity. Freedom becomes objective only in the state because in it all particular individuals become reconciled with the ethical substance of the collectivity. Individuals must, therefore, subordinate themselves to it, since it is only through the state's mediation that they can become conscious of themselves, of what they want, and of their destiny insofar as they are members of one nation. For the state is not an abstract entity that confronts individuals, as contractualist theory has it, but rather it exists in and through culture. In this sense can one understand the words of the German philosopher when he asserts that

> The general principle which manifests itself and becomes an object of consciousness in the State—the form under which all that the State includes is brought—is the whole of that cycle of phenomena which constitutes the *culture* of a nation. But the definite *substance* that receives the form of universality, and exists in that concrete reality which is the State—is the Spirit of the People itself.[17]

We see then that in the philosophy of history elaborated by Hegel and Herder, culture has been construed as an idiographic object of knowledge. As Wallerstein has shown, idiographic ways of knowing are distinguished from those that are nomothetic in that the former make the laws that govern human life into a product of the *historical development* of humanity. The philosophy of history in Herder and Hegel may be regarded in this sense as idiographic knowledge for two fundamental reasons: first, it makes *time* the basic factor over which the social and cultural life of human beings unfolds; and, second, it pretends to be scientific—a pretension, to be sure, very peculiar to German idealist philosophy from Herder to Schelling's last phase.[18] Thus, the idiographic concept of culture functioned as a chart *(Tableau)* destined to order, classify, and codify persons, assigning to them not only a role in the flux of history but also a function insofar as they are organic members of the nation and obedient citizens of the disciplinary techniques of the state.

We should not think, however, that idiographic discourses on culture remained consigned to one hundred or two hundred books, destined to be stored in libraries to satisfy the curiosity of a literate elite. Both Giddens and Wallerstein have convincingly shown that knowledge of social life transmitted by those and other discourses was incorporated into the structure of modern societies, in such a manner that people began to see themselves in those images that offered a determinate *type of representations* on culture.[19] The ontological security that guaranteed these representations started generating community identifications, norms, feelings, and a sense of belonging. The rituals, values, images, and mythologies generated by the nation-state were internalized by wide sectors of the population and produced wide identities founded on political projects of collective reach.

The questions that we must tackle now are the following: What happens when the nation-state loses the capacity to agglutinate interests and to create a collective will? What type of epistemological displacement causes idiographic discourses on culture to cease being "reflexive" (Giddens), that is, to stop functioning as representations interiorized by social actors? Once there has been an erosion of the ontological security that representations on national culture offered, what types of identities are generated by the new discourses on world culture? Such questions lead us to the core of the new agendas elaborated by social theory in the times of globalization.

## THE RETURN OF THE REPRESSED: GLOBALIZATION OR THE END OF THE PROJECT OF MODERNITY

We have conceptualized modernity as a series of *practices* oriented toward the rational control of human life. Some of these practices are the institutionalization of the natural and the social sciences, the capitalist organization of the economy, the colonial expansion of Europe, and above all, the juridical-territorial configuration of nation-states. Modernity is a project because the rational control over the contingencies of human life is exercised from a central instance, namely, the nation-state.

In this order of ideas, the following question arises: To what do we refer when we speak of the *final* project of modernity? Our response is that modernity ceases to be operative as a project insofar as the social sphere begins to be configured by instances that escape the control of the nation-state. In other words, the project of modernity comes to an end when the nation-state loses the capacity to organize the social and material lives of persons.[20] It is, then, that we can properly speak of globalization.

Of course, we should understand globalization not as the beginning of a new (postmodern) epoch of human history but rather as the unforeseen result of the tensions that were developing within the modern project itself. All the elements that characterize what we call today globalization were part of the dynamics that characterized modern societies from the nineteenth century onward. The change stems from the fact that those elements have lost their "Archimedean point"; that is, they are no longer coordinated with each other by means of a central category, namely, the nation-state, and, therefore, no longer constitute a project. It is in this sense that we can speak of the end of modernity or, if you prefer, we can now speak of a postmodern cultural condition. To be precise, we may say that the concept of globalization makes reference to the *dispersion* of those practices of control that were before coordinated by the nation-state.

Thus, for example, while modern capitalism ensures the material reproduction of society by means of labor and fiscal policies controlled by the state, global capitalism undermines the foundations of national economies; this unleashes a process in which economic growth ends up eroding the social relations of labor.[21] In fact, multinational enterprises withdraw from the framework of the nation-state and abandon any commitment to the social policies of their countries of origin. Companies such as Mercedes-Benz and Volkswagen, to give only two examples, have moved their factories to Latin American countries, where labor is cheaper and, in this way, have avoided the taxes that they would otherwise owe to the German state, not to mention that they also pay ridiculously low subsidies to the host countries.

As a consequence, the following contradiction develops: While sovereignty in fiscal matters is linked to the modern concept of state control within a concrete territory, multinational enterprises are linked to communication networks, market relations, and forms of life that completely transcend the territorial frontiers of the nation-state. In this way, the gigantic economic benefits of these enterprises stop circulating through the social network of the nation-state, which observes with impotence the scandalous increment in unemployment rates. The gap between rich and poor widens uncontrollably because there is no longer a common framework capable of implementing redistribution policies. We are witnessing, then, what Lash and Urry called "disorganized capitalism," in which the hegemony of economic power is detached from the nation-state and becomes fragmented in a plurality of deterritorialized agents.[22]

The ontological insecurity that this situation produces is reinforced by the loss of trust in the capacity to maintain control through knowledge. As we have seen, that trust had been one of the pillars of the modern project. The thinkers of the enlightenment and their followers had believed that the greater their accumulated knowledge about nature and society was, the greater their capacity for controlling the contingencies of social life would be. In fact, they believed that an increase in this type of control was the key to the attainment of human emancipation and happiness: The greater the state's competence to transform history in accordance with its interests, the greater the possibilities for realizing the ideals of liberty, equality, and fraternity. What seems evident, however, is that this increase in knowledge, far from eliminating the contingencies of life, has instead produced and increased them. The bewilderment that we experience today does not arise because of lack of knowledge, but rather *because* of knowledge. A clear example of this is the destruction of the ecological environment. The rational exploitation of natural resources continues to be a phenomenon unchained by the nation-states' deployment of their technical-industrial capacities, in their mad dash to achieve progress and development; however, the *consequences* of this deployment—for instance, the global warming of the atmosphere—are running completely out of our control. Teleological rationality, oriented by the state toward the diminution of risks and the calculation of advantages, has generated a situation of global incalculability and generalized risk. The logic of order and control has led to chaos and uncertainty, by virtue of its own dynamics.[23]

Once the pincers that held together all the modern technologies of social control have been pried open, these technologies scatter and create a situation of incalculability that spreads over all the realms of society. Mechanisms, which were used for order and ontological protection and for the function of which had been defined by the nation-state—such as the bourgeois family, political parties, geographic territorialities, labor unions, civil rights, and the policies for the social redistribution of wealth—burst open.

The nation-state is unable to protect us from a nuclear confrontation, an unexpected "crash" in the stock market, the impoverishment of large sectors of the population, or the global expansion of organized crime. We are being left to the mercy of global influences that we are no longer able to control but that directly affect our identity, our way of seeing the world, and our here and now. Social life becomes more and more plural, decentered, and interdependent, but at the same time more abstract, ambiguous, and unmanageable. The contingencies that the project of modernity set for itself to eliminate have returned with added fury, riding over the very ramparts that modernity had designed to ward them off. We witness a social situation very similar to the one described by Blumemberg in the case of the decadence of the Roman Empire or the end of the great Christian synthesis achieved during the European Middle Ages.

What happens in this context to idiographic discourses on national culture? To the extent that the nation-state loses its capacity to configure social reality, the binding force of the discourses that set out to posit an organic identity between nation, people, and culture also dries up. In Latin America, these discourses were part of the political arsenal of both the political right and the political left well into the 1970s. The former used them as they searched for populist modernization on the basis of import substitution, and the latter used them as they promoted a "resistance to modernity" on the basis of the revolutionary potential of popular culture. Beginning in the 1980s, however, it starts becoming clear that this crusade for the recovery of the values of the people is illusory, since neither the state nor any other instances are capable of controlling that global expansion of information and symbols that the theoreticians of the Frankfurt School called the "cultural industry."

The market breaks with the organizational framework of social reality that had been established by the modern state, and it subjects personal and collective identities to sudden changes in supply and demand. The rapid succession of fashions, the banalization of the sacred, the spectacle of carefree consumerism, and the always-changing production of references to identity, far from provoking a new regimentation and homogenization, generate instead a *multiplication* of the ways people appropriate symbolic goods for themselves.[24] Instead of taxonomization, the cultural industry has favored diversification and decentralization of meaning; meaning has now been transformed into a matter of individual selection and preference. But this implosion of meaning becomes distressing to the extent that nobody can aspire to a totalizing comprehension of reality, which has become, as Baudrillard teaches, *hyperreality.*

The political-cultural ground that allowed nomothetic and idiographic ways of knowing how to understand themselves as taxonomies, that is, as sets of propositions destined to "found" the social world, has cracked open. Once the project of modernity has ended, there also ends the idea of science as *foundation.*

Does this mean, however, that we can no longer think scientifically about the social and the cultural? Have cultural studies succumbed to the temptation of abstract and disciplinary scientism, as some suspect? Neither is the case. Instead, a significant part of contemporary social theory, even the one that is being developed by cultural studies, has not been able to release itself from the paradigms inherited largely from the nineteenth century. Although globalization has made obsolete the category of "society," we still speak of "world society" (Luhmann), the "society of risk" (Beck), "global society" (O. Ianni), and "civil society" (García Canclini). But society is a category that comes from the time when sociology identified the limits of its object of knowledge *("Die gesellschaft")* with those of the territorial state. Also, we speak of globalization as if it were a "system" (Wallerstein), but the processes of social transformation that we are experiencing today cannot be trapped within our eighteenth-century schemata of order and calculability. Finally, we also speak of a "world culture" (R. Ortiz) or "hybrid cultures" (García Canclini)—in contraposition to the type of homogeneous culture dramatized in the nation-state—without noticing that the very concept of culture is rooted, as we saw before, in the teleological historicism characteristic of modernity.

There is no doubt that detaching oneself from the epistemological paradigms inherited by modern social science is not an easy task, for globalization is not a phenomenon that one finds "outside" or "over there," or observable as if it were an object. In fact, what has become problematic is the methodological posture that simultaneously creates subject and object and that in its time was useful for generating a repertory of epistemic rituals and ontological certainties [*seguridades*]. It seems as if the speed with which reality changes has outrun our theoretical categorizations. What is evident, however, is that we need new epistemological frameworks that while renouncing the role of foundational *tribunals* of the social sphere can nevertheless continue to function as scientific discourse. The Portuguese theorist Boaventura de Sousa Santos speaks of a "postmodern social science," capable of representing itself as socially produced and, by the same token, agonistic and contingent. This would be a social science that takes its results to be products of a correlation of forces, a constant negotiation of meaning, and a struggle for the control of meanings.[25]

I think that despite all its categorial limitations, cultural studies have already begun the march toward a social science that thinks of itself as an integral part of the contingencies about which it reflects and not anymore as the epistemological *foundation* of a project called on to control contingency. The invitation that cultural studies extend to us is to think of globalization as a way of thinking about ourselves at those moments of the fugue when memories, the shared imaginary, and small histories appear and disappear, beyond the metaphysics of subjectivity. This seems to be also the challenge that social philosophy and the philosophy of culture face at the dawn of the twenty-first century.

## NOTES

1. See, for example, the exposition on culture set forth by Raymond Williams in his book *Sociología de la cultura* (Barcelona: Paidos, 1994). For the specific case of Latin America, see Nelson García Canclini, *Consumidores y ciudadanos: Conflictos multiculturales de la globalización* (Mexico: Grijalbo, 1995); and J. J. Bruneer, *América Latina: Cultura y modernidad* (Mexico: Grijalbo, 1992).

2. For the case of Latin America, see especially the critiques by John Beverly and Nelly Richard. Cf. John Beverly, "A little azúcar. Una conversación sobre Estudios Culturales," *Estudios* 8 (1996): 79–95; Nelly Richard, *La insubordinación de los signos. Cambio político, transformaciones culturales y poéticas de la crisis* (Santiago de Chile: Editorial Cuarto Propio, 1994).

3. For documentation on this debate, see Eduardo Mendieta and Santiago Castro-Gómez, eds., *Teorías sin disciplina. Latinoamericanismo, poscolonialidad y globalización en debate* (Mexico: Editorial Porrúa, 1998).

4. Cf. Hans Blumenberg, pt. II of *Die Legitimität der Neuzeit* (Frankfurt: Suhrkamp, 1997).

5. This concept of "ontological security" is one of the pillars in the sociology of Max Weber, and it continues to have importance in contemporary social theory. Anthony Giddens shows that the preservation of habits and routines serves as a protective shield against anguish, that is, against the risks that the very task of living carries with it. Even though there are traditions in all human cultures offering a repertory of securities that make the organization and control of social life possible, modernity establishes a *sui generis* type of ontological security that Giddens calls "post-traditional." It is characterized by the fact that basic trust is no longer placed on the certainties that the religious images of the world offer, but rather, on the *knowledge* generated by abstract systems. With the onset of modernity, the framework of action starts being defined by the philosophical presuppositions transmitted by the natural and social sciences, to wit, the perfectibility of man, the certainty of scientific-technical knowledge, the preestablished harmony between theoretical reason and practical reason, etc. Cf. Anthony Giddens, *Modernidad e identidad del yo. El yo y la sociedad en la época contemporánea* (Barcelona: Ediciones Península, 1995).

6. Cf. Francis Bacon, *Novum Organon*, ed. James Spedding, Robert Leslie Ellis, and Douglas Denning Heath (New York: Hurd and Houghton, 1878), nos. 1–33.

7. Cf. Ernest Gellner, *Nations and Nationalism* (Oxford: Blackwell, 1983).

8. Cf. Immanuel Wallerstein, *Unthinking Social Science: The Limits of Nineteenth-Century Paradigms* (London: Polity Press, 1991), 20.

9. Nonetheless, I do not share the thesis by the first Foucault that the ways of knowing [*saberes*] that I call here "idiographic" arise from the crisis of the *mathesis* configured by the classical *episteme*, in which nomothetic knowledge would have its *locus*. Rather, I think that both idiographic and nomothetic "knowledges" are generated from the *same* field of knowledge-power, which the second Foucault identifies as the field of "governmentality." Cf. Michel Foucault, chap. 7, in *The Order of Things: An Archeology of the Human Sciences* (New York: Vintage Books, 1973); and Michel Foucault, *La verdad y las formas jurídicas*, translated from Portuguese by Enrique Lynch (Barcelona: Gedisa, 1991). [*La verdad y las formas jurídicas* brings together the five lectures given by Foucault in 1973 at the Universidad Católica de Río de Janeiro in Brazil—*Ed.*]

10. Cf. Reinhart Koselleck, "Volk, Nation, Nationalismus, Masse," in *Geschichtliche Grundbegriffe: Historisches Lexikon zur Politisch-sozialen Sprache in Deutschland*, ed. Otto Brunner, Werner Conze, and Reinhart Loseller, vol. 7 (Stuttgart: Cotta, 1992), 147.

11. Johann Gottfried von Herder, *Ideas para una filosofía de la historia de la humanidad* (Buenos Aires: Losada, 1952), 279–80 [Spanish translation of *Ideen zur Philosophie der Geschichte der Menschheit* (Riga: Johann Friedrich Hartknoch, 1784–1791); *Outlines of a Philosophy of the History of Man*, English trans. T. Churchill (New York: Bergman Publishers, 1966)].

12. Herder, *Ideas para una filosofía de la historia de la humanidad*, 255–56, 283–84. According to Herder, Prussia is, as Rome, a state incapable of constituting itself as a nation, and the only destiny for which it is perfect is bureaucracy and military machinery. This is one of the causes of the estrangement between Herder and his teacher Kant.

13. Herder, *Ideas para una filosofía de la historia de la humanidad*, 285–86.

14. Herder, *Ideas para una filosofía de la historia de la humanidad*, 273. For Fichte also, the loss of the maternal language implies necessarily an estrangement from one's cultural roots and, together with it, the loss of freedom. Cf. Johann Gottlieb Fichte, *Addresses to the German Nation*, trans. R. F. Jones and G. H. Turnbull (Westport, Conn.: Greenwood Press, 1979), Addresses 6 and 7.

15. George Wilhelm Friedrich Hegel, *The Philosophy of History*, trans. J. Sibree (New York: Dover, 1956), 17–19.

16. Hegel, *The Philosophy of History*, 17–25, 45.

17. Hegel, *The Philosophy of History*, 50.

18. One should remember that Herder interprets his philosophy as a "system of history," as he asserts it in the eight books of his *Idees*: "The philosopher of history cannot base himself on an abstraction, but only on history; and, if he does not order the countless isolated facts under a common point of view, he is in danger of coming up with incorrect results" (Herder, *Ideas para una filosofía de la historia de la humanidad*, 219). As for Hegel, he thinks that, unlike historiography, the philosophy of history is a universal philosophical science, the point of view of which is not the empirical description of isolated events, but rather the conceptualization of the universal spirit, which is the soul that directs the historical process (Hegel, *The Philosophy of History*, 103–10).

19. I have dealt more extensively with this theme in the following articles of mine: "Los vecindarios de la ciudad letrada. Variaciones filosóficas sobre un tema de Angel Rama," in *Angel Rama y los estudios latinoamericanos*, ed. M. Moraña (Pittsburgh: Uni-

versity of Pittsburgh Press, 1997), 123–33; and "Latinoamericanismo, Modernidad, Globalización," *Cuadernos Americanos* 67 (1998).

20. Cf. Martin Albrow, *Abschied vom Nationalstaat. Staat und Gesellschaft im Globalen Zeitalter* (Frankfurt: Suhrkamp, 1998), 87 ff.

21. Ulrich Beck, *¿Qué es la globalización? Falacias del globalismo, respuestas a la globalización* (Barcelona: Paidos, 1998).

22. Scott Lash and John Urry, chap. 11, in *Economies of Sign and Space* (London: Sage Publications, 1994)

23. Ulrich Beck, *Risikigessellschaft. Auf dem Weg in eine andere Moderne* (Frankfurt: Suhrkamp, 1986).

24. Cf. J. Martín-Barbero, *De los medios a las mediaciones. Comunicación, cultura y hegemonía* (Barcelona: Gustavo Gili Ediciones, 1991).

25. Cf. Boaventura de Sousa Santos, *De la mano de Alicia. Lo social y lo político en la posmodernidad* (Santafé de Bogotá: Ediciones Uniandes, 1998).

# 2

# The Ethics of Globalization and
# the Globalization of Ethics

*Eduardo Mendieta*

In this chapter, I will begin by offering a typology of globalization theories. Then
I will articulate some reasons why globalization should be taken neither as the latest intellectual fashion of think-tank technocrats and ideologues of rogue states
nor as the latest "post" that comes after postmodernism. Rather, I will argue that
globalization is and should be a dignified and legitimate object of philosophical
reflection. Third, I will offer some elements for the elaboration of a phenomenology of globalization. In the fourth section of this chapter, I will turn to the relationship between globalization and ethics and more precisely to the challenges
that the former entails for the latter.

## TYPOLOGY OF GLOBALIZATION THEORIES

Prima facie, it appears that the discourses about globalization have assumed very
polarized positions, vis-à-vis all the possible ways in which one may approach
the issue: its causes, its chronology, its scope and depth, its consequences, even
its contested novelty. In other words, some argue that globalization was and has
been catalyzed by technology; others that it was augured by cultural elements
which coalesced earlier than the material manifestations of the global system;
others argue that, in fact, globalization is but the latest mutation of capitalism.
Similarly, some argue that globalization, in as much as it has been discernable,
first began in the 1970s; some instead pick the 1980s as the chronological marker;
others argue that it was the dropping of the atom bomb that began it all; and still
others argue that a sense of global consciousness was first made evident when

people saw the earth from the moon. In the same vein, many argue that globalization is just the richer getting richer by being better interconnected and the poorer getting poorer by being systematically excluded from systems of information production and retrieval. To this extent, globalization is just an ideology of the wealthy that allows them to excuse their willful ignorance of those they cannot see because their communication networks make them blind and deaf to the destitute many. Yet, others argue that globalization means that an economic slump here or there sends ripples across the net of interconnected financial markets and that the collapse of an ecosystem in Amazonia sends shock waves across the entire planetary ecosystem. At the same time, some argue that globalization is an imperative of human history, and to that extent, it is both uncircumventable and inevitable. If it turns out to be a tragedy, then it is no less tragic than the rise and fall of nations and political systems. In opposition, some think that some political and economic measures can be implemented that cannot just halt but reverse the processes of globalization. On another level, some are sanguine enough to suggest that, in fact, globalization is not entirely new, or new at all. From this perspective, then, globalization is merely a self-serving name for old forms of oppression made more sophisticated, and petrified ideas about privilege and injustice are given a postmodern and ultramodern veneer. Some others wonder about the relationship between modernity and postmodernity on the one hand, and postcoloniality and globalization on the other.

This theoretical pandemonium and quantitative proliferation of data has spawned massive scholarly production on globalization. These analyses of globalization have reached such high levels of differentiation and even specialization that we probably have reached the stage in which we need to venture a typology of theories of globalization.[1]

Theories of globalization can be divided into three types in accordance with their (1) diffusionism or integrationism; (2) theoretical reflexivity; (3) degree to which they are able to offer insights into the autonomy of social subsystems without creating a hierarchy or teleological model that may be merely a function of unanalyzed theoretical biases; and (4) degree of empirical concreteness and theoretical complexity. The more empirically detailed and textured a theory of globalization is, the more it tends to emphasize the particular process or structure it analyzes.

The three types of globalization theories are as follows:

## Monometastructural

These are theories of globalization that explain the rise of globalization in terms of the expansion of one societal subsystem. In other words, these theories see world integration as having been catalyzed by the world expansion of one particular subsystem of social interaction. Every other subsystem develops and reconfigures under the pressure of the dominant globalizing subsystem. So the political subsystem develops and globalizes under the pressure of the economic or cultural. Religion and culture in general, similarly, are seen as undergoing transformation under the modernizing pressures of the economy or the globalization of certain modes of economic relations. To this extent, what we have is less an integrationist perspective that wants to think the new global order and more a diffusionist perspective that sees globalization as the logical consequence of the diffusion of a particular modernizing agent. In this sense, most of these theories of globalization are really just other versions of theories of modernity, that is, of the expansion of modernity. For these theories, globalization is just modernity pursued at a more accelerated pace. The difference between globalization and modernity is one of quantity and not of kind or type. To this extent, they perpetuate the ethnocentrism and Eurocentrism of most of Western social theory. The critical options before these processes of catalyzation and accelerated modernity are of two kinds: euphoric celebration and cynical rejection. The possibility for radical critique is undermined by the ineluctability with which the process is thought to develop. Under this rubric, we can gather the theories of Amin, Wallerstein, Frank, Barber, Meyers, Barnet, and Cavanagh.[2]

## Matrix Rearrangement and Differentiation

Under this rubric fall those theories of globalization that do not depart from the idea of the catalyzing function of one particular social subsystem, nor do they depart from the idea that globalization ought to be understood in terms of subsystems that enter into new quantitative levels of deployment and differentiation. Instead, globalization is seen as a radically new order in which the fundamental building blocks of social interaction enter into radically new relations, sometimes mediated by new social subsystems that in many ways give entirely new meanings to these building blocks. These theories, in fact, are articulated at higher levels of generality and abstractness. Instead of trying to think of world societies from the standpoint of a series of sometimes unique Western social structures and processes, these types of theories try to circumvent such ethnocentrism by attempting to reach a different level of abstraction. In this case, then, these theories are less about the diffusion of one particular type of social structure or process and more about the conceptualization and visualization of the new social order in terms of an integrationist perspective. These theories therefore take issue with the debates concerning whether globalization is an extension of modernity. In the case of Robertson, for instance, modernity is seen as a consequence of globalization. There is a way in which the ideas of the differential expansion of modernity, the rise of global modernities, or different paths through modernity, already presuppose the idea of a planetary whole. These theories also seem to be motivated by self-consciousness about Eurocentrism and ethnocentrism that would like to challenge the primacy of certain Western structures and modes of social development. Here we would include Arjun Appadurai, Roland Robertson, Bryan S. Turner, Anthony Giddens, and Martin Albrow.[3] With varying degrees, some of these theories are plagued with a lack of clarity and reflection about their own theoretical standpoint. In other words, if the point is not to fall into Eurocentrism and ethnocentrism, why are these categories and not others used? For instance, Robertson works on the givenness of the categories of self and humanity in his theory of the matrix of globalization, while Turner departs from a philosophical-anthropological perspective that takes for granted the idea of the exocentric character of human existence. In both cases, however, such categories are already detritus of globalization, and they are explaining the whole in terms of the parts that are in need of being explained in the first place. A self, and whatever content we assign to this term, is already a function of a global order in which individualities must be discretely determined and differentiated. So the social order called globalization is prior to the self as a unity in the global matrix. One last point about these types of theories of globalization is that they apparently are unable to answer the question, How is the particular theory of globalization being offered, itself reflecting on its own globalization? Or, more precisely, to what extent is a particular theory of globalization itself a necessary perspective on globalization?

## Metatheoretical Reflexivity

Under this rubric I gather those theories of globalization that see the new global order from an integrationist perspective. The global order is different not just in quantity and order but in kind from what has preceded it. This type of theory sees the diffusion or expansion of one subsystem as already a function of a global order. If the economy expands and extends to every corner of the planet, this is because we are already part of a planetary whole, similarly with the cultural and religious realms. Religious revolutions, reformations, and so-called regressive fundamentalisms are not just defensive or counterreactions to the effects of economic globalization. Instead, they are already aspects of a global culture. In the same way, if individuality, particularism, cultural diversity, and in general particularization become relevant and more pressing, it is because they are already part and parcel of a global order in which the new social system calls for such differentiations and distinctions. From this theoretical perspective, then, global modernities are already forms of the world order of a globalized social system. For them, the issue of globalization is not even an empirical issue, it is above all a conceptual and theoretical challenge that requires that we understand not just why a particular system seems to dominate but why such a subsystem is thought to be the agent of globalization at the very moment when we are able to see other subsystems struggling for supremacy. In other words, this type of approach tries to think its object and subject at the same time. In Luhmann's terms, metatheoretical reflexivity requires that we observe the observer. For this reason, this type of theory of globalization is a second order observation, in which we are trying to see ourselves looking at ourselves. These theories begin from the standpoint of theoretical self-reflexivity. This is to be understood as the observing of observers or as an analysis of who is observing what and for which reasons. Put differently, globalization is a way in which society observes itself as an integrated system. From this perspective, namely, of society as a self-observing system, society itself can no longer conceive itself as an aggregation of somewhat interrelated parts and elements, such as humans, selves, societies, cultures, and so forth. Were this to be the goal, the self-description and self-observation of society would become paradoxical and incomprehensible.[4] Consequently, to think globalization requires that we think the unity of society in different terms. In fact, we must think society anew. Under this rubric, therefore, I gather the theories proposed by systems theorists, like Niklas Luhmann,[5] Richard Münch, and Jürgen Habermas.[6]

## GLOBALIZATION AS A PHILOSOPHICAL PROBLEM

Out of the cacophony of positions on globalization and out of the typology just delineated above, I would like to highlight two central aspects. First, that sociology, media studies, political theory, economic theory, historical studies, in fact, the social sciences in general have already contributed extensive amounts of work on the topic; and, second, that philosophy's absence in these discussions is notorious. What would a philosophical position on globalization look like? Can philosophy take globalization seriously as a philosopheme, as a philosophical theme of reflection? Has philosophy anything to add to the discussions that have been led by the social sciences over the last two decades?

Let me begin answering some of these questions by challenging their assumptions. In fact, philosophy is not a latecomer to the debate on globalization. Moreover, there is a way in which the argument can be made that the question of globalization as an epochal marker, as a new state of consciousness, and as a new self-awareness of humanity, was inaugurated, articulated for the first time by philosophers. What has subsequently happened is that the social sciences picked up the philosophical project, and then secularized it and scienticized it. Let me mention briefly the names of some philosophers who I think did this kind of work: Karl Jaspers, Martin Heidegger, Ortega y Gasset, José Gaos, Darcy Ribeiro, Arnold Toynbee, Enrique Dussel, Paul Ricoeur, Niklas Luhmann, Karl-Otto Apel, Hans Jonas, Hans Küng, and more recently, Gilles Deleuze, Felix Guattari, and Jacques Derrida. Allow me to illustrate by talking about some of these figures. Karl Jaspers wrote in 1949, shortly after World War II, and shortly after having written the important book *The Question of German Guilt*, a prescient book *The Origin and Goal of History* (1953 translation). In this book, Jaspers develops his ideas about the Axial Age, that period in which universal consciousness first developed across the ancient cultures. In this book, Jaspers writes, "Today, for the first time, there is a real unity of mankind which consists in the fact that nothing essential can happen anywhere that does not concern all."[7] In this book, however, Jaspers sought to compare those incredible conceptual, epistemological, spiritual, and structural breakthroughs of humanity during the height of the empires of antiquity, with the new radical metamorphosis of humanity during the middle of the twentieth century. Jaspers finds that, while the new Axial Age of the twentieth century is more universal than the first Axial Age because it is planetary in its scope and it is taking place with a "consciousness of universality," it is nonetheless different from the first Axial Age in that from the standpoint of inwardness, that is, from the angle of the moral growth of humanity, we are faced with emptiness, a great hollowness, and lack of spiritual creativity. Jaspers went on to write more on this new global consciousness, this new thinking, and with a great sense of urgency. See for instance his book on the Atom Bomb.

Martin Heidegger also contributed to an incipient philosophy of globalization when he wrote in 1938 "The Age of the World Picture," in which he seeks to characterize the modern age in terms of its planetary dominion, which it exercises primarily through technology. In fact, Heidegger suggests that to reflect on the modern age means to ask about its world picture *(Weltbild)*, and he tellingly suggests that every epoch has its own world picture. In the case of the modern age, its *Weltbild* is that of the picture itself. This means, proximally, that for the modern age the world is a totality for which humans are ready; they make themselves into objects while objectifying the world. Two totalities are juxtaposed. Heidegger writes:

> Hence world picture, when understood essentially, does not mean a picture of the world but the world conceived and grasped as picture. What is, in its entirety, is now taken in such a way that it first is in being, and only is in being to the extent that it is set up by man, who represents and sets forth. . . . The Being of whatever is, is sought and found in the representedness of the latter.[8]

José Gaos, one of Ortega y Gasset's most famous disciples, the translator of Heidegger into Spanish, as well as the father of the historicist school of philosophers in Mexico, also contributed to a theory of globalization, along Heideggerian lines, when he sought to explain the *History of Our Idea of the World (La Historia de nuestra idea del Mundo)*, which was a lecture course he gave in Mexico during the late 1960s. In this course, Gaos discusses the rise of a planetary and universalist consciousness along the lines of hermeneutical philosophy. This course was to be very influential in the development of Latin Americanism, which is most easily identifiable with Leopoldo Zea.

Enrique Dussel, an Argentine philosopher exiled in Mexico during the 1970s, wrote in the late 1960s a series of lectures of the place and meaning of Latin America in world history. Curiously, however, while he began by using Heideggerian concepts, he soon discovered Levinas, which led him to talk about totality and exteriority. It is not frequently known that liberation philosophy, one of Latin America's most original philosophical currents in the twentieth century, is a confrontation among, and synthesis of, dependency theory, Levinasian phenomenology, Ricoeurian hermeneutics, Latin American forms of historicism, and Freirian pedagogy. Nonetheless, already in the 1960s and 1970s, Dussel was developing a discourse about the world, the world system, the totality, and its periphery. Indeed, about a quarter of his massive *An Ethics of Liberation* from 1998 is devoted to a philosophical analysis of world totalities and their corresponding ethical outlooks. In the process, he develops an ethical analysis and critique of globalization.

I wish I had the time to write about Niklas Luhmann's fascinating work on globalization, or what he calls World Society, *Weltgesellschaft*, or to write about Deleuze and Guattari's ideas about geophilosophy in their book *What is Philosophy?*, but I will not strain you any further with this litany of names and encyclopedia entries on philosophers. I think that I have shown how there is a very solid and worthy tradition of philosophers who have thought about globalization and how their work can be incorporated and reclaimed for future work on the idea. Furthermore, I think that I have insinuated how and in which ways these works can contribute to the debates about the character or nature of this new epoch. I would like now to strengthen my case for a philosophical approach to globalization by illustrating how a phenomenology of globalization might proceed.

## TOWARD A PHENOMENOLOGY OF GLOBALIZATION

Globalization is the umbrella name for a series of processes. Generally, globalization is seen as economic, political, cultural, religious, and even ecological processes, in which sometimes one or a combination of some of them guides the others. At this level of abstraction, however, we are not able to capture the depth and extent of what is characterized as the "global condition." We need to move to a lower level of concreteness and specificity. With this in mind, I will describe what I take to be four factors, or processes, that allow us points of entry into a phenomenology of globalization. They are, first, what I call the megaurbanization and unprecedented demographic expansion and stabilization of humanity; second, the institutionalization of the continuous revolutionizing of the means of production; third, the shrinking of the world through the collapse or compression of space-time; and fourth, the permeation of technology and science into every level of social interaction. Now, let me discuss each one briefly.

First, one of the most important, although often overlooked, aspects of contemporary humanity is that it has ceased to be predominantly rural and that, at the same time, in comparison to other periods in the history of humankind, humanity has reached the most pronounced growth with an unprecedented rate of the prolongation of life spans. More people are being born, while fewer people are dying of natural causes. Demographics and urbanization, and population growth and megacities—these are two related processes with unimaginable consequences. Now when we actually look at where most of the megaurbanization and population growth are taking place, we will note that it is in what is generally known as the Third World. Most megacities in the twenty-first century will be in India, the Far East, and Latin America. At the same time, India, China, and parts of Latin America are becoming some of the most densely populated areas of the globe. In contrast, there are some countries in Europe that have actually experienced negative population growth: Germany, Norway, Switzerland, and France. While most of the poor world is growing more populated, younger, and poorer, the rich world is growing older, less populated, and richer. Oligarchical and finance capitalism is turning into the gerontocracy of the Whites in the fortress of the North Atlantic corridor.

Second, one does not have to be a Marxist to recognize that axial periods in the history of humanity have gravitated around revolutions in the modes of production, in the actual techniques for the production and reproduction of society. First there was fire, then agriculture, then a long hiatus, then the steam engine, and more recently, engines using fossil fuels and nuclear energy. The long eighteenth and nineteenth centuries and the prolonged reign of industrial capitalism could be explained in terms of the stability of the modes of energy production and transformation mechanisms and techniques. But one of the distinctive characteristics of contemporary societies is that the production of social wealth and the reproduction of society in general have become uncoupled from material production. In other words, we have become what Daniel Bell called the postindustrial society and, more to the point, what Castells calls the information society. We have become a society in which the means for the production of society and social wealth are continuously revolutionized through continuous technological and scientific innovation. Production is not separated from technological innovation; in fact, production has become the production of innovation. This is most clear in what is called the information economy, where wealth and survival are directly proportional to being ahead or at the vanguard of the newest and latest technology.

Third, the size of the world, and the cosmos in general, is determined by the time it takes to transverse any two points in it. Strangeness and familiarity are directly proportional to distance, be it temporal or spatial. The farther, temporally and spatially, someone or something is, the stranger, or more alien, something or someone is. Conversely, the closer, both temporally and spatially, someone or something is, the more familiar something or someone is. Presence, to put it in Heideggerian terms, is a function of spatio-temporal distantiation. For a long time, the partial unsurveyability and opaqueness of the world was determined by the time and space that conditioned presencing. Today when we can have almost instantaneous communication across the planet and with outer space—remember the excitement of receiving photos from Mars and having them broadcast across the world instantaneously—the sense of the world as being one place in one instant has led to the collapse of the notion of a foreign and distant world or worlds. The world has become a place of simultaneity and almost immediate presencing. As long as space and time were distended, presence could be delayed or maintained by artificial means. Presence, in fact, is a matter of deferring or distancing. Heterogeneity and homogeneity could be maintained fairly distinctly through the idea that the other could be distanced spatially and temporally. Today, however, after the collapse of space–time, after their compression, after their so-called elimination, heterogeneity and homogeneity have become difficult to disaggregate. Alterity, as well as sameness, can no longer be thought of in terms of presencing or its other, absence. The shrinking of the world has meant that the temporal continuum of the human experience has now become shot with the simultaneity of the noncontemporaneous (to echo Ernst Bloch).

Fourth, technology inundates every aspect of social life. This is perhaps the very first time in the history of humanity when technology has come to mediate every aspect of social existence. Technology, in other words, has become capillary to the social body. This is related to what I call the institutionalization of the revolutionizing of the means of production, but it also has to do with the transformation of our relationships to both our bodies and nature. On the one hand, we can talk longer about the discernable distinction between nature and society, for the reaches of technological intervention and mediation determine both. The most extreme picture of this codetermination of nature and society through the umbilical cord of technology is provided by the twin technologies of nanomechanics and genetic engineering. On the other hand, we can no longer talk about the "natural human being," for we have already become so much like our technological innovations and alternations of what was given to us by our human history that it is hard to say what is nature and what is the trace of human history. Let me be a bit colorful, although not glib or flippant; the struggle is no longer between something like unmodified natural humanity and diabolical cyborg creatures. The struggle is rather between those that have been left untouched by technology and those that are their technology. It is not that we should and can resist the Borg, but that we have been and are Borg.

These processes and transformations of human society, the world, our sense of what is natural, and our relationship to time and space have resulted in at least the following three challenges: first, the detranscendentalization of otherness; second, the acceleration of history and the concomitant question of the plasticity of tradition; and third, the foregrounding of the task of developing a political economy of knowledge. I will discuss theses challenges briefly. The unprecedented concentration of people in megacities, as well as the permeation of the means of communication and the attendant transformation of cognitive orientation of urban dwellers toward either tolerance or disregard for otherness, has meant that otherness is routinized. I take it that one of the positive aspects of urbanization is precisely the level of acceptance and management of otherness. In the city, in other words, alterity is routinized and made into an everyday event and aspect. This results in what I like to call the "detranscendentalization" of alterity. Alterity is no longer metaphysical, but incidental, a fact of the human condition in cities. Everyone is a stranger in the city; however, strangers are made, not born or discovered. I think this is a major conceptual reorientation for humanity. I think that most of the twentieth-century philosophy has been trying to come to terms with the question of the other precisely because we can no longer conceptualize otherness as metaphysical (as either ontological, religious, racial, or sexual otherness . . . all these states of otherness are social, and not immutable or metaphysical).

The perpetual revolutionizing of the means of production and of the consequent informatization of society, along with the collapse of space and time—or rather their compression—has resulted in what I would like to call the detraditionalization and retraditionalization of human time. Another way of putting it would be to say that traditions have become plastic, that is, malleable. Tradition, namely, that which gave coherence and identity to communities' experiences across time, has become itself subject to human manipulation. Tradition is that which could not be tampered with, but the fact that presence has become almost simultaneous and that heterogeneity and homogeneity have become difficult to distinguish due to the introjection of the noncontemporaneous into contemporaneity has made tradition as fluid as any other temporal region of the human experience. The insight could also be articulated in the philosophical language of nineteenth-century historicism, and thus we could say that historicity itself has been historicized. Our experience of time has itself become available for temporal tampering and manipulation.

Finally, and this is the perhaps the least obtuse point of my exposition, given the depth of the intervention of technology in our lives, the extent of our dependence on it, the unimaginable adverse, as well as positive and benign, effects of technological innovations and transformations, more than ever, it has become necessary to open up the sciences to deliberate deliberation. Also, given that so much of the future of humanity hangs on continuous technological and scientific innovations and the degree to which these are made available to all humans, it has become imperative that we develop a critique of the political economy of knowledge. The most extreme case that illustrates the imperative character of this critique is what Vandana Shiva has called biopiracy, but less extreme cases are, for instance, the claims of African countries before the World Trade Organization for deregulation of certain AIDS drugs for production and sale in Africa. Given that the twenty-first century is going to be the biotech century and that genetic engineering as well as nanomechanics can have such a profound impact on societies, just as nuclear weapons had on human society during the twentieth century, it is imperative that we put the human genome as well as the genotypes and gene maps of all plants in public domain. Oppenheimer's idea of public disclosure of nuclear secrets is perhaps yet to have its day, but maybe now it will in the next millennium, with respect to the information of life and the structure of matter.

The ethical questions already insinuate themselves in a pressing way, so let us turn to the fourth and final part of the chapter.

## ETHICS AND GLOBALIZATION

It will be schematic, although I hope neither cryptic nor banal. The new planetary condition of humanity that globalization entails can be and has been approached by ethicists in at least three ways.

First, one of the results of globalization has been the provincializing of the European and/or Western tradition. This has resulted in the imperative that philosophy itself be deprovincialized and de-Europanized. In fact, one can argue that one of the areas where there is most cosmopolitanism is precisely in the area of ethical and moral theory. This new imperative has made it necessary to develop a comparative philosophy, in which different philosophical traditions from different areas of the globe are brought into dialogue about issues like responsibility, duty, respect, dignity, conscience, and so on. Thus, one of the ways in which the ethical challenge of globalization has been met is through a comparative method.[9]

Second, following on the coattails of the comparative philosophy, a series of philosophical positions have developed that seek to elaborate a world ethic, or an ethics for the planetary age. These projects have taken two forms, as far as I can see. One is the *Project Weltethos* line of approach, generally identified with Hans Küng, that calls for a dialogue among the world religions to distill a series of overlapping core ideas for a world ethics.[10] The other line of approach is that which I think can be identified with Karl-Otto Apel, which seeks to derive in a Kantian manner, the most bare and elemental principles to guide a planetary ethics.[11] So one line advocates an overlapping consensus approach, the other an axiomatic and rationalist line that argues that we can discover the principles of a world ethic through transcendental reflections.

Third, sometimes in tandem and sometimes in utter disregard with the just-mentioned approaches, there is a third line of approach that seeks to talk about world ethics in terms of issues. This line focuses on discerning what global moral problems are, why they are global moral problems, and what kinds of attitudes we should opt toward them. This line of approach is more interested in applied moral philosophy than in metaethics or moral theory *qua* philosophical analysis of the possibility of moral systems.

Here one may have to pause and ask about the recent debates in moral theory, namely, the debates between communitarians and universalists or between neo-Aristotelians and neo-Kantians, and whether these debates have attempted to deal with the challenges of globalization to moral theory. For the moment, I would like to say that these debates have been debates internal to Western philosophy; one could even say it is the North Atlantic marketplace of ideas, and their provincial character therefore mars them. At the same time, the questions of globalization, of a new global order, have not been addressed directly by the participants in these debates, notwithstanding the amazing ability of a few national philosophers to project immense global shadows.

I think that the three lines of approach I just delineated have failed to properly develop a sophisticated moral analysis of globalization, although if we were to turn our theoretical gaze toward work in comparative religious ethics and work in comparative religions in general, we might find both substantive work and highly nuanced approaches that can help us deal with these failures in "mainstream" philosophy. Conversely, the way in which globalization challenges the central categories of moral agency have remained underthematized. In light of this, I would like to conclude this chapter by discussing some elements of my own research agenda that seek to remedy these failures.

First and most important, globalization has unleashed a dialectic of, what I would like to call, cosmopolitan reflexivity. By this I understand that all traditions are relativized and made contingent vis-à-vis global history. But as ethical traditions are relativized, their historicity is foregrounded. Simultaneously, traditions are required to look at themselves from the standpoint of other ethical traditions. Not only must we be attentive and tolerant of other traditions, but we must also seek to make sense of our traditions from the standpoint of those with whom we are now in dialogue. In this way, cosmopolitan reflexivity might be another name for a global dialogical hermeneutics in which we try to understand others and ourselves through a dialogue with others in which the other is an equal.

I think that this new methodological demand for cosmopolitan reflexivity on the part of moral theories requires that we engage in what I would call a genealogy of Western moral concepts, which would proceed by way of a marriage of Foucault and Schneewind (and Robert Spaemann), to mention some of my inspirations.

Second, and due to some of the consequences of globalization as they are disclosed by a phenomenological analysis as I have just profiled, we need to turn to an inspection of the conceptual and experiential matrix of moral action. This matrix includes philosophemes such as:

*a.* autonomy
*b.* conscience
*c.* responsibility
*d.* will
*e.* imagination
*f.* dignity
*g.* duty
*h.* reasonableness

As we look at this matrix, we can easily see that this is underwritten, or sustained, by a more elemental matrix. Let me illustrate by focusing on two elements of this more elemental matrix of moral agency:

Autonomy has to do with subjective sovereignty, or deliberate self-legislation. At the center of the sovereignty and self-legislation of the subject is the issue of what is deemed foreign and alien. The content and character of autonomy is directly linked to alterity. This alterity has been not only conceptualized metaphysically as the wholly other, in the case of Levinas, but also

psychoanalytically as the abject other, and so on. Now if one of the consequences of globalization is the transcendentalization and demetaphysicaliza-
tion of alterity and its concomitant routinization and quotidianization, then we
have to rethink the logic of enmity on which a moral agency has been predicated. Here, I am finding Kelly Oliver's recent work on *Witnessing* extremely
important because it seeks to develop an ethics beyond the dialectic of recognition that presupposes the alterization of the other, the abjection of others.[12] I
do not seek to mention Oliver's work gratuitously, but rather because it does
indeed evoke something I had had a glimpse of when I read the work of someone like Dussel, and most recently, the work of Spanish philosopher Reyes
Mate. Dussel argues for an ethics of liberation in which the other remains distinct, which is never assimilable. Mate talks about an ethics of *compassionate
tolerance*, which he paradoxically develops out of Heidegger, Benjamin, and
Agamben. What is common to Oliver, Dussel, and Mate, however, is that they
are arguing out of a global problematic: how to deal with moral responsibility
in an age of such profound suffering, without banalizing and dismissing the
uniqueness and unusurpability of the victim, and without, at the same time,
ceasing to keep present those extremes that mark the limits of morality.

Responsibility has to do with an agent's relationship to temporality. In fact, all
moral agency and consciousness has to do with the temporality of memory and
remembrance and the futurity of promising and fulfilling commitments. At the
heart of the moral agency is our relationship to *Vergangenheit*, what has been,
*was gewesen ist*, and futurity, what is yet to be and to come, *was geworden wird*.
Indeed, the discernability of moral responsibility is related to the temporal stability of moral agents, to what Nietzsche called their calculability.[13] But if one
of the consequences of globalization is the collapse of our modern notions of
temporality, then how must we rethink the notion of responsibility? In fact, we
already have a sense of the kind of consequences that the *deteleoligization* of
temporality can have. We are talking about responsibility for the past and the future, in ways that hitherto we have found unacceptable and even unimaginable.
Related to this transformation of temporality is the shift in moral discourse from
talk of danger to talk of risk.[14] I mentioned this because while *danger* has an in-
eluctable quality that diminishes accountability and culpability, *risk* refers us
back to the foreseeable and forecastable, and thus harkens us back to issues of
collective responsibility.

## NOTES

1. See Ulrich Beck, *Was ist Globalisierung?* (Frankfurt am Main: Suhrkamp, 1997), see
also the wonderful book by Malcolm Waters, *Globalization* (London: Routledge, 1995). See
also, the recently published comprehensive work by David Held et al., *Global Transformations: Politics, Economics, and Culture* (Stanford, Calif.: Stanford University Press, 1999); the
synthesizing Jan Aart Scholte, *Globalization: A Critical Introduction* (New York: St. Martin's

Press, 2000); the readers by David Held and Anthony McGrew, *The Global Transformations Reader: An Introduction to the Globalization Debate* (Cambridge, U.K.: Polity, 2000); Patrick O'Meara, Howard D. Mehlinger, and Matthew Krain, eds., *Globalization and the Challenges of a New Century: A Reader* (Bloomington, Ind.: Indiana University Press, 2000).

2. Samir Amin, *Capitalism in the Age of Globalization: The Management of Contemporary Society* (London: Zed Books, 1996); Benjamin R. Barber, *Jihad vs. McWorld: How Globalism and Tribalism Are Reshaping the World* (New York: Ballantine Books, 1995); Richard J. Barnet and John Cavanagh, *Global Dreams: Imperial Corporations and the New World Order* (New York: Simon & Schuster, 1994); and Richard J. Barnet and J. Cavanagh, "A Globalizing Economy: Some Implications and Consequences" in *Conceptualizing Global History*, ed. B. Mazlish, B. and R. Buultjens (New York: Westview Press, 1993), 153–72. See also the following works by Immanuel Wallerstein: *The Modern World System: Capitalist Agriculture and the Origins of the European World-Economy in the Sixteenth Century* (New York: Academic Press, 1974); *The Capitalist World-Economy* (Cambridge, U.K.: Cambridge University Press, 1979); *The Modern World-System II: Mercantilism and the Consolidation of the European World-Economy 1600–1750* (New York: Academic Press, 1980); *Unthinking Social Science: The Limits of Nineteenth-Century Paradigms* (Cambridge, U.K.: Polity Press, 1991); *Geopolitics and the Geoculture: Essays on the Changing World-System* (Cambridge: Cambridge University Press, 1991); and *After Liberalism* (New York: The New Press, 1995).

3. Arjun Appadurai, *Modernity at Large: Cultural Dimensions of Globalization* (Minneapolis: University of Minnesota Press, 1996); Roland Robertson, *Globalization: Social Theory and Global Culture* (London: Sage, 1992); Bryan S. Turner, *Religion and Social Theory*, 2d ed. (London: Sage, 1991 [1983]), and Bryan S. Turner, *Orientalism, Postmodernism & Globalism* (London: Routledge, 1994).

4. See Niklas Luhmann, "Deconstruction as Second-Order Observing," *New Literary History*, 24 (1993), 763–82, especially 774. See also Niklas Luhmann, "The Two Sociologies and the Theory of Society," *Thesis Eleven*, 43: 28–47; and "The Paradox of Observing Systems," *Cultural Critique*, 31 (fall 1995): 37–55.

5. Luhmann has been dealing with the concept of the global society at least since the early 1970s. For theoretical reasons, it stands at the center of his work. See these works by Luhmann: Niklas Luhmann, "Die Weltgesellschaft," *Archiv für Rechts-und Sozialphilosphie*, 57: 1–15. *Soziologische Aufklärung 2: Aufsätze zur Theorie der Gesellschaft* (Opladen: Westdeutscher Verlag, 1975); *The Differentiation of Society*, trans. Stephen Homes and Charles Larmore (New York: Columbia University Press, 1982); *Essays on Self-Reference* (New York: Columbia University Press, 1990); *Die Gesellschaft der Gesellschaft*, 2 vols. (Frankfurt am Main: Suhrkamp Verlag, 1997). See the recent translation of Luhmann's important work *Observations on Modernity*, trans. William Whobrey (Stanford, Calif.: Stanford University Press, 1998).

6. See Richard Münch, Sociological Theory, 3 vols. (Chicago: Nelson-Hall Publishers, 1994); Richard Münch, *Globalen Dynamic, lokale Lebenswelten: Der schwierige Weg in die Weltgesellschaft* (Frankfurt am Main: Suhrkamp Verlag, 1998); Jürgen Habermas, *The Postnational Constellation: Political ssays*, trans. Max Pensky (Cambridge, Mass.: MIT Press, 2001).

7. Karl Jaspers, *The Origin and Goal of History*, trans. Michael Bullock (New Haven, Conn.: Yale University Press, 1953), 139.

8. Martin Heidegger, *The Question Concerning Technology and Other Essays*, trans. William Lovitt (New York: Harper Torchbooks, 1977), 129–30.

9. See Sumner B. Twiss and Bruce Grelle, eds., *Explorations in Global Ethics: Comparative Religious Ethics & Interreligious Dialogue* (Boulder, Colo.: Westview Press, 2000).

10. Hans Küng, *Global Responsibility: In Search of a New World Ethic* (New York: Crossroad, 1991) and Hans Küng, ed., *Yes to a Global Ethics* (New York: Continuum, 1996); see also the critical volume by Gerd Neuhaus, *Kein Welfrieden ohne christiliche Absolutheitsanspruch* (Freiburg: Herder, 1999).

11. See Karl-Otto Apel, *Diskurs und Vertanwortung: Das problem des Uebergangs zur postkonventionellen Moral* (Frankfurt: Suhrkamp, 1988) and, most recently, Karl-Otto Apel, Vittorio Hösle, and Roland Simon-Schaefer, *Globalisierung: Heausforderung für die Philosophie* (Bamberg: Universitäts-Verlag, 1998).

12. Kelly Oliver, *Witnessing: Beyond Recognition* (Minneapolis: University of Minnesota Press, 2001).

13. Friedrich Nietzsche, *On the Genealogy of Morals*, trans. Walter Kaufmann (New York: Vintage Books), 58.

14. See Niklas Luhmann, *Risk: A Sociological Theory*, trans. Rhodes Barrett (New York: Aldine de Gruyter, 1993), especially chap. 1. See also Ulrich Beck, *Risk Society: Towards a New Modernity*, trans. Mark Ritter (London: Sage Publications, 1992).

# 3

# Transnationalization, the State, and Political Power

*Rafael Cervantes Martínez, Felipe Gil Chamizo,*
*Roberto Regalado Álvarez, Rubén Zardoya Loureda*
*(Translated by Mario Sáenz)*

Rulers of developed and underdeveloped countries, government and party lead-ers, representatives of transnational monopolies, the authorities of supranational institutions, small and middle businesspersons, intellectuals, and even represen-tatives of political currents considered to be on the left express "a great preoccu-pation for the future of democracy," and they issue diagnoses that oscillate be-tween the verification of a "profound and broad crisis in politics as a human activity" and references to a "mere disenchantment by citizens with the way of doing politics." In a detailed and fragmentary way, some of these diagnoses get close to the objective problems of contemporary capitalist society, such as the "decline of the electoral powers of the state and the strengthening of the so-called factual powers," the "strong power of concentration of the productive processes," the "progressive diminution of state activities and resources," the "weakening of traditional popular organizations," the "decisions that are not taken in the elec-toral institutions over which citizens may exercise some influence by means of the vote," the "conditions established by the World Bank and the International Monetary Fund," the "recent changes in the distribution of economic and politi-cal power, and their anti-democratic consequences," the "increasing vulnerability of the Latin American economies in the face of the behavior of financial markets, and the political instability that it brings."[1]

In the face of the worsening economic, political, and social crisis, imperialist governments, as well as those of dependent countries; institutions of the system of the United Nations, such as the PNUD and UNESCO; thinktanks of the con-servative, liberal, Christian Democratic, and Social Democratic internationals; and *ad hoc* groups, such as the Montevideo Circle, zealously look for formulas of *governance*—that inaccessible omega point of domination by monopoly transnational capital—that is, for techniques and decrees capable of avoiding the explosion of the economic, political, and social contradictions that the imperialist process of concentration and transnationalization of wealth and political power carries with it. In other words, what is looked for is a way to guarantee the necessary political conditions for the development of the transnational process of concentration of wealth and power at the expense of the oppression—that is, the exploitation and marginalization—of most of humanity.

The formulas for governance, which have flooded the market during the past few years, inundated the book markets and absorbed the attention of multiple international forums, appeared during the 1960s as a response to the erosion experienced by imperialist power.[2] It is not coincidental that the basic "great design" which serves as an unimpeachable pattern for its practical prescriptions becomes the fruit of the works done during the 1970s by the Trilateral Commission—representing the ideology of the "global corporations" of the United States, Europe, and Japan—dismayed, as it was, by the boom since the prior decade of social protests, the demands for a New International Economic Order, and the national liberation movements of the Third World. Nevertheless, although conservatism is the current of political thought most inclined to study the functioning of the system of domination in "democratic societies," liberalism, Christian Democracy, and Social Democracy, preoccupied in their own way in the maintenance of the status quo, have also assumed the theme as their own.

The fundamental ideological terms of theories of governance are *legitimacy* (achieved by the governing political party through free and democratic elections) and *efficiency* (derived from a government administration that satisfies the interests of the citizens). Their creed is articulated around the cult of the *political form* (so-called representative democracy: free elections, multipartyism, freedom of expression and association, etc.) devoid of *real content* (i.e., of an effective capacity to decide on fundamental issues of political, economic, and social character).[3] Their economic, political, and ideological complement is *neoliberalism,* despite the fact that recently its own promoters and patrons have begun to treat it as their bastard child. If neoliberalism promotes the concentration and transnationalization of political power, as well as the fragmentation and dispersion of all dominated social classes and sectors by the aristocracy of world finance, the dominant theories of governance construct the political paradigm that legitimizes the appearance of democracy in an increasingly antidemocratic state organization.[4] Also, they provide the recipes for the goals that are to guarantee "quality control in politics" [*sic*].[5] Theories of governance and neoliberal doctrine share the same origins and purpose: they constitute organic moments of the deepening rift between real power and the political mediations of the bourgeois state, even though diverse political currents of the center-left intend in a rhetorical and utopian manner to build a nonneoliberal and even antineoliberal project of "democratic governance" within the framework of capitalism. The theoretical weakness and the conscious or unconscious apologetic character inherent in theories of governance are revealed when one understands that their objective is to trace a schema of global domination that guarantees the subordination of oppressed social classes and sectors. These are at the margins of the socioeconomic contradictions generated by the process of the reproduction of transnational capital; that is, by means of the application of projects of democratic governance and models of social control capable of neutralizing the political effects of the socioeconomic crisis, they seek to facilitate the process of concentration and transnationalization of capital that constitutes the objective foundation of the so-called crisis of governance in which all the nation-states are immersed, especially those of the underdeveloped world.

If we begin with the assumption that political power in bourgeois society constitutes the form *par excellence* in which the force of capital manifests itself, it becomes evident that the scientific understanding of *political transnationalization* is possible only if it is conceived at the decisive moment in the deployment of an *integral metamorphosis* in the relations of power; these are linked to a *new historical form* in which the economic reproduction of imperialism is realized. In the course of this metamorphosis, accelerated by the collapse of the Soviet Union and the European socialist bloc, the specific features of an emerging sector of the finance bourgeoisie and of new mechanisms of domination and subordination begin to take shape. The fundamental components of those mechanisms are the nation-states themselves and the supranational institutions that represent and defend the interests of imperialism.

The dominant social force in contemporary capitalist society is the *transnational finance oligarchy*.[6] It is the bourgeoisie that directs its capital on the road to transnational concentration, for which it is a matter of life or death to occupy all the spaces, each time more reduced, on the planet, so that it can guarantee its material and spiritual conditions of existence. This elite—a parasite in the organic body of the social division of labor—carries out its economic activity fundamentally by speculation. Furthermore, in the midst of the bitterest contradictions with the national bourgeoisies and the workers, it has been configuring a transnational domination through which it appropriates the largest share of the world's surplus. It is supported to such a degree by the concentration of capital that it has been able to negate free competition in the decisive links of its increased reproduction. Thus, Claude Meillassoux notes the following:

> At the international level, economic power tends to devolve to a limited sector of the capitalist class, i.e., the *big bourgeoisie*. It pretends to arrogate for itself exclusivity not only against the proletariat, but also against all other sectors of capitalism, whether to gain advantage from them or because it is afraid of competition. . . . Essentially, the power of the capitalist class is situated in the faction linked to large concentrations of capital, and it rests on its ability to deploy high-level organizational and financial management.[7]

To the extent that its interests become different and enter into an antagonistic relationship with the interests of the remaining sectors of the bourgeoisie, the new aristocracy is taking steps toward the formation of its own identity. The monopolization of the bourgeois nation-state by the finance bourgeoisie—with the consequent control of its functions—accentuated its separation from society to a hitherto unheard of degree. The transnationalization of monopoly tends to give an antinational character to this oligarchy, although for the moment this determination is muffled in some of its sectors, in particular the United States; it is set upon globalizing the prerogatives of its own nation-state. In the darkness of transnational monopolies, all the capitalist cats, regardless of citizenship, turn grayer and grayer: The national differences existing among them manifest, nonetheless, a tendency to integrate themselves into the cosmopolitan substance of monopolies. The conflict of interests to the interior of this bourgeois elite does not essentially obey national differences, but instead it is due to interimperialist and intermonopolist contradictions in the process of extortion and redistribution of surplus value. In this sense, the nation is the big fig leaf with which the transnational financial oligarchy covers itself in each imperialist country; it is the shield with which it defends itself from its rivals and the spear with which it attacks them. We should stress that we are dealing with a social caste in contradictory unity that even in the midst of the bitterest internal struggles is compelled to come together against other sectors of the bourgeoisie, as well as any other class, human community, or social group that dares to hamper its domination; this concerns, in particular, the bourgeoisies of the neocolonial countries.

During the whole history of neocolonialism, the national bourgeoisies had counted on certain spaces for their reproduction as a social class. These spaces had not been disputed by imperialism because of the association of those bourgeoisies with the dominant financial powers and their capacity to find refuge in the economic gaps left for them. They also held an undisputed portion of the power of the nation-state. Political transnationalization and denationalization tend to reduce to a minimum these local spaces. Those bourgeoisies find themselves today on the road to absorption and destruction by the transnational finance oligarchy and, consequently, the share of political power that they can exercise has become reduced. This process is taking place in the midst of the intensification of interimperialist competition for regions, subregions, countries, localities, and branches, industries, and services that meet the indispensable requirements to guarantee the extended reproduction of monopoly capital, as well as having the infrastructure, the capacity to assimilate new technologies, the labor force, and the necessary markets for juicy profits. This shameless feast sharpens, on the one hand, the contradictions between the financial oligarchy and the national bourgeoisies and provokes, on the other, the stratification and fragmentation of the latter insofar as the banquet's leftovers are, with each day that passes, less able to guarantee the substance of local capitals, compelled as they are to compete against the monopolies and among themselves.

Thus, in the war of all against all that capitalist production entails, one may confirm a tendency toward the appearance of common economic and political interests. In the defense of these interests, the transnational financial oligarchy of each imperialist country coincides more fully with the transnational financial oligarchy of the other imperialist countries than with the remaining layers of the bourgeoisie, and the social classes and sectors of its own country. This community of interests is derived from the necessity to guarantee the rotation of global capital under conditions of heightened internal stratification within the bourgeoisie, accelerated pauperization of the proletariat and peasantry, and increased marginalization of a growing number of the world's population.

This community of interests among the sectors of the big bourgeoisie expresses itself politically in the immanent necessity, consciously assumed and with important practical accomplishments, to build a machinery of violence able to fulfill transnational policies and to dissolve anti-imperialist contradictions. The categorical imperative of the national financial oligarchy had been to take control of the reins of an *already constituted* nation-state; the categorical imperative of the transnational financial bourgeoisie is to *create* a transnational state capable of consolidating its political power on a regional scale, with a tendency toward a global level.

The establishment of capitalist relations of production in Europe and North America led to the union of the old independent provinces "into one nation, with one government, one code of laws, one national class interest, one frontier, and one customs tariff."[8] To the extent that the process of concentration of property and rotation of capital goes beyond the jurisdiction of the nation-state, the transnational finance oligarchy needs to bring the world under "one government," "one code of laws," "one class interest" (in this case, *transnational* imperialist), and "one frontier"—a frontier that prohibits the remaining types of world economy from participating in the benefits of the transnational rotation of capital. This immanent finality constitutes one of the fundamental laws of its historical development; toward this maximum objective, the bourgeoisie that is emerging in the arena of history mobilizes all its efforts as a class.

Nevertheless, the designs of contemporary imperialism find insurmountable obstacles for their realization. These are the contradictions between imperialism—with North American imperialism in the foreground—and the countries of the so-called Third World; interimperialist contradictions; the contradictions between the transnational finance oligarchy and the national bourgeoisies, between the sectors of these national bourgeoisies associated with transnational capital and those that see themselves threatened by it, and between these latter bourgeois sectors and the universe of wage earners—organized or not—and the marginalized, whose increasing pauperization foments ungovernability and social explosions that have the capacity of generating authentic revolutionary situations. In particular, no less than thirty-seven thousand transnational enterprises and a significant number of financial groups dispute daily among themselves every single millimeter of economic and political terrain, including the labor force and markets, and the national state machinery. These contradictions tell us that the transnational finance bourgeoisie, although it is committed to exclude the absolute majority of the world's population—namely, the small and middle bourgeoisie, the proletariat, the peasantry, and the marginalized—from any participation in decision making, it is nonetheless incapable of eliminating political confrontations at the national and international levels insofar as it is impossible for it to create a sole monopoly. To the interior of this oligarchy there are numerous contradictions, the most important expressions of which are the formation of rival regional blocs—and the antagonism created between its most powerful sector, the United States above all, which is oriented toward total globalization—and those sectors that need to shelter themselves in regional spaces to ensure their transnational economic and political positions. These antagonisms explain in good measure the important role that the imperialist nation-states still play in the process of transnationalization of monopoly capital. They are—particularly the North American state and, to a lesser degree, the Japanese, German, and other European states—the main political (i.e., military, judicial, and police) supporters of transnational monopolies.

The contradictory relation of competition and cooperation existing among the three fundamental groupings forming the transnational finance oligarchy, and their respective imperialist states, is determined, on the one hand, by the objective necessity of setting up mechanisms for political domination and economic regulation that are adequate to the transnational level of the rotation of capital. On the other hand, it is determined by the specific interests of each of the three imperialist centers: first, the fluctuating correlation of forces among "panglobalist," "regionalist," and "nationalist protectionist" interests of the U.S. bourgeoisie, who after the signing of the North American Free Trade Agreement, hindered the carrying out of the project of a Free Trade Zone of the Americas; second, the Western European imperialist integration, with the German Federal Republic as its center, destined to counteract the political, economic, and military hegemony of North American imperialism; and, third, the "aggressive export" policies of Japanese imperialism, characterized by a relatively small geographic extension and population, which have made it depend, to a much larger degree than its main partners–competitors, on the location of its enterprises beyond its national borders (especially in the territories of the Pacific basin) and on external markets.

So powerful is the tendency toward the constitution of a transnational machinery of power that one gets the strong impression that contemporary humanity is witnessing a process of configuration of a global state starting from old and new supranational mechanisms and institutions, which, like mushrooms after the rain, have emerged and consolidated themselves since the end of World War II. These are, in the economic sphere, the World Bank, the International Monetary Fund, the Organization for Economic Cooperation and Development, and the World Trade Organization; on the political plane there are the Group of Seven (G-7) and the Security Council of the United Nations; and in the military order, we have the

North Atlantic Treaty Organization and all the other treaties that function to further imperialist domination.[9] There is no doubt that in all cases we find ourselves before institutions and mechanisms that administer determinate and, in some cases, important and even decisive shares of public power. Thus, with the objective of keeping off the threats that stalk contemporary capitalism, such as inflation, unemployment, and financial crises, the Group of Seven fulfills the function of setting guidelines for the regulation of the economy and the money supply at an international scale; it also acts as a mechanism for the reconciliation and negotiation of interimperialist rivalries.[10] The International Monetary Fund and the World Bank create mechanisms the objectives of which are to guarantee the free rotation of transnational capital and transform the permanent renegotiation of the foreign debt of the underdeveloped countries into an instrument for the absorption and destruction of their national capitals. For its part, the Security Council of the UN reveals itself as a means for interference by imperialism and the intervention of its "peace forces" in the internal affairs of nations; NATO and regional military pacts with or without the approval of the UN Security Council also perform this function.

Moreover, there is no doubt that among all these organizations and institutions, there is a certain level of organic interrelation in the exercise of their functions, which has given to this process the appearance of a state structure—in this case a supranational state structure. Nevertheless, that is an external resemblance only, linked to the representation that an eventual world-state would have to have an analogous organization as well as count with institutions that are similar to those of a nation-state. In contrast, the fundamental element of the transnational machinery of political power is constituted, in our judgment, by the nation-states themselves, both the imperialist states, which assume transnational attributes, and the dependent states. The former is an attempt to convert the latter into mere transmission belts of the will of the transnational finance oligarchy within their respective nations.

It is important to insist on this point: The transnational bourgeoisie cannot yet in any way do without the services of the nation-states, however weak they are, just as a knight cannot manage without his grooms. Thus, Miren Etxezarreta writes:

> The economic interests of the large transnational groups do not necessarily coincide with the interests of the political capitals of their nations of origin; but, on the other hand, states are necessary to transmit the power of the transnational entities in those ways in which the large economic conglomerates cannot do so directly.[11]

The gigantic financial operations of these conglomerates require the intervention of the institutions of the nation-states, as well as the military, political, and judiciary apparatuses, for the sake of those conglomerates' full freedom of movement and, especially, political control over the workers, the marginalized, ethnic and social minorities, and even the national bourgeoisies.[12] The support that nation-states give for the ideological legitimation of transnational capital is not negligible. From this perspective, the supranational institutions to which we have referred do not go beyond the performance of state functions that are complementary to those carried out by the imperialist states. *The whole riddle consists of ascertaining to what extent this political metamorphosis strengthens the power of transnational monopoly capital and creates new and sharper international and social-class contradictions that undermine the basis of the imperialist system of domination considered as a totality.*

It is necessary to identify with clarity which functions of the imperialist states are being transnationalized; which functions of dependent states have become atrophied and which ones remain tied to their diminished institutions; which functions have been assumed by supranational entities, both those left over from the Cold War and those that are "legitimate children" of the epoch of dominance by transnational monopoly capital; which supranational political functions are searching for new structures; and which ones cannot be structured as a consequence of the colossal contradictions unleashed by the process of transnationalization of imperialism.

The imperialist megamachinery that is in the process of historical assemblage is characterized by an increase in the direct coercive capacity of the economy and, in particular, of monetary relations and financial speculation; the transnationalization of the executive, legislative, and judicial functions of the imperialist states and the transnational projection of their military power and public force; the exacerbation of the totalitarian, domineering, and antidemocratic character of the capitalist mode of production; the shameless way in which ideology is placed at the service of the interests of transnational capital; and the sharpening of the antagonism among the imperialist states, especially because of the disappearance of the Soviet Union. All these determinations of the process of political transnationalization present the double character of being instruments of domination and sources of destructive contradictions for the capitalist system in general.

The enormous degree of concentration achieved by transnational monopoly capital considerably enlarges the power of the politico-economic relationships characteristic of capitalist society[13] in terms of both the mechanisms of economic domination set in motion and the breadth and diversity of classes, social groups, and nations over which the form of domination it implicitly carries with it is exercised. The principal instrument for political subjection used by the transnational oligarchy, which makes it into a giant with feet of clay, is *financial speculation*; it is based on the control of the aggregate mass of the world's money, the public and private debts, and the global redistribution of the national patrimony. One must add to this the political subordination to transnational banking's impositions, protectionism, unequal exchange, payment of the foreign debt,[14] and manner in which the transnational division of labor evolves, which places those economies that operate with local currencies in a condition of inferiority. The

recipes of the International Monetary Fund, the conditions established for grant-
ing loans by the World Bank, the unfair terms imposed by the Paris Club for the
renegotiation of the foreign debt,[15] the World Trade Organization's regulations,
and, in general, the dictates by supranational institutions—which represent capitalism as a whole—constitute a fundamental complementary power to the direct
use of force by the imperialist nations. In particular, the financial oligarchy's
domination rests on the control that it has over the main financial transactions and
over national banking systems, its monopoly on dividend gains, unequal exchange, capital flight, the political manipulation of credit, the capitalization of the
foreign debt, and the requirement for the convertibility of local currencies. From
the perspective of social classes, the disproportionate excess of the labor force
with respect to the demands of variable capital has acquired particular importance. Although the rise in unemployment, underemployment, and job insecurity
causes, in the short term, a weakening of the labor movement, this rise expresses,
nevertheless, the clearest indication of the sharpening of the contradiction between capital and labor that, *in objective terms,* has become a veritable powder
keg at the very foundations of the capitalist mode of production. In contrast,
transnational monopoly heightens the absorption, destruction, and marginalization of the small and middle bourgeoisies, as well as the stratification and fragmentation of the dominant class.

The transnationalization of the legislative, executive, and judicial functions of
the imperialist states, especially of the North American state, constituted an authentic crusade against the principles of sovereignty, self-determination, and independence of the nation-state, on which are imposed a growing number of
transnational juridical norms and the corresponding coercive mechanisms that ensure compliance.

One should notice the essential difference between public international law—
as it has developed since the formation of the bourgeois nations—and the transnational law that the imperialist nations are attempting to build in the epoch of
transnational monopolies. In the first case, we have a set of principles, usages,
treaties, and agreements brought into existence to regulate relations between sovereign states, above which no supreme tribunal is recognized. In the second case,
however, we are dealing with norms imposed on the subordinate states by the imperialist states, regarding both international law and the internal functioning of
the subordinate states.

It is increasingly evident in the contemporary world that transnational law tends
to supplant international law. In this sense, "unilateral" transnational laws (often
called "extraterritorial" laws) are worthy of mention. These include the following:
dispositions for the transnational action of the executive and judicial powers of the
imperialist state; laws imposed by means of international treaties and supranational
institutions (whether global or regional), accompanied by mechanisms of "verification," control, and sanction of the "offender"; and the laws adopted by the legislatures of the dependent nations, as a "requirement" for the signing of political,

economic, and military accords or as the result of direct or indirect pressure by the imperialist powers. The international opposition to the U.S. promulgation of the Helms-Burton and the D'Amato-Kennedy laws constitutes evidence that this road also has its stumbling blocks, and it also contributes to the worsening of the interimperialist contradictions and the exacerbation of the nationalist sentiments of oppressed peoples, with their invaluable revolutionary potential.

We notice something similar when we observe the direct relation maintained between, on the one hand, the magnitude, sophistication, and concentration of transnational military power and public force with a degree of sharpening of the economic and social-class contradictions and with, on the other hand, the level of potential development of the anti-imperialist struggle. With the end of the Cold War between the military superpowers, imperialism has not only *continued* investing a huge number of resources into the development of military, repressive, intelligence, and counterinsurgencecy technology and doctrines—oftentimes hidden behind the mask of the fight against terrorism and the drug traffic, it has also decided to subordinate the armies and the public forces of the neocolonial states to its interests. In these adventures, imperialism relies on the most novel systems of armaments, communications, and transportation, on the widening and strengthening of its planetary network of military bases and pacts, and on the use of international organisms—particularly, the UN Security Council—to clean up its acts of piracy and military aggression. Imperialism stumbles in this goal with opposition from nationalist sectors of the armed forces of neocolonial nations, alarmed by the imperialist intention of transforming them into police agencies at the service of foreign powers and by the process of privatization of military enterprises, which have been traditional sources of lucrative positions. No less important, however, is the opposition by some military sectors that are motivated by genuine patriotic ideals.

Transnationalization intensifies the antidemocratic character of the capitalist mode of production and the historic tendency toward the progressive separation and alienation of the state from the rest of society. Insofar as economic power increases its direct coercive force, political power—including the military machinery and public force—is concentrated and transnationalized, and growing numbers of the population are marginalized from the labor market; thus, *capitalism attains the most antidemocratic political organization of its history.*

Under the banner of the struggle against "democratic egalitarianism," which overburdens the state and compels it to raise taxes and use some of its funds for diverse social programs (funds that supposedly would be better employed by the "private sector of the economy") transnational powers demand a "moderation" of democracy. This would, on the one hand, prop up government by the elite and, on the other, create apathy in the rest of the population by means of a reduction of expectations among the poor and the middle classes. Hiding behind these demands is the recognition—made explicit some time ago by the Trilateral Commission—that every democratic society *needs a marginal population that does not partici-*

*pate actively in politics.* The more vast and diverse this population, the more effective the functioning of bourgeois democracy will be. It is not coincidental that
the financial oligarchy, from which the people had to wrest with blood and fire the
right to universal suffrage, is today the big promoter and defender of the government system based on "free elections." After all, if the main political decisions are
taken and adopted in the centers of transnational power outside the political institutions of the nation-state, it is evident that most of humanity, confined as it is to
national territorial spaces, is deprived of having an effective political participation.
That becomes evident especially when one analyzes the functioning of supranational organisms, the high functionaries of which do not have any links whatso-
ever with the populations subjected to their dictates.

In a society in which economic power is in the hands of speculative financial
capital, bourgeois politics can only be managed as if it were a stock exchange.
What become operative are the fictitious politics of manipulated projections of
winners and losers, use of polls and manipulation of the mass media, and dis-
sembling and disguises. The winners are generally those with the biggest resources to create a "believable" image, despite the noticeable loss of prestige of
executive, legislative, and judicial institutions, the increase of contradictions
within political parties and currents, the rapidly increasing mistrust in the electoral systems, the increase in abstentionism, the quick tarnishing of recently
elected government officials, the proliferation of corruption scandals, and the
decadent practice of demagoguery as a resource for capitalizing on the frustration
and despair of the population.

The antidemocratic character of the capitalist system manifests itself even
more acutely in the underdeveloped countries: Their inhabitants cease being
mere citizens of their respective countries and, therefore, subjects of national
bourgeois aristocracies, only to become subordinated, by means of multiple mediations, to a finance oligarchy that exerts dominion within the space of the
transnational rotation of capital; this oligarchy does so with noticeable contempt
toward a country's symbols, historical loyalties, cultural traditions, or people's
idiosyncrasies. Those sectors of the national oligarchies that have become in-
serted into transnational monopoly capitalism as straw men of transnational powers displace the political and economic groups still oriented by the old logic of
national capitalism. As a just prize for their fidelity and complicity, sectors of the
national oligarchies of the dependent countries receive as their assignment the
task of making their territories attractive for the inversion of transnational capital by means of all sorts of attacks on the rights of workers and by confronting
the crisis of modernity provoked by the imperialist plunder. They only count for
this mission with the ghosts of the old nation-states and with a party system that
persists in staging old and tired regional plays in which the political parties play
at representing the voters.

Privatizations have left the states without the means to obtain the resources they
used to have at their disposal for co-optation and patronage *[clientelismo]*: There are

no longer funds to permit rulers to maintain privileges reserved for the middle strata so that they can act as a buffer for the system, nor can they be attentive to unions and other officialist organizations that served the function of dividing the popular sectors. The progressive refunctionalization of the nation-state limits the activity of legislatures to the formal approval of legislation of transnational provenance, while the executive organs and the tribunals of the state, tied by hand and foot, commit themselves to preserve macroeconomic stability, despite the abuses of financial speculation and the onerous payment of the foreign debt. Under such conditions, the traditional parties are fractured, consensuses are broken, and the alliances that were functioning during the postwar period are disarticulated. Political and economic groups, which had established more or less stable rules for sharing out the government and the national wealth, find themselves today on opposite sides; there is also an increase in the discrediting and decomposition of state institutions, as well as in the dissociation between real politics and electoral processes.

Contemporary imperialism attempts to confine those exploited by capital and those exiled from the kingdom of material reproduction inside its temple of spiritual reproduction; it does so through the monopolistic control of the means of mass communications, favored by the confusion among the revolutionary ranks and the momentary retrogression in the political consciousness of oppressed social classes and sectors. A chorus of pagan idols surrounds the altar of the Market, the only God and universal Father to which ailing humanity owes absolute devotion. Spurious ideas, inverted images, and manipulated values, preconized to the four winds by the monopolies of communication and sold wholesale in all the corners of heaven and earth, are superimposed with Olympic hypocrisy over prosaic reality: postmodernity, end of history, technocratic civilization, efficiency, competitiveness, ethical values of democracy, pluralism, tolerance, dialogue, consensus, freedom of the press, freedom of expression, freedom of conscience, disideologization, cultural autonomy, individual self-realization, prosperity, humanitarian aid, fight against corruption, refocusing of social programs, and so forth. The inhabitant of the transnational *polis*, the citizen who buys, sells, or auctions his or her labor power, finds ready for consumption a spiritual food prefabricated with those and other enchanted substances, sustenance that he or she is compelled to consume and that pretends to model his or her inner world, aspirations, and social activity. The growing separation between virtual and real capitalism attains its *non plus ultra* in the peculiar way in which all ghosts are reproduced and "adapted" by the ideologues of transnational capitalism in the so-called Third World.

Through their impetus and control by transnational monopolies, the new technologies of information—above all, satellites and fiber optics—have facilitated the creation of universal communicative spaces and a virtual simultaneity in the transmission and reception of images: films, television series, news, publicity, polls, educational series, and circulation materials are articulated in political, religious, ethical, and artistic spaces and processes; these have become fused in an authentic transnational industry ruled by the law of value. Behind the fallacies of the "free circulation of ideas" and "freedom of expression," and the "independence," "neutrality," and "objectivity" of information, an authentic transnational monopoly of mass communication is enthroned, which through forms of censorship ever more sophisticated rejects information generated in other venues.[16] In addition, it prevents the majority of countries in the world from using communicative strategies based on national, economic, political, and cultural relations. The distinctive notes of this transnationalizing process are banality and manipulation; its most characteristic result is the establishment of a genuine tyranny over world consciousness. Four transnational monopolies, United Press International (UPI), Associated Press (AP), Reuters, and France Press, whose correspondents work all over the planet, give an account of world events from a perspective of domination that is also alien to local, regional, and national perspectives; also, they make a norm out of falsification and omission. To the multiplication of channels of communication, transmitters, and broadcasting stations, there corresponds a *transnational concentration of centers of production* under the rule of the financial powers, especially the U.S. finance oligarchy. By means of the fragmentation and segmentation of communication, voting consumers are intentionally kept away from any socially significant action, and people are also intentionally led to see themselves and those who dominate them through the prism provided by transnational press agencies, movies, radio, and television.

Nevertheless, in spite of what we are led to believe, the plan for transnational ideological domination is unable to erase from the face of the earth alternative modes of communication that are proper for peoples and for the use to which they put their cultures, values, and traditions. Also, it cannot erase the persistence of popular rebellion, despite the authoritarianism of communicative relations, techniques, and strategies of manipulation and banalization, and the campaigns unleashed to demobilize peoples.

The process of political transnationalization does not take place in a homogeneous way because of unequal economic and political development and worsening interimperialist contradictions. This can be confirmed by examining, for example, the differences existing between the United States and the European Union: The North American state has the requisite force to act by itself as a transnational power, while the European states find themselves compelled to form a transnational (regional) machinery that integrates their political and economic forces, in order to preserve their own areas of supremacy and to manage to keep themselves afloat in the interimperialist fray.

In the European Union, we find evidence of protoforms of a transnational, regional state to which the member nation-states cede part of their sovereignty, despite the preponderant role and growing power of the German state. In this process, through economic, monetary, and military union, the national structures become a mediating instance between citizens and transnational powers; also, they tend to disappear and integrate themselves into a regional unity—rife, nonetheless, with contradictions among different financial groups and the bureaucracies of the nation-states—which sets out to establish a more favorable balance of forces in relation to the power of U.S. imperialism and aggressive economic competition from Japan.

The United States, for its own part, has the ferocious vocation to become all by itself a transnational state—a state that pretends to institutionalize its "right" to exercise transnational legislative, executive, and judicial functions; by these means, it even tries to impose itself over the remaining imperialist powers. The consolidation of its transnational action is manifested openly in the following: the approval of the Helms-Burton law, the processes of certification for good conduct (or decertification for bad conduct) of sovereign nations, the imposition of programs against narcotics traffic and terrorism (which include direct and unconsulted operations by the U.S. armed forces and special services), the faculty that the U.S. Congress gives to U.S. courts to judge and sanction foreign governments, the clauses on political conditionality that have been imposed on the other nations of the American continent in bilateral accords and agreements, the elaboration of reports on the human rights situation in other countries, and, finally, the ideological oversaturation that leads the states of dependent countries to "voluntarily" adopt U.S. legislation and recommendations.

Insofar as Latin America is concerned, U.S. imperialism has tried to consolidate a system of hemispheric domination, to complement its unilateral actions and displays of force against the rest of the nations of the Americas since the end of the nineteenth century. Patriotic, progressive, and revolutionary forces, and even some sectors of the national bourgeoisies met U.S. policy with great resistance. But the United States had relative success with the creation of the Pan-American Union in the first decades of the twentieth century. The outcome of World War II and the declaration of the Cold War created the conditions that proved indispensable for the realization of imperialism's early dreams: the building of the so-called inter-American system, in the web of which were woven the Inter-American Treaty of Reciprocal Assistance (ITRA), the Organization of American States (OAS), the Inter-American Defense Board (IDB), and the Inter-American Development Bank (IDB); all of them were instruments of the Cold War. Nevertheless, only at the end of the 1980s was the United States able to build a strong enough foundation to undertake the reform of inter-American relations, by means of a process that included the invasion of Grenada; the transformation of the foreign debt into an instrument for strengthening the domination over, and subordination of, the countries of the region; the neutralization of the revolutionary war in Central America; and the military aggression against Panama.

The possibility of the admission of Latin America and the Caribbean into the North American Free Trade Agreement (NAFTA), the renegotiation of the debt in the terms established by the "Brady Plan," and the launching of the "Americas

Initiative" generated in the Latin American and Caribbean bourgeoisies the vain illusion that they were going to count with the support of the finance oligarchy of the United States so that they could preserve their economic space despite the accelerated process of transnationalization of the capitalist relations of production. Little by little these bourgeoisies ended up accepting the new "rules of the game." This process achieved its most finished expression in the Summit of the Americas, held in Miami in 1994, where, after almost one century of neocolonialism (concentrated mainly in the Caribbean basin), by means of the vanished Pan-American Union, the creation of the OAS, and the successive processes of reform of the OAS's charter in response to the victory of the Cuban Revolution, U.S. imperialism was able to wrest from the governing elite in Latin America, the Caribbean, and Canada a commitment to the fundamental principles of its system of transnational domination. The fundamental ideological expression of the new system of domination is "collective defense of representative democracy," depicted in the doctrine of governance as some sort of universal panacea. Starting with the meeting of the General Assembly of the OAS in Santiago de Chile in 1991, this supranational institution was explicitly authorized to determine whether or not a government was "democratic"; it was also empowered to adopt coercive measures against any Latin American and Caribbean nation that did not bend to the ordeals of its "Holy Inquisition." Since then, North American imperialism has not stopped exercising bilateral and multilateral pressures so that all forums and institutions in which the governments of the Americas participate endorse the principles of this system.

Imperialism promotes, by direct means or through its most docile subordinates, the creation of an inter-American force with interventionist ends to complement the so-called collective defense of representative democracy. Nevertheless, in the face of the opposition of several governments in the region, it has had to content itself, at least for the moment, with promoting the Argentine government's initiative to create a body of "White Helmets" to confront situations of civil emergency; however, this initiative has not yet gotten the consensus of the governments of the region.

U.S. imperialism's success has so far been only partial. It has not been able to overcome the resistance that its discriminatory commercial practices provoke, nor has it been able to get approval for the creation of an inter-American military force. The generalized reaction of the Latin American and Caribbean governments against the Helms-Burton law—a reaction that became a resolution of the General Assembly of the OAS in Panama in open defiance of the U.S. delegation—the irritation provoked by the decertification of Colombia, bilateral pressures against Mexico, Brazil, Argentina, and other countries, and the tensions that developed in the meetings of Trade Ministers of the Hemisphere, all confirm the existence of strong disagreements.

With respect to the underdeveloped world, we can properly speak of a process of *denationalization of political power*, devaluation of the neocolonial states, atrophy of their national functions, and the acquisition of subordinate transnational functions that threaten to transform them into dependencies of monopoly transnational capital, insofar as the dependent national bourgeoisies have become absorbed or are being destroyed by it.[17] These states become progressively transformed into organic appendices of the machinery of transnational power, which imposes on them standards and codes of conduct they are compelled to observe. These are economic (i.e., privatization, convertibility of local currency, and suppression of tariffs), political (i.e., the prescription of norms of state organization and democratic mechanisms, limitation of state functions in the fight against terrorism and narcotics traffic, police control, and a stop to emigration), military (i.e., reductions in the armed forces and subordinate participation in the systems of "collective security"), social (i.e., cuts in expenses for health care, education, and social security), and ideological (i.e., imposition of neoliberal dogma, the mythology of globalization, and postmodern forms of discourse).

The curve of political dependence of nations shows us cases of states that are already nothing but veritable political subsidiaries of imperialism, in essence mere pieces of a new machine of transnational power. We are not dealing, of course, with a uniform historical movement, but with a process charged with extreme contradictions. The intensity and fullness of those contradictions depend, in different nation-states, on diverse concrete historical circumstances, but especially on the degree of development of capitalism in them. Besides these gradations, it is evident that the process of transnational globalization weakens the national links in the chain of bourgeois power, particularly those that bear the direct brunt of the formidable pressures from the class contradictions it generates and reproduces. At the opposite pole, the socialist state of Cuba and the Asian socialist states constitute genuine bastions of national independence and sovereignty, with vigorous state powers that have preserved and strengthened their attributes and functions. Imperialism is not wrong when it identifies them as the most powerful historical countertendency to its transnational domination.

## NOTES

1. See *Memorias del Seminario Partidos Políticos y Gestión Estratégica* (Santiago de Chile: ILPES-Dolmen Ediciones, 1997).

2. "*Governance* and *ungovernability* quickly acquired a place of considerable importance in the language of politicians and social scientists. . . . Originally, both referred to the phenomenon of stability in the economy and its fluid functioning, such as it was expressed in the period between wars, and according to a monetary instability-productive instability-social instability sequence, which required processing through institutions and social subjects. In social science, by contrast, 'governance' was used to refer to the political-institutional control over transformative social change; 'ungovernability' defined, then, the loss of governmental control over the mechanisms or forces that were the objects of government" (*Memorias del Seminario Partidos Políticos y Gestión Estratégica*, 8–9).

3. *Memorias del Seminario Partidos Políticos y Gestión Estratégica*, 9.

4. See Holly Sklar, "Trilateralism: Managing Dependence and Democracy—An Overview," in *Trilateralism*, ed. Holly Sklar (Boston: South End Press, 1980), 21–22.
5. See *Memorias del Seminario Partidos Políticos y Gestión Estratégica*, 15–16.
6. The transnational finance oligarchy is the prodigal daughter of what Marx had called "Bourse wolves," "bank kings," "state creditors," "*rentiers*." See Karl Marx, "The Class Struggles in France from 1848 to 1850," in *Marx & Engels: Basic Writings on Politics and Philosophy*, ed. Lewis S. Feuer (Garden City, N.Y.: Anchor Books, 1959), 296. See also Karl Marx, *The Eighteenth Brumaire of Louis Bonaparte*, 1995, 1999, at www.marxists.org/archive/marx/works/1852-18b/ch06.htm (accessed March 8, 2002).

By the aristocracy of finance must here be understood not merely the great loan promoters and speculators in public funds, in regard to whom it is immediately obvious that their interests coincide with the interests of the state power. All modern finance, the whole of the banking business, is inter-woven in the closest fashion with public credit. A part of their business capital is necessarily invested and put out at interest in quickly convertible public funds. Their deposits, the capital placed at their disposal and distributed by them among merchants and industrialists, are partly derived from the dividends of holders of government securities. If in every epoch the stability of the state power signified Moses and the prophets to the entire money market and to the priests of this money market, why not all the more so today, when every deluge threatens to sweep away the old states, and the old state debts with them?

7. Meillasoux goes on to say: "The volume of private capital and its insertion in the national and world economy of this capitalist segment with international stature affects in a decisive way the internal and foreign policies of states, as well as the policies of international public institutions (such as the International Monetary Fund, the World Bank, or the European Economic Community). Small and mid-size capital does not count with this political ascendancy" [Claude Meillassoux, "Clases y cuerpos sociales," in *Marx y el siglo XXI. Una defensa de la historia y del socialismo*, ed. Renán Vega Cantor (Santa Fe de Bogotá: Ediciones Pensamiento Crítico, 1997), 57].
8. Karl Marx and Frederick Engels, *The Communist Manifesto* (New York: International Publishers, 1948), 13.
9. Cf. Noam Chomsky and Heinz Dieterich, *La sociedad global* (Mexico: Joaquín Mortiz, 1995), 53–91.
10. "There are also private organizations, powerful pressure groups with abundant resources, which try to have influence in the running of societies both, at the global level and at the level of specific states. As examples of these, we could mention institutions such as the Trilateral Commission—at this time, remaining more in the shadows than during the time of President Carter's administration—, the large world foundations—such as the Rockefeller and the Ford foundations—, or institutions such as the Club of Rome" [Miren Etxezarreta, "Globalización e intervención pública," in *Propuestas desde la izquierda. Los desafíos de la izquierda transformadora para el próximo siglo*, ed. Manuel Monereo (Madrid: Fundación de Investigaciones Marxistas, 1998), 185].
11. Miren Etxezarreta, "Globalización e intervención pública," 185. See also, Juan Francisco Martín Seco, "Economía y democracia," in *Propuestas desde la izquierda*. "While certain aspects—such as mercantile, monetary, and financial aspects—are supranationalized, others—such as political and fiscal aspects—remain within the narrow confines of the nation-state, impotent already to limit and compensate for economic power, or to correct the failures and huge inequalities that are generated in the markets when these are left to their own laws."

12. "In the political-military and economic-monetary fields, [supranationality] is leaving the *management* of the internal class struggle in the hands of each national government" [F. Vercammen, "¿Un estado supranacional en marcha?" *Viento del Sur* (1996): 28].

13. Since the birth of the capitalist social-economic formation, economic power is expressed, without any other adornments than ideological ones, as the immediate content of all political forms. This peculiar organic interaction between the economic and political engines of society, characteristic of bourgeois civilization, attains maturity in the epoch of formation and consolidation of national state monopoly capitalism. Already Lenin had noted that "the power of capital is everything, the stock exchange is everything, while parliament and elections are marionettes, puppets" [Vladimir Ilyich Lenin, "The State: A Lecture Delivered at the Sverdlov University, July 11, 1919," *Collected Works*, trans. Jim Riordan (in Lenin), vol. 29 (Moscow: Progress Publishers, 1964), 487].

14. Fidel Castro was pointing out in 1985 that "as of late, an unprecedent expansion of transnational banking has been taking place in the underdeveloped world. The causes of this expansion are related, in one way or another, with the very development of transnational enterprises, the internationalization of production, and especially, the economic crisis and its effects in both, developed and underdeveloped countries. . . . It has been precisely the private banking sector, by acting especially through relatively new mechanisms such as the Euromarket, that has put pressure, in full concordance with the IMF, on the debtor nations to apply measures of economic policy that harm the most vital interests of the peoples of the Third World. The underdeveloped countries have thus been trapped in the web of a market of highly speculative and restrictive capital. This fact, together with the deficits in their commercial transactions and payments, has provoked a critical situation in the attempt to achieve compensation for the accumulated negative balance." Fidel Castro Ruz, Cuban TV Appearance, February 2, 1998; also in *Granma* (February 5, 1998): 85.

15. "A mere glance at Latin America's reality makes evident the current importance of the problem of the debt which, from being a premise for the introduction of the transnational schema of dominations, has become one of the fundamental instruments on which imperialism counts to maintain and increase the flow of resources toward the centers of world power, as well as the economic and political subordination of the underdeveloped countries. If in 1970 the "obligations" of the subcontinent were as high as $60 billion, already by 1980 the total sum of the foreign debt had reached $225.5 billion and, in 1996, $607.33 billion, despite the fact that the region had made payments for $739.9 billion. Only in 1995 and 1996 did the debt of the countries of the area increase by $73 billion to $974 million. Between 1986 and 1988, the annual transference of resources by means of the debt was $53 billion, and in the period between 1991 and 1996, it went up to the astronomical figure of $86 billion yearly, which jeopardized 30 percent of regional incomes. The processes of renegotiation continue mortgaging the future of the Latin American *and* Caribbean nations, and they stress the collection of the debt from the few assets that have not been privatized. See "Por una alternativa popular para América Latina," paper presented by the delegation of the Communist Party of Cuba in the VII Encounter of the São Paulo Forum, *Cuba Socialista* 7, 46–63.

16. We read in the documents of the V Summit of the Non-aligned Movement that this situation "creates a situation of dependence and domination in which the greatest number of countries are reduced to passively receiving insufficient and deformed information full of prejudices. To recognize themselves better and to affirm their national and cultural identity, it is necessary to remedy this great disequilibrium and to urgently take

measures that give a stronger impetus to mutual cooperation in this area. The emancipation and development of national information media are integral to the global struggle carried out by the greater number of the world's peoples to attain their political independence in the economic and social spheres, and for that it is necessary to inform and be informed objectively and correctly. Self-sufficiency in sources of information is as important as technological self-sufficiency. For dependency in the area of information puts a brake in turn on economic and political development" ["Declaraciones aprobadas en la V Cumbre de Jefes de Estado o de Gobierno de los Países No Alineados," *Colombo* (August, 1976): 16–19, para. 2. 160–63 of the political declaration].

17.

I must state some things in which I really believe: States, that is, the nation-states created in a historical period, will disappear. They are already disappearing; it is a difficult parturition, but they are disappearing. The sovereignty of states had already been disappearing as an inevitable sequel to the hegemony of U.S. imperialism, of the unipolar world, and the order and institutions that it has established. These deplete and erode more and more the independence of states and countries, in the first place of those that are midsize or small. But I was referring to the other aspect of the process, namely, the states that will disappear simply as a consequence of the necessity to survive, as is happening today in Europe. These countries fought against each other for centuries, but they march today in an inexorable process towards integration and their disappearance as nation-states. They do not have any other alternative. The same is taking place in other regions of the world. There will be also disintegrations, reintegrations, assimilations, ferocious competitions, a struggle for markets and resources, economic wars, perhaps bloody conflicts, interregional and world agreements wrapped up at the same time in an unstoppable process of globalization. Why, if not because of this, does the United States perfect and increase with new weapons the efficiency of its powerful military apparatus? In short, the nation-states will disappear; *it is a law of history and a process that is accelerating.* (italics ours) (Fidel Castro Ruz, Cuban TV Appearance, February 2, 1998; also in *Granma*, February 5, 1998)

# II

## RETHINKING IDENTITY

# 4

# Globalization and the Borders of Latinity

*Walter D. Mignolo*

## I

"Latin American Thought" and globalization invite a series of considerations that go beyond "Latin America" proper and beyond the scope of "Latinoamericanism" in their past and present forms. In the past and in Europe, it was fundamental for France to create a community with southern countries to confront the two competitors in the new imperial world order: England and Germany. In the past and in the Americas, "Latinité" served the same purpose in the colonial order: to confront the expansion of "Anglicité" (in this case the United States) toward the Latin countries, that is, Latin countries that had not been colonized by France, but by Spain and Portugal. Today Latinoamericanism in the United States has become a location for critical discourses in literary and cultural studies.[1] But also, it has been transformed into "Latin/o Americanisms" to embrace the growing and influential presence of Latino/as in the United States and the fact that Latin America is no longer, from the demographic perspective of the United States, a reality "down there," offering possibilities of expansion of the market; it is also "up here," transforming the socioeconomic configuration of the United States.[2]

Latin America means a group of continental and insular countries that have been colonized by Spain, Portugal, and France; Spanish, Portuguese, and French are their basic languages (with the exception of Haiti, where French Creole is the official language). Consequently, Latinoamericanism or Latin/o Americanisms (in plural) either do not make sense or, if they do, do not have the same meaning. I adopt here the expression, Latin American Thought, for a genealogy of intellectual production (equivalent to "European Thought") for which Latin America is never the only and final destination. The world, as well as Europe or the United States, can be the object of Latin American Thought while at the same time these practices can never be confused with Area Studies either. Area Studies is not an academic or scholarly practice in Third World countries! It is precisely the geopolitics of knowledge that brings the universality of Reason back to modern/colonial histories, that is, to the geopolitical articulation of modernity/coloniality.

Thus, Latin American Thought refers, in my understanding, to the intellectual production in Spanish, Portuguese, and the French Caribbean, as it was shaped by global designs (French "latinité") in the history of the colonial as well as the nation-building periods. Today global designs are guided in different directions to the fringes of "Latinidad," to its borders. There are other borders of Latinidad that I will not consider here, but that should be mentioned. For instance, the borders between French Latinidad and North African Arabic and Berber, or the European Latinidad and the Balkans, where Latinidad encounters the history of the Ottoman Empire and that of the Slavic countries. Finally, what shall we (the participants in this volume and the eventual reader) understand by "Thought"? Why thought and not, for instance, philosophy, social sciences, and so forth. *Is* there a Latin American thought? Is there *a* Latin American thought? Is there a *Latin American* thought? Is there a Latin American *thought*? Whatever question we (the participants in the volume and the eventual reader) choose to answer, I assume that there are a few starting points. First, the Latin part, the Latin substratum, and the vernacular languages derived from it shall be considered. Second, there is the question of coloniality, that is, the fact that Latin American thought and European thought are at different ends of the colonial spectrum and separated and linked simultaneously by the epistemic colonial difference. The colonial difference can account for the fact that, for instance, European Thought does not need Latin American Thought, but Latin American Thought cannot be such without European Thought. They are separated but at the same time linked by the coloniality of power and the colonial difference. It is precisely the asymmetric relation of power implied in the simultaneity of separation and linkage that makes border thinking possible. Thus, thinking about Latin American Thought presupposes Eurocentrism and coloniality, and by coloniality, I mean the constitutive and darker side of modernity. That is, Latin American Thought cannot be thought without thinking coloniality and the colonial difference. And third, Latin American Thought has to be conceived as intertwined, on the one hand, with the colonial difference and Eurocentrism, and on the other hand, at the intersection of coloniality and internal colonialism; that is, the reproduction of the coloniality of power by the "native" (Spanish/Portuguese Creole and mestizo elite that replaced the colonial power after independence) and the marginalization of Amerindian and Afro-American "Thought."

My contribution here offers further explorations on border thinking, and it is, simultaneously, a dialogue with a similar project advanced by Raul Fornet-

Betancourt. He calls his project "Interculturalidad y globalización," and proposes it as "Ejercicios de crítica filosófica intercultural en el contexto de la globalización neoliberal." In one of his recent publications, Fornet-Betancourt[3] called attention to the fact that "Latin American philosophy" has built itself a subaltern dialogue with a continental philosophy (thus, the question: Is there a Latin American philosophy?) simultaneously with its back to Amerindian and Afro-American contributions and to (Latin) American intellectual (in the larger sense of the word, not in the restricted sense that implies a certain kind of official and institutional education to be able to "think") production and imaginary.

The thesis that I propose and defend here is a continuation and expansion of the one formulated about a decade ago in an article by Anibal Quijano and Immanuel Wallerstein entitled "Americanity as a Concept or the Americas in the Modern World-System."[4] However, an important modification shall be introduced here in order to understand *Latinidad* in the colonial horizon of modernity, or, if you wish, in the horizon of coloniality at large. I will imagine the "modern/colonial world-system" and assume that modernity cannot be understood without coloniality. Also, the success of the self-definition of modernity consisted in creating the illusion that coloniality was something that belonged to the past and that modernity was destined to supersede it.[5] In reality, modernity cannot supersede coloniality because coloniality is constitutive of modernity. Although my focus is on Latin America, from the south to today's Latino/as in the United States, the larger frame is Latinidad in the colonial horizon of modernity. Latinidad played and was played out with a European imperial difference (the Anglo-Protestant world in conflict with the Latin-Catholic world). It did so by making the colonial difference (Latinidad and the Arabic/Islamic world in the Mediterranean) and also within the borders of Slavic-Turkey to the east (e.g., Rumania). Last, but not least, Latinidad in the south was introduced to mark the frontier of Anglo-America and ended up silencing, in a different way, the indigenous and Afro-American population whose relationship with the glory of Latin was never enthusiastic. At least, they did not have the same enthusiasm that is shown today by French intellectuals. *Globalatinization* (see following paragraph) was indeed a global design that now *est tombée et desuetude*, to use Marcel Proust's sentence referring to a glorious past that has turned gloomy.

The first configuration of the modern/colonial world system was the imaginary that was forged, consolidated, and transformed within the history of capitalism and geopolitically located in the western Mediterranean (Florence, Venice, Genoa, Seville) and in the passageway from the Mediterranean to the Atlantic beginning in the sixteenth century. Today we live in the most recent stage (global coloniality) of a long process of globalization inaugurated precisely by the emergence of the Atlantic commercial circuits and the foundation of modernity/coloniality. At stake today is the concept of Latinidad both in its global scope and in its local dimension in Latin America and in the Latino/a demographic configuration in the United States. Let me begin by remembering a historical narrative not always remembered. Latinidad is, indeed, a creation of the second stage of globalization (roughly since 1860), that is, of the colonial horizon of modernity and a creation of French imperialism. It is no longer obvious today that Latin America should be an identification to be defended and that *latinoamericanismo* shall be a project to be embraced. Raúl Fornet-Betancourt has advanced several arguments about the fact that Latin American philosophy has been blind to Amerindian contributions to Latin American social and philosophical thoughts. Latinidad, from the nineteenth century on, did not greatly improve much of the situation that was already mapped out in the sixteenth century: Amerindians were there to be educated and brought into Western philosophy and rationality. Vine Deloria Jr., a lawyer, intellectual, and activist from the Osage tribe points out several times that Native Americans have "visions," while Anglo Americans have "science" and "philosophy."[6] Jamaican-born philosopher Lewis Gordon makes a similar claim with respect to Afro-Americans. Afro-Americans in general (and not just Afro-Americans living in the United States) are considered to have "experience," while Anglo-Americans are provided with "theory."[7] Latin, before English, was the language of theology, philosophy, and theory. Thus, it is not clear in which sense the Amerindian, Native American, and First Nations would see themselves as Latin. Similar observations could be made about how Afro-American populations from Brazil, Colombia, the Caribbean islands, and French Canada consider themselves Latin. However, people of European descent are seen, from the outside, as Latins. And some of them would also see themselves as such. Pierre Nepveu has coined the expression "L'Amerique Latine du Nord" to describe French Canada.[8]

Thus, Latinidad continues to be a fiction that has been embraced in the nineteenth century by Spanish Creoles and mestizo intellectuals and that has also been embraced toward the second half of the twentieth century by immigrant intellectuals as well. The examples, in Argentina, of H. A. Murena, Alberto Gerchunoff, or Enrique Dussel illustrate how immigrant intellectuals joined the national (in the case of Gerchunoff) and the Latin American imaginary (Murena, Dussel), a fiction that, above all, has been restricted to the legacies of Spanish and Portuguese early colonialism. It is not altogether clear that Guadaloupe and Martinique are part of Latin America and that they belong to latinoamericanismo, an equivalent to orientalism in the imperial imaginary. There is no question that Cuba, Santo Domingo, and Puerto Rico belong to Latin America and to the *latinoamericanista* imaginary. Therefore, what is at stake here? Latinidad was a name proposed by French intellectuals in consonance and agreement with nineteenth century intellectuals in Spanish America and, therefore, Latinidad in Spanish America is not quite the same as Latinidad in French America (like Guadaloupe and Martinique) or British America (like Barbados, Antigua, or Jamaica).[9]

In a nutshell, Latinidad was part of the global designs and imperial conflicts of northern Europe in the late nineteenth century. The fact that Latin America emerged as a distinctive entity from imperial conflicts and that it was embraced by Spanish Creoles and mestizos in Spanish America and by Portuguese-born intellectuals is quite significant. At that period in time, northern Europe was distinguishing itself from southern Europe (and, therefore, Spain and Portugal missed the train for the second stage of modernity and for being identified with the Renaissance but not with the Enlightenment). Latin America was, and still is, for better or for worse, the America colonized by Spain and Portugal and, therefore, distinguished from the Latin America colonized by France, the Caribbean islands colonized by the British empire, and the Anglo-America that gained independence from England at the end of the eighteenth century. But, of course, all these "Americas" are not quite yet the same for Amerindians, Native Americans, and First Nations, nor are they the same for the Afro-American population whose memory has been construed between an Africa and different faces of imperial expansion (Spanish, Portuguese, French, and British) during the period of global expansion identified as modernity/coloniality. That is why four apparent different religions are so similar: Candomble in Brazil; Santería in Cuba, Venezuela, and Puerto Rico; Vudoon in Haiti; and Rastafarianism in Jamaica, Barbados, and Antigua. These "new" religions are the outcome of the early stage of globalization, and they have emerged at the intersection of African spiritual traditions and European colonialism (Spanish, Portuguese, French, and British).

But why should all of this matter? Why do we not ("we" the educators, scholars, intellectuals, politicians, bankers, economists, journalists, as well as all those who feel the need to be identified with a territorial unit) just forget about it? Why do we not, like the announcers of CNN News, keep Latin America, without further question, as the name of an existing entity, a subcontinental divide identified by the connections between the sign and the referent and not by the coloniality of power and the colonial difference? Therefore, why do we not proceed to identify "ourselves" (that is, those who are willing to be identified as such) as other than Latin Americans or Latino/as? By doing so "we" would not play that game of global designs imposing an identity on "us" that "we" are no longer sure of. Would indeed an identity that is based on a French idea and accepted by White Creoles in South America be an identity to be proud of and be embraced? Or is there something else in such an identification? Thus, if identity matters, it does so because of two reasons: The first is that Latinidad had indeed a double function in nineteenth-century global, imperial designs. On the one hand, France had a need to confront and stop U.S. expansion toward the South, particularly after 1848 and the Guadalupe Hidalgo Treaty. On the other hand, France needed to establish alliances in southern Europe with Latin countries (Italy, Spain, and Portugal mainly), both to assert its power vis-à-vis Germany and England and to have a buffer zone for its colony in Northern Africa (Argelia, Tunisia, Morocco). One can understand today how important it was for José Martí to claim "Our America." By the same token, one can surmise how difficult it would be today to make the same claim, not knowing whether Amerindians or Afro-Americans would identify with it. And the reasons are several beyond the growing presence and claims by Amerindians and Afro-Americans (no longer invisible).

Cartographers from the European Union and from the United States are re-
defining Latin America in the new map of globalization. Hubert Védrine, Foreign Minister of France, has it all figured out. Asserting the relevance of France
in the new global order, he divided the world into five categories: the "hyperpower"—United States; powers with "worldwide influence"—France, Great
Britain, Germany, Russia, China, Japan, and India; simple "powers"—Mexico,
Australia, Egypt, Spain, and Italy (and notice that Brazil is not here); "powerless
states" (or mere states)—Belgium, Sweden, Portugal, and Austria; and "pseudostates," which allude to Asia, Africa and, most likely, Eastern Europe.[10] Védrine
concedes to some of the "powers" a regional postcolonial influence, like Spain
in Latin America, Italy in the Mediterranean, and Greece in the Balkans. But that
is not all. To read Védrine's cartography is to read an update of the cartography
of modern imperialism (Western Europe after the eighteenth century). Védrine
considers France, England, and Germany among the "powers with worldwide
influence." He mentions them all and then immediately disqualifies Germany,
since Germany never was a colonial power and its language is hardly spoken beyond Europe. Thus, that leaves England and France, the two colonial powers
from the post-Napoleon era up until decolonization after World War II. However, the more we advance in the cartography, the more we learn that France and
"Latinidad," have an edge among the powers with worldwide influence. But of
course, we learn—indirectly—much more from reading this cartography. And
which is the missing country that fills the category of hyperpower? The United
States. As far as Védrine's work is concerned, France ends up being the future
promise of the European Union, and the United States, the friendly enemy. Are
we still not in the same nineteenth-century matrix that produced a Latin America to keep France's imaginary alive outside of France, as a country with worldwide influence? From Védrine to the attacks against U.S. mass culture (Ignacio
Ramonet) and scholarship (Pierre Bourdieu) in *Le Monde Diplomatique*,[11] there
is of course one difference: Védrine is on the side of neoliberalism while Ramonet and Bourdieu are against it. However, the idea that Latin America can
help France in maintaining its position of power within the imperial conflict
seems to be out of the question. There is already a revival of Latinidad in Europe that is at the core of the future constitution and governance of the European
Union. What would prevail, the "Machiavelian moment" and its influence in the
constitution of England and the United States or "la loi/voie Romaine" that
grounded the constitution of the Latin countries?[12]

On the other side of the imperial conflict, we have the imaginary of Latin
America being rearticulated from the United States. In the 1990s, Harvard political scientist Samuel Huntington[13] anticipated that wars in the future would be
provoked by the clash of principles and values of different civilizations rather
than by economic competitions. Consequently, he proceeded to identify nine existing civilizations in the post-Cold War order:

1. Western, which includes Europe, the United States, Australia, and New Zealand;
2. Latin American, from Patagonia to the northern frontiers of Mexico, and excluding the Folks Islands and Suriname (of course, the entire Caribbean is, for Huntington, Latin America);
3. African, which includes Sub-Saharan Africa only;
4. Islamic, which includes Northern Africa, the Middle East, although not much of India;
5. Sinic, which includes mainly China;
6. Hindu, which is basically India and certain corners of South Asia;
7. Orthodox, which covers the former Soviet Union;
8. Buddhist, namely, certain corners of China; and
9. Japanese.

Some people would argue that Huntington's classification is obsolete. Huntington's particular map may be, since books and maps become disposable commodities. However, the idea is still there, and what Huntington did was to remap an idea that is around in the common knowledge and belief of millions of people, at least in the North Atlantic. Huntington's classificatory logic reminds us of Jorge Luis Borges' description of the classification of the world in the Chinese Encyclopedia. Some of the classifications, perhaps most of them, are based on religion (Sinic, Islamic, Hindu, Orthodox, Buddhist). However, Western Civilization is not characterized by the dominant religion, Christianity, but instead by the secular identification: the West. Japanese is a civilization identified with a nation. And, alas, Sub-Saharan Africa and Latin America are identified as subcontinental divides, clearly enough, the most marginal in the post-Cold War centers of capitalism.

On the other hand, there are fewer and fewer voices in Latin America claiming a lost identity or trying to recast the remains of nineteenth-century days. Latinoamericanism seems to be more a nostalgic theme in the U.S. academy or in France's need for "dernière gadget d'outremer," than of Latin Americans based in Latin America. There is not time in Latin America to think about identities, national, or subcontinental. There are instead other pressing issues such as memory (of the indigenous people in the Andes, Guatemala, and southern Mexico or in postdictatorial regimes, like Chile and Argentina), the future and destiny of the university, and how to survive globalization economically and democratically. And these three major topics, which involve regionalization (MERCOSUR and NAFTA), foreign intervention (like the Plan Colombia) to control guerrilla as well as indigenous insurgencies, and the new articulation of ALCA (Area de Libre Comercio de las Americas). Thus, "Nuestra America" began to look like Simón Bolivar's dream of the Gran Colombia extended to an Hispanic American confederation that José Marti fiercely attempted to recast from Cuba, but that may no longer be available or desirable. Beyond the economic and military rearticulation, massive migrations from South to North, including, of course, Amerindians as well as Haitians, Jamaicans, Barbadians, and, of course, Cubans and Puerto Ricans who have U.S. citizen rights, Latin America does not correspond any longer with a territorial space. There may be a Latin culture that has spread all over the Americas, but that no longer coincides with South and Central America and portions of the Caribbean. Latinidad, furthermore, may be interesting to revisit as a possible identity claimed by a large number of people. However, it should be kept in mind that an identity that may serve for the identification of people belonging to a group of "mere states" or "pseudostates" only refers to a certain group of people (White Creoles, mestizos, and European immigrants) but not to others (Amerindians and Afro-Americans). Furthermore, the notion of Latinidad is also being used in the new world capitalist order for various other purposes: one would be to justify the exploitation of labor and of nature (oil in Mexico and Venezuela, the Amazon's natural resources); another, to appropriate the natural resources in vast areas of Colombia occupied by the indigenous population, as well as those of the Black population on the Pacific coast, that is, Ecuador and Bolivia. Latinidad in the Americas has been, particularly, since the Spanish-American war of 1898, the backyard of the United States, both when it refers to Latinos in the United States or Latin America in the South. But Latin America is also an international post to be reconquered by France, and now in complicity with Spain, in its constant and vigilant attitude toward the United States. Briefly, Latinidad in the Americas has a racial connotation that contributes to support the arguments and the economic and political interests of the neoliberal philosophy I just sketched in the previous sentences. The fact that France and Spain value Latinidad should not be confused with a disinterested recognition for the people of Latin America but, rather, as a place for economic investment and a territory to be defended from Anglo influence *(Anglicidad)*—the United States and England. That is, Latin America is one of the places in which imperial conflicts and the imperial difference are being reenacted at the beginning of the twenty-first century.

Next, I will sketch the historical processes that brought Latin America to life, and up to this point. Latin America emerged at the crossroads of the new imperial local histories, in the nineteenth century (involving mainly France and the emerging United States), and the local histories of the Spanish Creole and mestizo statesmen and intellectuals, in Spanish America, building new nation-states with their backs toward the indigenous and the Afro-American population. I will conclude by showing the need for imagining the possible futures beyond Latin America and, of course, latinoamericanismo in the Western colonial image. However, I will not propose a new name, an empty signifier that "includes" everybody. I will, instead, suggest that the Latin as well as the Anglo be uncoupled from territorial and national identification and that the Americas shall be rethought from several perspectives but, above all, as a historical crossing of imperial forces and hegemonic designs. There was, and still is, a racialization of subcontinental divides that I will attempt to map in the following pages.

During the sixteenth century, several commercial circuits were formed in the Atlantic that connected for the first time in human history: the commercial centers of Beijing, Baghdad, Venice, Cairo, and Seville to Cuzco of Tawantinsuyu, and to Anahuac (i.e., Mexico-Tenochtitlan of the Aztec Empire). Up to that point, Tawantinsuyu and Anahuac were disconnected from the rest of the commercial circuits from Beijing to Seville. Furthermore, toward the end of the sixteenth and during the seventeenth century, the plantation economy in the Caribbean began to develop and set the stage for the upcoming surge of trade with Holland, England, and France.[14] The plantation economy would eventually both displace Spain and Portugal from the hegemonic control of the Atlantic and contribute to the surge of the Anglo-Protestant in the North and prepare for the divide with the Latin-Catholic in the south of Europe. Furthermore, it introduced a strong Afro-American component that was divided between Anglo and Latin America, in continental as well as insular America (the Caribbean). We have here a scenario that Spanish Creole and South American mestizos will erase when Latinidad becomes the signature of nation building and subcontinental identity.[15]

Today Amerindian and Afro-American communities are making their voices heard, in continental South America and the Caribbean and among the Latino population in the United States with its thirty-five million people who are contributing to a new configuration of Anglo-America. It is time, then, to take seriously Fornet-Betancourt's claim[16] of the need for an intercultural philosophy that will help in imagining a future across continental divides that were set two hundred years ago by the projects of Simón Bolivar and Thomas Jefferson.[17]

My argument develops in three parts: The first part is the narration of the configuration and transformation of the ethnoracial imaginary within modernity/coloniality. The second part of the argument introduces the massive migrations as moments of transformation and *mestizaje* of communities identified with particular territorialities. The third part connects "cultural mestizaje" with "multiculturalism," both being consequences of cultural classifications related to states and socioeconomic structures. Cultural mestizaje involves questions of power inscribed in the hierarchical classifications of languages and forms of knowledge, in as much as both contribute to legitimizing ethnic cultures and citizens in hierarchical orders. For example, consider the fact that philosophy and science, today, are written in German or English, yet it would seem strange if they were written in Aymara or Hindi. Finally, the argument will be organized around a specific case, that of Latinidad as an identity category that enables the explanation of the fabrication of differences as well as the placing of those differences into hierarchies. Thus, I will explore the idea of the Americas in the modern/colonial world system also as a constitutive part of it. As O'Gorman convincingly argued in the 1950s,[18] America did not exist as such previous to the discovery of America. After his devastating arguments, which decolonized the image of the Americas forged during 500 years of colonial discourse, it is time to move the agenda forward and look at Latin America in the colonial horizon of modernity. I will do so by focusing on the concept of race. There are two assumptions underlying my argument: The first is that there is no America, Latin or Anglo, without modernity/coloniality. The second is that the very image of both Americas is heavily entrenched in the concept of race, an epistemic instrument in the modern classification of the world as its necessary colonial foundation. In order to imagine possible futures, it is necessary to look back, and in different ways, to what is and has been taken for granted and to think about Latin America's possible future from the perspective of coloniality. The Zapatista uprising and the increasing visibility and force of indigenous social movements are telling us, daily, that we have been paying too much attention to the Atlantic and modernity and have forgotten the Pacific, the Andes, and coloniality.


## II


Not long ago I heard a Korean intellectual say that in East Asia the concept of race, as we understand it today in Europe and the Americas, only entered Asian vocabularies and ideologies after contact with the West. Of course, I do not mean to suggest that differences, based on some criterion to distinguish certain human communities from others, did not exist. The Aztecs of the Valley of Mexico differentiated themselves from the Chichimecs to the north by not recognizing in them an adequate command of the Nahuatl language, which was spoken in the *tollan*. I have heard it said that something similar happened in ancient Greece, when the Athenians classified as "barbarian" those who did not correctly speak the Greek of the *polis*. The Korean intellectual's observation contributed to establishing a hypothesis that is not easy to prove but that is worth the effort to maintain as a horizon for reflection. The hypothesis is that the concept of race as it is conceived and discussed today is a concept that began to be constructed in the sixteenth century. Two sets of events contributed to the formation of this idea: the triumph of Western Christianity in Europe and the emergence and consolidation of the Atlantic commercial circuit in the sixteenth and seventeenth centuries. In the first case, the long-standing conflicts between Christians, Moors, and Jews acquired a new configuration with the triumph of Christianity on the Iberian Peninsula, which resulted in the expulsion of the Moors to North Africa and the Jews to northern Europe. In the second case, the emergence of Indians in the Christian consciousness forced a reflection on the limits of the human. Meanwhile the contingents of African slaves brought to the Americas became synonymous with "blackness" and "slavery." "Purity of blood" and "true religion" were two of the principal criteria through which the "religious-state" began to be constituted and based on religious criteria, racial differences, and the criteria of homogenized communities. Mixed blood was linked to religious ambiguity and the "convert" was the paradigm for the complicity between blood and belief.

It was through the complicity of purity of blood with true belief that the "religious-state" was transformed into the nation-state that was complemented with a restructuring of the coloniality of power, under the leadership of England and France. While the colonization of India and Africa transformed ethnoracial configurations, it was over a foundation laid in the sixteenth and seventeenth centuries. Meanwhile, primarily in the more populated regions of the Americas, terms began to appear to designate possible combinations of ethnicities. In the eighteenth and nineteenth centuries, terms such as Christians, Whites, Africans, Blacks, Amerindians, and olives reconfigured the ethnoracial matrix itself, which was the basis for the ethnoracial and territorial distribution of the planet. We owe this configuration in part to Immanuel Kant, who, in his little-known lectures on anthropology from a pragmatic point of view (given between approximately 1760–1790), classified the planet into four continents and four colors. The Kantian ethnoracial tetragon placed Blacks in Africa, Reds in America, Yellows in Asia, and Whites in Europe. Of course, for Kant, Europe was already Europe north of the Pyrenees, the Europe of nations after the Treaty of Westphalia (1648). The Europe of nations that implemented new forms of coloniality was also linked to another stage of the expansion of capital by means of the industrial revolution, the conditions of possibility for which had been created in the sixteenth and seventeenth centuries. The Atlantic commercial circuits supplied Europe with the reserves of gold and silver that allowed some countries to insert themselves, from the margins of the world-system, into the still dominant Asian markets (principally China and India, before colonization by England). However, another important transformation occurred during this period. The confluence of the accumulation of capital and the Protestant Reformation, north of the Pyrenees, also produced the distinction between White Anglos and Protestants on the one hand, and White Latinos and Catholics on the other. To be sure, the establishment of this difference is a crucial moment in the ethnoracial configuration of the modern/colonial world, the repercussions of which we are still living with today, particularly with respect to Latinidad and Hispanidad.

The Spanish-American War of 1898 was a crucial moment for the rearticulation of the ethnoracial roots of the modern/colonial world, as well as for the current debates in the United States surrounding Latinidad. In truth, beginning with the end of the eighteenth century, the question of the purity of blood was already not so much associated with religion as nation and, certainly, with the (in)compatibility between citizen and foreigner, instead of between Christian and pagan or infidel. In the next part of this chapter, we will see how my narrative concerns cultural mestizaje, hybridity, double consciousness, and different forms of state identifications and misidentifications from subordinated positions, as well as the ethical and political consequences involved in these processes. However, let us continue a little further with the narrative of modernity/coloniality.

In 1898, a strong and interesting reconfiguration of the ethnoracial sources that had gestated and consolidated in Europe since the sixteenth and seventeenth centuries occurred. It could not have been otherwise. The United States was in the process of ceasing to be a colony and a postcolonial country and was transforming itself into a leader in the new world order. A nation that was the beneficiary of the White, Anglo-Saxon, Protestant legacy, as well as a place in the structure of power and all that it implied, enabled the United States to confront Europe, at the same time, to mark its difference from the "Old World." Thomas Jefferson used the idea of the "Western Hemisphere" to indicate such a geopolitical difference. Let us recall that Anglo-Creoles as much as Latino Creoles, in the north and south of the Americas, respectively, marked their difference from Europe, after decolonization and during the nation-building period, in geopolitical terms. This is the being "raised" in the Western Hemisphere that granted themselves the right to difference (with England, in one case, and Spain, in the other) that was not racial or national, but geopolitical. Clearly, however, the apparent symmetry between the North and the South was not so, since the structures of power had already been established before the independence of the colonies in the North and the South. And one of these differences was ethnoracial. Being Anglo-Saxon meant being whiter than being Latino did. The ethnoracial difference was parallel to the ascendance to economic power of the North Atlantic, on both sides of the ocean. Thus, South America, which separated itself from Spain in the process of national construction, was associated at the same time with France, England, and Germany: countries that had already outlined the imperial difference with regard to southern Europe, principally with the Iberian Peninsula. To be Latino and Catholic (e.g., White Creole) in South America meant being in a third space in a global imperial order organized through ethnoracial differences. Clearly, this happened in the world of White and Latino Creoles who, in turn, marginalized mestizos, mulattos, Indians, and Blacks (and, of course, women of color) in the process of national construction. White women were admitted into the circles established by color, although they suffered a subordinated role awarded by the White patriarchy.

Whereas the preceding is a sketch of the reconfiguration of power in the Atlantic between Europe and the Americas during the nineteenth century, it should be noted that the triumph of the United States in 1898 was secured precisely over this process of reconfiguration. Simultaneously, this victory stimulated a new and decisive turn on two fronts. On one front, the U.S. victory structured the play of forces of the modern/colonial world. Political, economic, and military power began to be displaced from England to the United States, just as in the previous centuries power had been displaced from Portugal and Spain to Holland, France, and England. This turn of events brings to light the extreme importance of the American Revolution in 1776, as being as important as the French Revolution was in 1789. The fact that the latter is in a prominent position in all the histories of Western civilization is simply due to the narrow-minded chronological and linear view of history imposed by European modernity. Once you look at things and history from a geo-historical rather than from a chronological perspective, then you would understand that 1776 and 1789 are equivalent and decisive dates in the history of the modern/colonial world. The passing of a former colony to a postcolonial country and then to a leading nation in the new world order marked the change. That is to say, the change affected the entire structure of the modern/colonial world-system. On the second front, the discourses that supported the action and intervention of the United States in Puerto Rico (as well as in the Philippines) against Spain were decisive in reconfiguring the ethnoracial pentagon. In the first place, the distinction between Whites, Anglos, and Protestants, on the one hand, and Whites, Latinos, and Catholics, on the other, that had already been established in Europe moved to the United States in a complex and parallel manner. Complex, because the racial discourse in defense of "white supremacy" worked to erase the fact that Whites in the United States were Creoles. In a parallel manner because, just as the eighteenth century produced the "south" of Europe, 1898 produced the "south" of America—that is, Latin America. In the second place, the discourse of 1898 displaced and replaced the discourse around the events of 1848, when the United States took possession of lands that had belonged to the Mexican state. While on the one hand, in this case, the conflict involved two nations, on the other hand, the happenings of 1898 situated the United States in a prominent place in the structure of the modern/colonial world-system, and, therefore, in the field of imperial conflicts that until that moment had only been waged in Europe, between the sixteenth and eighteenth centuries. In the third place, 1898 established the basis for what is known today as the ethnoracial pentagon in the United States. Until the 1970s, the official formulas for ethnoracial classification were White, Asian-American, Afro-American, and Native American. Since that time, "Hispanic" has been added. For all these reasons, the identification of Hispanic was generated from and by the state, but also a thorny issue for those who found themselves identified as such. Chicano, Cuban American, and Puerto Rican are certainly three strong national categories derived precisely from relations between the United States and Mexico in 1848 and between the United States, on the one side, and Cuba and Puerto Rico, on the other, in 1898. Hispanic (i.e., the Castilian part of Latinidad), on the other hand, is a general category that identifies by means of a cultural-linguistic root and that finds its reason for being in 1898 when an old empire's moment of decadence coincided with a new one's moment of ascendance. Beyond these coordinates, the identification includes the rest of the immigrants from Hispanic America, including the increasing immigration of indigenous peoples from the Andes, Mexico, and Guatemala. Nevertheless, as Hispanic America began to be identified, beginning in the second half of the nineteenth century, as Latin America, Hispanicidad became confused with Latinidad. As it is well known, France introduced the idea of Latinidad in the second half of the nineteenth century for two reasons: one was to defend a Franco-Latin identity that was threatened by growing Anglo-Germanic power; the other was to prevent the southward advance of the United States after 1848, as evinced by the presence of Maximilian in Mexico. Latinidad, in the last instance, is a consequence of globalization in its nineteenth century phase, although with a double Christian background, that is, the Christianity in which western Europe was founded, and divided between Catholics and Protestants, and the Christianity that led the colonization in the sixteenth and the seventeenth century.

## III

*Globalatinization*—or *mondialatinisation*—is a term introduced by Jacques Derrida (1996) to describe the first dimension and, indirectly, to put on the table the force of Latinidad in the current play of forces in the European Union. There are some striking correlations between the *Ministre des Affaires Etranger*, Hubert Védrine, on the one hand, and "les historiens des gauches, en France et en Europe" (*Le Monde Diplomatique*, Pierre Bourdieu, Jacques Derrida, Žižek, etc.), on the other. Mondialatinisation is the name of the global dimension of Christianity that has its foundation in Latin. Nevertheless, while Derrida endorses and takes advantage of a reemergence of Christianity and Slavoj Žižek promotes a return to Christianity, in the Americas, however, the Theology and the Philosophy of Liberation came forward both in the South and in the North (as Black Theology of Liberation and in philosophy mainly through the work of Cornel West) and, as such, cast doubts on the Latinidad of Christianity and the Christian side of Latinidad. Vudoon, Santería, Candomblé, and Rastafarianism brought to the foreground memories that are no longer Christian, even if Christian elements can be found in them, and collectivities that until recently have been made invisible by Mondialatinisation and other forms of global designs. In what follows I will contrast the recast of Christian Latinidad with countermovements and emerging forms of identifications no longer reducible to the master plans of Christian and Catholic Latinidad or Christian Protestant Anglicidad. Furthermore, the racial underpinnings of Latinidad and Anglicidad are being revealed by intellectual projects no longer anchored in the identification between territory (America) and macrocultural markers such as Latinidad and Anglicidad. In his article "Faith and Knowledge" Derrida writes:

> We met, thus, at Capri, we Europeans (Derrida's accent), assigned to languages (Italian, Spanish, German, French) in which the same word, religion, should mean, or so we thought, the same thing.[19]

I am less interested in pursuing the etymology of *religio*, from Latin to modern vernaculars than I am in the "we Europeans" and the languages mentioned. English is not there, and, of course, neither is Polish, Portuguese, or Rumanian. English, as far as it is connected with the United States, already appears in Derrida's argument as the mask of Latin. "[W]e must formally take note of the fact that we are already speaking Latin (Derrida's accent). We make a point of this in order to recall that the world today speaks Latin (most often via Anglo-America when it authorizes itself in the name of religion).[20] If the world speaks Latin through English it is because Christianity underlines 'modernity' and, therefore, "modernity/coloniality." There is, however, a distinction to be remembered. If Christianity is indeed the ideological matrix of the modern world, then modernity is linked to Christianity, not through its Roman genealogy but, rather, through coloniality, which is the other side of modernity. But if this argument can be sustained, then the geoculture of the "modern world-system" is not anchored in the French Revolution, as Wallerstein has proposed[21] but, rather, in the Christian foundation of the modern/colonial world at the end of the fifteenth and the beginning of the sixteenth century. The expulsion of the Moors and Jews from Spain; the encounter with dubious "religions," called idolatries, in the Americas; and the still dubious practices of African slaves, in the Americas, gave to Christianity a central place in the emerging idea of Hispanidad. Thus, when Immanuel Kant reflects on *Religion Within the Limits of Reason Alone* (1794),[22] he is thinking at the threshold of the secular concept of Reason although maintaining the superiority of Christianity as the religious foundation of modern Europe and, eventually, the Western world.

This particular foundation is not necessarily available to Latin Americans, including of course the Indigenous and the Afro-American population with a long history ingrained with colonization, and the later immigration from Asia, in the nineteenth century. In fact, what would be a statement parallel to Derrida's if we remember not just the shadow of English for certain sectors of the European Union but also "the other borders" of Latinidad, those sides that remain hidden by the colonial difference that Latinidad produced and globalatinization continues to reproduce? Let's imagine one of the borders by imagining the following: "We met, thus, at Jamaica (or La Paz, Martinique, Puerto Rico, Chiapas, etc.), 'we' Latin Americans, assigned to languages (Spanish, Portuguese, Aymara, Quechua, Maya, Totzil, Nahuatl, French, English, Benue-Congo, Wolof, Fulani, etc.), in which the same word *religio*, should not mean, or so we thought, the same thing [emphasis mine]." Africa obviously contributed to a range of Caribbean and South American religions, that is, religion becomes, on the one hand, a hegemonic word that has Christianity as the parameter of religion, and on the other hand, it is a word that implies and names the colonial difference. Latin American and Afro-American religions and languages include Candomblé, Umbanda, and Portuguese in Brazil; Santería and Spanish in Cuba; Shango and English in Trinidad; Obeah and Myalism in Jamaica; and Voudou and French in Haiti. There is more, however; these religions have been invented at the intersection of imperial designs from different languages and countries, on the one hand, and African histories, on the other. And let us pass over the complex history of religion in the Andes where Latin and Spanish interacted, and still do, with Aymara and Quechua. It is not obvious here that Aymara and Quechua speakers speak Latin through English, as Derrida suggests! Perhaps he has in mind the northern part of the Mediterranean and the North Atlantic when he sees Latin as the Archi language beneath. His globalatinization may be indeed valid for a good sector of the North Atlantic, and the North Atlantic only, but not all of it. Indigenous and African components have been always tangential and edge-lined in the Latin world. (I do not think that in China or in India "we" all speak Latin through Christianity.)

What distinguishes religion in these countries from religions in the United States is the high ratio of Black inhabitants in the Caribbean and South America.

Moreover, the religions that are most easily identified with West African sources are practiced in colonial domains that received sizable numbers of enslaved Africans until far later than did the United States (Jamaica, Martinique, Barbados, Guadaloupe). The late importation of captives allowed the continual reinforcement of African forms of knowledge in the corresponding African American community. The limit of Latinidad appears when we think that if it is true that the prevalence of Roman Catholicism reinforced parallels between the Catholic saints and the multiple gods of, especially, the Yoruba, then it is not altogether clear that contact meant Christianization. Briefly, Latinidad is being tested within the borders; these borders are between Christianity and Afro-Caribbean religions, Andean religions and languages, and so forth, but also beyond the Americas, with Islam and Arabic, Hinduism and Hindi, and so forth. If the world is speaking English, as Latin was the global language of the Roman Empire and early Europe, and Sanskrit of ancient South Asia, speaking a language does not mean "being [in] that language."

Let me give you one more example and let us focus on a Native American lawyer, scholar, and activist, Vine Deloria Jr., instead of backing up our arguments with figures from the pantheon of the Greco-Roman and modern European history. (They are equivalent, are they not?) Are we not saying constantly that "difference" shall be overcome by the "similarity" of all of "us" ("we" Europeans, Latin Americans, Caribbeans, Native Americans, Afro-Americans, etc.)? Thus, as a Native American, Deloria speaks English, but he speaks more than Latin and Christianity through the English he speaks. He speaks Native American languages and also another *religio*, that is to say, a system of beliefs, view of the world, attitude toward life, and ethics and politics of social organization. Among Osages, these concepts and ideas received the name of *religio* because of Christianity. Certainly, *religio* became hegemonic and is a Latin word that tied up language and belief systems and was imposed as a reference to name similar practices in different communities that were named in different languages. Thus, *religio* is not a connector but, rather, an empty signifier that has the capacity and the power of subsuming under its master meaning the religions of the world.[23] Deloria's native tongue is Native American, although he speaks English. But when he speaks English, he does it from the perspective of Native American religions and toward Christianity as the unavoidable enemy. For Deloria the enemy is not English, but Christianity. English is his language, the language that overpowered Native American languages many centuries ago. Deloria is not in the position of a French or European intellectual in general, who, today, has to support the state public policy to ban English from school, from business, from advertising, from television, and from everyday life. Latin was like English, and if Latin and Christianity are being spoken through English today, it is because we are still within the modern/colonial world, within the imperial ideology that Christianity imposed throughout Spain and Portugal since the sixteenth century. Deloria is not concerned with the etymology of the word *religio*, but rather with Christian ideology seen from the receiving end. He states: "That Christianity takes special pain to ask whether we are friends or foes, to me, betrays the fact that Christianity is an imperialistic religion and so polarizes religious communication in a hostile manner,"[24] or "The Christian notion of religion seems to be commemorative in the sense that its ritual repeats and reenacts the sacred story of its founder's life."[25] "We now come to the nature of religion. The majority of tribal religions, as far as I can tell, look at religion as a healing and balancing process, whereas I understand the Christian tradition as a commemorative, historical, institutional phenomenon."[26]

Globalatinization—yes, but to a certain extent the borders of globalization are becoming increasingly vociferous. English, of course, is being used both as an instrument of neoliberalism but also as an instrument of liberation. Was it not the same with Latin? Latin was the instrument of the imperial designs of the Roman Empire, but it was also used at its borders by subaltern communities that ended up with vernacular languages, regional monarchies, and, later on, nation-states. Thus, liberation came not only from the borders of the Roman Empire but also from the borders of the Islamic and the Ottoman Empire. Christianity and Latin joined forces to build, on the one hand, a vernacular Europe and, on the other, an imperial Europe. Today the struggle is within the modern/colonial empire, the locus of enunciation of the network society. But it is difficult to anticipate where a change of direction would take place, as it may have been difficult to anticipate, in the fourteenth century, that one of the margins of the Roman Empire, Spain, would become a bastion of Christianity and a new empire. It would have been difficult in the fourteenth century, in China, to anticipate that in the western, unknown margins of the commercial trades, an economic power would grow.

## IV

Today we are in a new phase of globalization that is no longer dictated by the conflicts among nations that were or were not becoming imperial states, but characterized by its reorganization into a networked society. It is precisely the passing of the nation-states into a networked society that has motivated discussions about mestizaje, hybridization, double consciousness, mestiza consciousness, and other similar expressions. Why is this?

During the stage of the religious-state and mercantile capital, the commercial circuits, more than the cities of the metropolis, constituted the reference point for the economic transactions and the displacement of peoples. However, at the same time, only beginning with 1850, with the intervention of the steamship and the installation of railroads throughout the planet, was it possible to displace large contingents of peoples in different directions. During the sixteenth and seventeenth centuries, the only massive displacement of peoples was the trafficking of African slaves to the Americas. Perhaps, because of this, Kant was able to imagine that there was a relation between human communities and the continental division of the planet. At the same time, Kant could also imagine the configuration of European nations and nationalities and describe their national characters: Germans, Spaniards, French, Italians, and so forth. It was precisely in the eighteenth century when the concept of culture began to acquire its current meaning. Culture is defined in two complementary directions. First, culture referred to "national cultures" in Europe. The other definition is "colonial cultures" in Asia, Africa, and the Americas. National cultures were imagined with as much homogeneity as colonial ones. The same logic of homogeneity of national cultures, which were also imperial and hegemonic (England, Germany, and France), came to consider colonial cultures as homogeneous. It was necessary to construct the homogeneity of national culture, and, precisely for this reason, it was necessary to imagine the homogeneity of the "other" cultures, the colonized cultures.

The appearance of the steamship and railroad began to change the calm waters of national and colonial cultures, and mestizaje changed their characteristics. In the Americas, for example, the mixing among Iberians, Creoles, Amerindians, and Afro-Americans, in the South and among Britons, Creoles, Native-Americans, and Afro-Americans in the North began to become more complex with the arrival of new contingents of immigrants, mostly from Europe. However, such contingents of immigrants did not alter the model that had been established during the colonial centuries. The differences can be found in terms of class, but in ethnoracial terms things continued as they were; in the United States, the melting pot could be discussed as a sort of biological and cultural mestizaje. However, starting in 1970 the direction of massive migrations changed. No longer were the massive migrations composed of Europeans crossing to America. Rather, contingents from what was classified as the Third World during the Cold War (in practical terms, the former colonies of the imperial states), began to move toward the First World. In the United States, the melting pot was transformed into "multiculturalism" insofar as the new cultural mestizaje acquired a markedly political shade because of major changes in immigration laws in the 1960s. This history was not foreign to Europe, as reports of the increasing distaste for foreigners who have arrived from former colonies or areas considered marginal to Europe attest (i.e., areas that were once the Ottoman and Soviet empires). Cultural mestizaje is highlighted today by a new phase in the expansion of capital, in which the primacy of the market is displacing colonial differences toward other terrains. If race, gender, and sexuality continue to be important markers of identity, the fundamental device now is inclusion or exclusion according to the capacities of persons to integrate themselves into the new order of labor. The intellectual capital of the new economy displaces the manual capital that the old economy required. Cultural mestizaje is one thing, for example, when it involves groups of people that arrive in Europe from India or Pakistan in order to perform manual labor. It is another thing when groups of computer experts go to Germany, for example, to solve the problem of a lack of cultural capital so that they can compete in the new economy.

It seems reasonable to assume that persons and communities have always been mixed or hybrid. Not only in terms of biological reproduction, but different communities exchanged forms of life, which is to say, culture. However, the mestizaje and hybridization about which we speak today should not be seen so much through the depth or distance of universal human history as through the closer history of the configuration of the modern/colonial world. The imaginary of the modern/colonial world imposes an ethnoracial classification that gives a new meaning to the old differences between Christians, Moors, and Jews, since these differences had to be reconciled with the entrance into the same imaginary of the Indians of the West Indies and of the African slaves who were transported there. Later, in the course of time and with the expansion of England to the Pacific, the matrix of ethnoracial differences was brought up to date but with the same logic imposed in the sixteenth century.

Technologically, the possibilities for mobility created by the voyages of global exploration that began in the sixteenth century, by the industrial revolution, and by the processes of decolonization created a particular type of mestizaje, which is biological and cultural, that is, the mestizaje in and of the modern/colonial world. Latinidad emerged in these processes of imperial conflicts and was assembled to identify France with southern Europe and South America as a form of differentiation from northern Europe and North America. However, the concept of Latinidad created another structure of power insofar as France was, on the one hand, a constitutive part of the second modernity (since the French Revolution) and, on the other hand, built a discourse of differentiation from Iberian Latinidad, and, moreover, from South American Latinidad.

Well then, I think that the celebration of mestizaje and the hybridization has to do with the strong ideology of homogeneity that originated in the process of the construction of the nation-state. It came forward as a consequence of the Peace of Westphalia and the ascent of the bourgeoisie during the French Revolution, on the one hand, and of the first wave of decolonization in the Americas (United States, Haiti, various republics in Hispanic America), on the other. Without a doubt, there are various differences in the process of national construction in Europe, the United States, and Latin America. Significantly, while the United States and Europe constructed national homogeneity with white supremacy as their trademark, Latin American national homogeneity took an oxymoronic turn: it was conceived on the basis of mestizaje as purity and a guarantee of national homogeneity. The weakness of states is part of the last stage of globalization guided by the ideology of the market, which does not respect national ideologies or values. With the weakening of the state as a legal and administrative structure, the idea of national homogeneity built on the values of one nation (the dominant nation) also began to crack. With the breaking up of *the* nation, nations appear, that is, the minorities; hence, the migratory processes from south to north accentuate this process.

Things being thus, I would not try to celebrate mestizaje and hybridity for their contribution to the dismantling of national ideologies or criticize them for their excessive presence in the academic and journalistic languages of the last few decades. Rather, I want to understand, in the first place, the complicities between economic structures that permit and force the displacement of peoples and the values of the market that reward or punish determined behaviors and commodities. Something similar happens with "multiculturalism," a word that alludes to another type of phenomenon that has its roots in the disarticulation of the nation-state and the emergence of nations.

Certainly, national ideologies are not limited to particular nations, but they participate in the configuration of continental or subcontinental unities. So, for example, while the idea of Latinidad configured a transnational area identified by certain types of languages, certain types of memories, and certain forms of life (what we call culture), this configuration coincides with the strong stage of the formation of nation-states. Today Latinidad is acquiring another meaning in response to the economic restructuring of the global order. The south of Europe (the area identified with Latinidad and therefore with a slow rhythm, love, songs, and food) finds itself in a process of transformations, of mestizajes, and of double hybridizations. On the one hand, integration into the European Union creates the conditions for new articulations and for the modification of the old idea of the Anglo-Saxon and Protestant north and the Latino and Catholic south. On the other hand, the massive migrations from North Africa to southern Europe rearticulate the relations and borders established during the sixteenth century by Spain and France and during the nineteenth century by England and France.

In the United States and Latin America, the transformations are no less radical, although they have a specifically different historic economic configuration. Latinidad served France, as much in Europe as in the Americas, to characterize an area of contention against the advances of the North. For the Creole intellectuals of South America, Latinidad was a means of establishing an identifying discourse. It is clear that this discourse of identity elided South America's Amerindian and Afro-American communities for whom Latinidad was foreign. While this happened in South America, the Spanish-American War of 1898 not only established new articulations among imperial powers but also created the conditions for what is today Latinidad in the United States. Now then, this new configuration of Latinidad is so far from the motives that France had, in the nineteenth century, as to suggest it as the name for the campaigns of the Spanish government and royalty to promote Hispanic culture (through cultural centers and universities) in the United States. In the United States, Latinidad identifies two subordinated positions that are defined by their differences as much from Anglo-Saxon culture as from Latin culture, as it is currently manifested in Europe. In the last instance, Latinidad is a word that cuts both ways. On the one hand, it contributes to maintaining the imperial difference in the economic and political conflicts within the European Union. On the other hand, Latinidad has contributed to creating the colonial difference in the United States, to the constitution of an ascending Hispanic minority with a memory that still does not correspond with the cultural configurations in those terms in Europe and Latin America. It is not so much mestizaje that distinguishes the latter from the former, but double consciousness. The Latinidad of Latinos/as in the United States is not so much a question of mestizaje, or hybridity, as of the double consciousness of being Latinos/as and in the United States at the same time. This situation is not found in Spain, France, or Latin America.

## V

Latinidad is not a name to be used to single out a group of people who are mainly in Europe and South America but also in the colonial possessions of Spain, Portugal, and Spain in Africa and in Asia. It is a name that in the second stage of globalization, secular and nonsecular, Christians used to draw a geopolitical configuration in which Christian-Catholics became clearly distinguished from Christian-Protestants. As a matter of fact, Latinidad was invented by a French intellectual, with the collaboration of Spanish and Spanish American ones, precisely to draw a cultural divide that, in other terrains, was being articulated economically and militarily. Latin America becomes Latin America only in the nineteenth century and as a by-product of the imperial conflicts, in Europe, between France on the one hand and England and Germany on the other. Imperial conflicts are still at work today, as Védrine's cartography shows. However, Latinidad seems to still have a role in the cultural structure of power, and in the philosophical and political play of forces, as Védrine shows, of ethnic concerns of the leading nations (England and France). Nonetheless, at another level, the level of the civil society, Latinidad is being challenged daily by the massive migration entering Europe from Africa and Asia.

On the other hand, Latin America is becoming Latino America. The existence of a population of about thirty-five million Latinos/as in the United States points more toward a demographic and cultural rearticulation of the postnational stage of globalization. Indeed, while the national stage of globalization created the distinction and the divide between Latino and Anglo-America and between Bolívar and Jefferson, "Nuestra America" is no longer a clear identification or place of belonging. Nuestra America is being claimed also by Amerindians, from Southern Chile to Southern Mexico and from Bolivia and Ecuador to Canada. And of course, what is happening here is no longer the emergence of Indo America, which was a creation of the well-meant Creole and Mestizo intellectuals. Now the name is coming from those who claim their own names. Xavier Albó has reminded us of the meaning of Abya-Yala:

> Abya-Yala is the term with which the Cuna, Panamá, Indians name the continent . . . in its totality. The choice of this term (which means "earth in full ripeness") was suggested by the Aymara leader Takir Mamani, who proposes that all indigenous peoples use it in their documents and oral declarations.[27]

I am aware that there is certain tendency in Latin America, among Latin Americanists in the United States, and the informed public sphere to remain silent or react with an almost imperceptible smile when "things Indian" from Latin America are invoked. Those who are prone to the forces of modernity, moving fast and forward, and leaving behind what is slow may suggest that only new agers, lovers of traditions, romantics, and idealists can really take seriously suggestions such as the one advanced by Takir Mamani. However, the issue is not what name is better, but the question that asks about the politics of naming. Something like the "due velocità" in the language of Italian promoters of modernization who would like to see the South disappear once for all. However, there is a growing tendency among political theorists in Canada and the United States, who do not believe any longer in the possibilities offered by Jürgen Habermas, Ernesto Laclau, Chantal Mouffe, John Rawls, Charles Taylor, Martha Nussbaum, and others, to look for a "third way." Now, this third way is not the one advanced by sociologist Anthony Giddens and embraced by England's Prime Minister Tony Blair. No, Giddens and Blair are thinking a third way between right and left (or beyond right and left, as Giddens would prefer). The third way is that of political theorists such as James Tully[28] and Romand Coles.[29] James Tully, for example, theorizes the future of constitutionalism and draws extensively from British Columbia's celebrated artist and essayist, Bill Reid, and his no less celebrated sculpture *The Spirit of Haida Gwaii*. Tully's point as a political scientist is similar to the issues Xavier Albó and others (e.g., Silvia Rivera Cusicanqui) have been dealing with. Thus, bringing forward a name for a continent that has the same right to be as (Latin) America is one way of scratching beyond the surface. One way of saying that the question is not: Let's redefine Latin America, taking globalization into account but, rather, How is it that Latin America became to be such in the process of Western expansion and colonization? Globalization is revealing the borders of Latinity precisely because it is making it possible to ask questions about the political constitutions of historical scenarios that became confused with ontological entities.

Readers with a practical bent will find the suggestion of an indigenous name farfetched. However, what is at stake is an identification that is related to the very foundation of the political, beyond the regulation imposed by the configuration of Latin and Anglo-America. And this is also being claimed by the diversity of Afro-Americans linked, as I said, to different imperial languages and different religious creations in the Americas, as I mentioned before. Thus, what is emerging here is an Afro-America with the same titles and rights as those who claim Latin America. I am not proposing a map of distinctive and isolated configurations, but, rather, the multiple borders of Latinidad. If, on the one hand, Latinidad is occupying today a subaltern position in relation to Anglicidad, in Europe and in the Americas, it is also true that the current stage of globalization (postnational) is characterized by significant reconfigurations of the ideologies that mapped the continental divides during the national period. Massive migrations from South to

North and voices that have been silenced in the past, by the images of and by the hegemony of Anglicidad and Latinidad, are no longer claiming the right to be included but, rather, their right to be different, because we, humans, are all equals. *The Droits de L'Homme et du Citoyenne* (Latinidad) and *Human Rights* (Anglicidad) are being claimed from the perspective of those that have been left out of the hegemonic versions of the very concept of "human" and "rights." In the final analysis, what is at stake in the global transformation of hegemonic identification is the question of rights and the planetary reformulation of the political proper beyond the confines of globalatinization, that is, beyond the complicity between Christianity and Latinity and its secular transformation, Reason and modern vernacular languages, that went together with the foundation of capitalism and of Western expansion.

## NOTES

1. Campa, Román de la Campa, *LatinAmericanism* (Minneapolis: The University of Minnesota Press, 1999).
2. Agustín Lao-Montes, "Latin/o Americanisms: Epistemological and Political Challenges," in *Nepantla: Views from South* (March 1, 2001); Juan Poblete, ed., *Rethinking Area and Ethnic Studies* (Minneapolis: The University of Minnesota Press, forthcoming).
3. Raúl Fornet-Betancourt, *Interculturalidad y globalización. Ejercicios de crítica filosófica intercultural en el contexto de la globalización neoliberal* (Frankfurt: Editorial DEI, 2000).
4. Immanuel Wallerstein and Anibal Quijano, "Americanity as a Concept: Or the Americas in the Modern World-System," *ISSA* 134 (1992): 549–57.
5. Walter D. Mignolo, "The Many Faces of Cosmo-polis: Border Thinking and Critical Cosmopolitanism," *Public Culture* (December 3, 2000).
6. Vine Deloria Jr., "Christianity and Indigenous Religion: Friends or Enemies?" in *For This Land: Writings on Religion in America* (New York: Routledge, 1999), 145–62.
7. Lewis Gordon, "A Problem of Biography in Africana Thought," in *Existentia Africana: Understanding Africana Existential Thought* (New York: Routledge, 2000), 22–40.
8. Pierre Nepveu, "Poderes do Estrangeiro," in *Literatura e História na América Latina*, L. Chiappini and F. Wolf de Aguilar, orgs. (São Paulo: EDUS and Centro Angel Rama, 1993), 163–72.
9. Arturo Ardao, *América Latina y la latinidad* (Mexico City: Universidad Autónoma de México, 1993).
10. Hubert Védrine, *Les cartes de la France á l'heure de la mondialisation* (Paris: Fayard, 2000).
11. Pierre Bourdieu, *Le Monde Diplomatique* (1999, 2000).
12. Rémi Brague, *L'Europe ou la voie romaine* (Paris: Fayard, 1999).
13. Samuel Huntington, *The Clash of Civilizations* (New York: Simon and Schuster, 1997), 36ff., 246–48, and 312–18. See also map 1.3, 26–27.
14. Eric Williams, *Capitalism and Slavery* (1944; reprint, Chapel Hill, N.C.: The University of North Carolina Press, 1994).

15. Ardao, *América Latina y la latinidad.*
16. Fornet-Betancourt, *Interculturalidad y globalización. Ejercicios de crítica filosó-fica intercultural en el contexto de la globalización neoliberal;* and Mignolo, "The Many Faces of Cosmo-polis: Border Thinking and Critical Cosmopolitanism," 127–71.
17. Mignolo, "The Many Faces of Cosmo-polis: Border Thinking and Critical Cosmopolitanism," 127–71.
18. Edmundo O'Gorman, *La invención de América. El universalismo de la cultura occidental* (México: Fondo de Cultura Económica, 1958); and Edmundo O'Gorman, *La idea del descubrimiento de América. Historia de esa interpretación y crítica de sus fundamentos* (México: Universidad Autónoma de México, 1951).
19. Jacques Derrida, "Faith and Knowledge: The Two Sources of 'Religion' and the Limits of Reason Alone," in *Religion,* ed. J. Derrida and G. Vattimo 33 (Palo Alto, Calif.: Stanford University Press, 1996), 1–78.
20. Jacques Derrida, "Faith and Knowledge: The Two Sources of 'Religion' and the Limits of Reason Alone," 26–27.
21. Immanuel Wallerstein, "Culture as the Ideological Battleground of the Modern-World System," in *Global Culture: Nationalism, Globalization and Modernity,* ed. M. Featherstone (London: Sage Publications, 1990), 31–56.
22. Immanuel Kant, *Religion Within the Limits of Reason Alone* (New York: Harper Torchbooks, 1960).
23. The distinction I am making here between "connectors" and "empty signifier" is the following: Empty signifier (cf., Laclau 1998) is a concept within the logic of abstract universals that has been concocted to accommodate multiculturalism. An empty signifier is a space in which diversity can be included, while the empty signifier appears to be empty of meaning. However, the empty signifier as proposed is shaped by the existing hegemonic narratives (Marxism and Christianity) maintaining a hegemonic position from the left or, at any rate, as an alternative to the macronarratives of neoliberalism. Connectors are, instead, words as instruments constantly revealing their double side, their double density. They are the seed and the spark of border thinking (Mignolo 2000b). The hegemonic meaning of a word jumps at you immediately (like *religio*), and it appears as the word is naming the world. The hidden meaning, its darker side, cannot be deconstructed. You can deconstruct *religio* within the same family of languages and cosmologies, but you have to decolonize it to show that the word is not an empty signifier within the Western tradition but a connector that speaks for and from all those meanings and belief systems that have been cast away by the imposition of a name, a generous name, *religio.* Decolonization requires double translation, translation in two directions, from the silenced meaning to the hegemonic empty signifier and vice versa (Mignolo 2000a, 2000b). An empty signifier is willing to accommodate all different religions in and of the world. In a sense, the link Derrida establishes between Latin and Christianity makes me think that that they, Latin and Christianity, operate as an empty signifier of sorts, open to the inclusion of the world as far as the substratum remains recognized and as a platform.
24. Deloria Jr., "Christianity and Indigenous Religion: Friends or Enemies?" 145.
25. Deloria Jr., "Christianity and Indigenous Religion: Friends or Enemies?" 155.
26. Deloria Jr., "Christianity and Indigenous Religion: Friends or Enemies?" 154. Thus, there is no need among Native Americans, Amerindians, and First Nation "religions" to go back now and find the founding father, like Alain Badiou and Slavoj Žižek have been doing recently with Saint Paul and with the European revival of Christianity.

See Slavoj Žižek, *The Fragile Absolute—Or, Why Is the Christian Legacy Worth Fighting For?* (London: Verso, 1999); Alain Badiou, *Saint Paul. La fondation de l'universalisme* (Paris: PUF, 1997).

27. Xavier Albó, "Our Identity Starting from Pluralism in the Base," in *The Postmodern Debate*, ed. J. Beverly, José Oviedo, and Michael Aronna (Durham, N.C.: Duke University Press, 1998), 29.

28. James Tully, *Strange Multiplicity: Constitutionalism in an Age of Diversity* (Cambridge: Cambridge University Press, 1995).

29. Romand Coles, *Rethinking Generosity: Critical Theory and the Politics of Caritas (Contestations)* (Ithaca, N.Y.: Cornell University Press, 1997).

# 5

# Going Home: Tununa Mercado's
# *En estado de memoria*

## *Debra A. Castillo*

$F$rederick Jameson defines globalization "as an untotalizable totality that intensifies binary relations between its parts—mostly nations, but also regions and groups, which, however, continue to articulate themselves on the model of 'national identities.'"[1] He further clarifies that "globalization is a communicational concept, which alternately masks and transmits cultural or economic meanings."[2] This somewhat neutral definition, as Jameson succinctly notes, elides very deep ambiguities and even contradictions in the use of the term, which is given very different emphases and valorations depending on how and by whom it is deployed. Theorists of globalization frequently fall into mutually exclusive positions, making the concept subject to what Jameson calls both "baleful" and "joyous" interpretations. Thus, for example, among some thinkers, the much-discussed phenomenon of globalization has been demonized as the latest metamorphosis of a corrupt capitalist system, and for others, it has been celebrated as marking the freedom of both the marketplace and the local actors in the political and economic realms.[3]

Beyond such ideologically charged positions of a phenomenon largely defined with relation to the international economy, Jameson also notes the reinscription of globalization as a philosophical and cultural concept. Interestingly enough, in the more typical analyses of globalization in recent years, the baleful readings tend to attach themselves—if ambiguously and complexly—to questions of the economic realm and the globalized capitalist market, whereas the joyous readings are most typically associated with the elaboration of opportunities for cultural exchange involving both mass and high culture, as well as for opening up new directions in philosophical discourse. Thus, for example, Martín

Hopenhayn asks us to think about the possibilities of a globalization that "could mobilize liberating energies. I am referring to transcultural enrichment, the encounter with the radically-other. . . . More than multicultural respect, transcultural recreation: To come back to us after having passed by the good savage, to put ourselves experientially in perspective, to have our bodies pass through the body of the South, the North, the East."⁴ Hopenhayn is in this respect a utopistic visionary, drawing us with him into the seductive, provocative celebration of cultural multiplicity as a new kind of freedom, achieved through international travel and through the near simultaneous exchanges at the speed of electrons in the contemporary communication net.

From where I stand here in the First World, both economic and cultural globalization seem a self-evident fact, with implications ranging from shopping mall construction to university curriculum development. Nevertheless, even if we accept the theory that globalization has inescapably and universally impressed itself upon turn-of-the-century modernity, numerous questions remain. What are the blind spots in globalization theory? How is globalization differently understood in the U.S.-European (or Eurocentric), and Third World(ist) theoretical locations? In a recent paper, Santiago Castro-Gómez comments, for example, that the normative understanding of modernity in Latin America is necessarily different in kind from the Euro-American and that this temporal belatedness reflects a qualitative distinction in theoretical structures of thought about modernity: "By contrast to what happened in Europe, the consolidation of cultural modernity in Latin America does not precede the cinema, radio, and television, but it arose precisely because of them. . . . Modernity in Latin America challenges, then, the theoretical framework generated by 'the project of modernity.'" It is precisely this antinormativist perspective that Castro-Gómez analyzes in his recent work delving into the still relatively unexplored territory of modern Latin America's philosophical difference from, and potential contributions to, the metropolis.⁵ There is in this argument a strong claim for a supplementary reading of this Euro-identified theory, one that comes from the South, from the peripheries of modernity. Even further: this southern take on this theory, suggests Castro-Gómez, not only will serve as a supplement to the metropolis but can provide the foundation for a countertheoretical stance that will challenge some of modernity's most basic and assumed premises.

Reading both Castro-Gómez and Hopenhayn together reminds us, too, that the "nosotros" [the "we"] and the "otros" [the "others"] in the latter's commentary are more ambiguous than they might look at first glance. From one point of view, the "us" is the international body of scholars who read and enjoy thinking about questions such as those raised in these fairly abstract, relatively dense, academic articles and books. Both Hopenhayn and Castro-Gómez, in this brief capsule, serve as exemplars of representative projects for Latin American engagement and dialogue with the challenges of thinking globally from outside the Euro-American axis. They are the "others" within the purview of the globalized theoretical network, the oppositional thinkers who frequently serve to remind metropolitan totalizing thinkers of the local particularities and regional realities that serve as an offset as they undergird theoretical analyses. The questions they pose are essential ones; furthermore, the nuanced engagement with thinkers such as these men reminds us of a crucial blind spot in much First World theorizing and provides a resource for deeper and more powerful thinking.

From another perspective, people like Hopenhayn and Castro-Gómez—along with other scholars such as Ernesto Laclau, Enrique Dussel, Gayatri Spivak, or Homi Bhabha, to name just a few—represent courtesy members of the First World "us," always marked by (and often celebrated for) a putative or real aura of otherness, that in turn and paradoxically makes them "other" to the intellectual institutions of their home countries as well as, obviously, "other" to the subalternized citizens inhabiting those local realities. Still further, in this playing off the global "us" versus the local "other," there are many, many others who inexplicably remain on (or even imperceptibly off) the margins of theory, who perhaps cannot globalize, even if they want to, because their experience does not fit conventions that allow for the first opening into a dialogue. Tendentiously, I would say that, by and large, this is women's case.

If, following Jameson, we agree that at the heart of discussions about globalization is the theorization of a totality, even if an untotalizable one, then a serious gap arises with respect to at least 50 percent of the human race who remain almost entirely absent except for passing references in the vast body of theoretical work associated with thinking through the implications of globalization in contemporary society. This is what Kaplan and Grewal, following Vivek Dhareshwar, call the predominant "male agon" in the international cultural debate, a largely unexamined ethos that, they theorize, may derive at least partially from the Marxist heritage of many prominent thinkers and from the well-known limitations of Marxism with respect to gender-conscious analysis.[6] Beyond the obligatory feminist article in any anthology on the topic, the extensive mainstream bibliography on globalization rarely engages rigorously with gender-conscious research and tends instead to vaguely acknowledge the importance of international feminism without doing close readings of, or entering into dialogue with, these works. Raquel Olea says it well:

> Women have been the subjects neither of the project of modernity nor of the crisis of this project; historically absent from the pacts of discursive, social, and political power, our recent incursion into the public sphere still situates us on the margin, outside of the spaces valorized by dominant culture. . . . Feminism comes from "nowhere" into spaces where its discursivity does not yet have a history, where it does not yet have the capacity even to negotiate or enter into alliances.[7]

Feminism and, indeed, women in general represent real problems for these theoretical exchanges, and as a result, they tend to be all but ignored as a complicating variable that somehow seems to be uncomfortably and, indeed, almost self-consciously displaced outside the boundaries of ongoing discussions. As Olea intimates, feminism seems to come from nowhere, and while its location in the public space has by now become technically unavoidable, the possibilities of engaged dialogue remain severely limited. Jean Franco would agree. She writes that "the class privilege of the intelligentsia has always posed a problem for Latin Americans, but in women's writing it becomes particularly acute since women writers are privileged and marginalized at one and the same time."[8] Likewise, Amie Parry's trenchant response to the presentations in the 1994 Duke University Globalization conference is apposite: "One of the ongoing concerns of the conference was the question of feminism and its role in resisting the effects of globalization, a concern that was brought up in various contexts but was rarely itself the subject of prolonged discussion."[9] Parry articulates a frustration that many academics have felt when participating in conferences and other intellectual exchanges; our colleagues openly and frankly acknowledge the importance of international feminist contributions to their projects, but they rarely go beyond the one-sentence reference to the essential importance of the advances in this theory by transnational feminists (a list of names typically accompanies this reference to feminists). The ubiquity of this throwaway acknowledgement in the glaring absence of any real engagement with feminist theories or women's texts seems to appear as a way to avoid an intractable problem without pretending that it does not exist.

This problem is, of course, too large to address in a single chapter, and the dearth of reciprocity in theoretical discussions can only be alluded to here. I propose to contribute obliquely to a potential dialogue through a discussion of Argentine's Tununa Mercado, paying particular attention to her remarkable 1992 text, *En estado de memoria (In a State of Memory).*[10] Without ever using the word globalization, Mercado addresses a kind of globalized, cosmopolitan experience akin and analogous to that theorized in recent work like that of Jameson, Hopenhayn, and others, and links it to a particularized consciousness and to a style redolent of old-fashioned storytelling. The author describes this book in a 1992 interview as a "conquest of the body of the text—the only thing that could stanch the flow of personal loss, of nation, people, memory."[11] In this book, ineluctably, the memory of an Argentina that has fueled personal identity during the long years of exile comes into conflict with the lived Argentina of a postexile returning home. This is a book that in some sense rigorously addresses the question asked a few years ago by Néstor García Canclini: "What does it mean to belong, to have an identity, in this end of the century?"[12]

In his perceptive study of this work, Idelber Avelar classes it among a body of "untimely" texts, works that take up the political and personal task of writing in a postdictatorial climate, confronting both "the imperative to mourn" and "the epochal crisis of storytelling and the decline in the transmissibility of

experience."[13] For Avelar, the impossible condition potentiating this work de-
rives from the author's personal need and her intellectual commitment to come
to terms with Argentina's recent past, in the recognition that the official strategy for redemocratization on the national level involved "the erasure and forgetting of the experience of the victims" of the Dirty War.[14] How, Avelar asks,
do committed writers go about the task of mourning—an active forgetting—
and a necessary personal and ideological task, in the face of a national process
defined by passive forgetting?[15] At the same time, this work of mourning and
remembrance is encumbered by the fact of the author's own absence from Argentina during those critical and terrible years, a period during which an imagined Argentina, constructed piecemeal in a foreign country, served her as the
touchstone to ground identity. Globalized despite herself, because of her pro-
fession as a committed Argentine intellectual and a writer living in exile, Mercado, thus, returns "home" after long years in France and in Mexico, to a
deeply loved and lovingly remembered Argentina that no longer feels comfortable and that is no longer entirely home.

Critics have differed considerably as to the genre of this work, and the slight
variations in genre ascription seem to me to be telling in terms of the uses to
which this text can/has been put. Jean Franco calls it simply a novel; Avelar refers
to it as "highly fragmented and reflexive memoirs,"[16] and as a testimonial
novel;[17] Patrick O'Connell talks about it as a novel,[18] as an autobiography in an
episodic style, autobiographical fiction,[19] and "personal testimony."[20] In any
event, readings of this text, and Mercado's own comments on it, generally reflect
an awareness of the close parallels between the first-person narrator of the series
of interconnected stories and the events in the author's life. This fundamental
slippage among fiction, autobiography, and meditative essay offers readers the
first and perhaps most radical message about this text, one we begin to absorb before even beginning to explore the book. In contrast to the comfortable norms and
expectations associated with academic writing in general, this text's *sui generis*
combination of fictional self-writing, on the one hand, and meditative essay, on
the other, keeps us off balance and hints at the contradictions associated with a
double-edged process when "others" deploy their knowledge in and against the
structures associated with "us."

Strategically, while retaining its fundamental, irrecuperable strangeness, the
text also suggests a modality by which a traditionally excluded subject can attempt to represent herself in a way that meets the demands of metropolitan
knowledge construction—if only as a kind of inversion of norms associated with
European-identified genres: travel writing (here Latin American woman explores the world), autobiography, trauma narrative, and personal essay. I have already noted the tendency in theoretical texts to use the abstract third-person discourse, as well as the fascination with, and almost obligatory allusion to, some
ill-defined and underanalyzed other outside the bounds of theoretical discourse.
At the same time, an essentialized concept of women and a vague gesture toward

feminism abound in globalization theory, subject to the displacements that are structural to the genre of the theoretical essay. Against this dominant tendency, Olea references a basic untranslatability of the woman's experience in the public space, the relative opacity of an embodied subject that seems to come out of nowhere and does not readily dissolve into existing discursive needs. In Mercado's text, we have the concrete working out of one response to this intermingling of expectations and exclusions with her simulation of witnessing in place of the re-creation of an imagined authentic other's voice. *En estado de memoria* fits neatly into the growing, and now better-recognized, subgenre of the "criolla gender essay" that Mary Louise Pratt succinctly defines with reference to Victoria Ocampo. The preferred form of the male essay, says Ocampo, is the monologue; conversely, Pratt suggests, the criolla gender essay structures itself implicitly or explicitly as a dialogue or conversation with its readers.[21] The Argentine writer, thus, implicitly takes issue with the traditional self-image of analytic thought as single, neutral, and objective, reminding us that the (returning) exile's consciousness is shaped inexorably by dialogue with other people and other cultures, by the class privilege that has allowed the narrator the option to choose exile, and by the overtly feminine voice that recalls the gender privilege attached to specific kinds of discourses.

Jean Franco has dedicated much of her recent work to exploring the expanding cultural repertoires that come with an increasingly intense and frequent juxtaposition, exchange, and displacement of peoples and cultures in a series of studies that have ranged from commentaries on mass culture comic books to analyses of Tununa Mercado's highly complex essays and fictions. She focuses on the profound transformations taking place at all levels of society and argues that in the Latin American context "this process can be described as 'deterritorialization,' although . . . in a sense rather different from that used by Deleuze and Guattari," one that not only takes into account the configurations of advanced capitalism but also recognizes the seductive power of the family and of the home as a "space of refuge and shelter."[22] The premise underlying *En estado de memoria* intersects directly with these concerns, in its unmistakable delineation of a peculiarly Argentine, specifically feminine, working through of the implications of a deterritorialized consciousness with respect to a problematic that is intensely personal, as well as both local and broadly universal, both rooted in a particular national history, and deracinated from the nation.

The problem Mercado sets for herself in this book is deeply hermeneutical, involving talking through a layering of culture on culture and text on text, learning how to think from the perspective of a Latin American woman displaced from her homeland into an alien cultural space (France, and later, Mexico), and then returning home in the aftermath of unthinkable traumatic violence. As Martín-Barbero says in another context, equally applicable to Mercado's problem: "A national memory built on a hereditary vindication explodes, divides, multiplies. It is the other face of the crisis of the national, a complement of the new lattice that the *global* constitutes: Each region, each locality, each group demands the right to its memory."[23] And yet, this fiercely defended right to memory encodes its own irrevocable refusals. Mercado's work, says Jean Franco, "confronts one of the major issues of our time—the issue of a pluralism that permits and even encourages difference. The narrator's obsession with a tramp . . . may, in fact, reflect a certain nostalgia for marginality that has, however, no social significance. For the marginal is merely an individual rebellion while, on the other hand, the social text has become unreadable except individually." In Franco's reading, one of the accomplishments of Mercado's text is to bravely confront such teasing or baffling intellectual and institutional uncertainties. In the last story in the volume, the narrator writes on a cracked gray wall and is, finally, absorbed into the text of her own self-inscription, which dissolves under her writing hand. Referring to this metaphor, Franco continues: "When the wall of gender difference comes down, it is not simply the center that is destroyed but also marginal positions, including that of 'woman' and 'woman writing as a woman.' . . . The woman intellectual must witness not only the destruction of the wall, but that of her own anonymous inscription on that very wall."[24] It is a difficult and arduous path that leads Mercado from dream text to this seemingly nihilistic dissolution.

The longest text in *En estado de memoria* is a thirty-page meditation entitled "Exposure" *[Intemperie],* staging the encounter between a woman who has come home from exile and her obsession with a homeless man. This man offers an intractable mystery; as Franco says, he is marginal and (cruelly) insignificant, yet the narrator's nostalgia and her yearning for meaning ends up constructing an encounter and elaborating a discourse between the two of them in the pages of this text. In this effort, Mercado reminds us of parallel efforts of the fellow southern cone activist, Chilean-born Diamela Eltit. Eltit has spoken forcefully about the importance of working at the level of discourse in order to effect social change and has been particularly committed to mobilizing and giving nuance to that which has been most marginalized within culture. She is the author of a series of technically dazzling novels beginning with *Lumpérica,* a novel she notoriously read in a brothel after staging readings in Santiago in which she cut and burned her own flesh, and including controversial works like *Por la patria, Cuarto mundo, Vaca sagrada,* and especially her *El padre mío*—a famously "unreadable" text consisting of a recompilation and edition of a homeless man's disconnected, severely traumatized, schizophrenic monologue. Eltit specifically associates a rigorous and politically committed recuperation of marginal voices with a rearticulation of the feminine, since, as she notes, that which in society has been most repressed and negated tends to be relegated to the feminine space.[25] The feminine, then, is not just the space of women; for Eltit, it is whatever has been muted and privatized at the margins of official culture. Then too, as both Eltit and Mercado know, the individuals and groups who occupy the interstices of the system also reveal its limits when official discourse is put under pressure.

In Mercado's text, the style is less scourgingly transgressive, but the commitment to a writing that combines intellectual rigor and aesthetic value is the same as the overlap between the space of the feminine and the politics of marginalization. Her narrator is a writer, trying to use her craft to write her way back into this place that is both familiar and strange, in an awareness of the accrued effects of all the other places she has resided in the interim. The homeless man seemingly has no fixed place to be, since he lives and sleeps in a plaza; yet he rarely moves more than a few meters from a single spot, whereas the writer comes and goes throughout her newly reannexed space, drifting from room to room in her house, going out to walk her dog, and getting into taxis and buses to move through the city. As the narrator struggles to write through her estrangement from her homeland, every morning she watches the homeless man writing in a notebook, and her distraction from her work provides an absolute contrast to his total absorption in his.[26] In this manner, her writing and his become inextricably bound together and linked to her return to Buenos Aires, a reincorporation into her homeland interrupted in the course of this work by a two-month return trip to Mexico. The act of writing itself is one of the dominant metaphors of the text, and the homeless man, who she later learns is named Andrés, occupies the cusp of this meditation. Thinking of her own interrupted writing and watching Andrés' concentration on writing in his notebook, she comments: "Doing things is a way of life; this may seem obvious, but it is not so obvious to people who fold and unfold their existence as if it were made of paper and then go on folding it smaller and smaller until there remains a thin scrap left to stand on. . . . But if there are no chores, if the folding and unfolding is performed on the basis of pure being and the absence of doing, contact with the universe will necessarily be stark and withering."[27] It is in the reciprocal fluctuation of these observations of, and later conversations with, Andrés that the narrator moves to a radical uncertainty about her own work, a hyperconsciousness about the tasks she assigns herself perhaps because the encounter with self in a stripped and pitiless universe would be too impossibly difficult. Says the narrator: "My interest in the man of the plaza would put me, whether I wanted it or not, in an exceptional state, if not in a state of urgency . . . of the kind that one feels when one comes across a forceful revelation in a text concerning the question of being."[28] Thus, Mercado insists on the contrast between working day life, lived minute by minute in a consciousness of the passage of time, and *vivir a la intemperie* ["the life of exposure"]. She explains: "In that state of exposure there are no concrete or practical chores, no small closures that block off periods of time. . . . It would be endless to enumerate all the things that have no end, all that does not have to be done and that has no place in the place of exposure."[29] More important, this concept of *intemperie* [exposure]—living it, the state of it, the place of it—connects to her imagination of the time and space of exile, which also has "pequeños cierres" [small closures], the imagined/constructed temporal and spatial parenthesis of a nowhere that marks time between the home before and the longed-for home after:

> Time spent in exile has a trajectory like a great sweeping brushstroke . . . but it is brushed aside, one prefers not to perceive it because one assumes that the banishment will end, that it has all been some kind of parenthesis unrelated to the future.
> Time is provisional, passing week by week.[30]

Exile, in this analogy, is like homelessness, like living under the elements, provisionally; it is like being folded tight into a scrap of paper, like occupying a parenthesis. The continuity of the homeless man's day-to-day existence comes to represent for her the experience of the discontinuities and disruptions of an exile's life.

It is no wonder that the narrator finds herself becoming confused: "I did not know what my own situation of exposure was, and I could not know, what his was either."[31] The narrator in this manner includes herself in the loose society of people living a la intemperie—but only in a metaphorical sense. Mercado, however, is pitiless with her narrator, who enjoys unreflectively the middle-class comforts that allow for a privileged abstraction without real commitment. There is still a further, necessary step in Mercado's account; the abstract becomes concrete when the narrator goes beyond speculation about the homeless man, when she learns about his past, gives him a name, and speaks to him. In the course of these conversations, it begins to rain, reminding both the narrator and her reader that the *intemperie* [exposure] that had become a metaphor in the text, anchoring abstract thinking about the situatedness of the gendered self, has its basis in a climatological phenomenon and is not merely the grounding for an existential speculation. Here, under the rain, her meditation breaks down—precisely when she tries to imagine bringing Andrés home, conversing with him in her house: "[I]f I was able to speak to him there, outdoors *[en la intemperie]*, then there was no apparent reason why I could not do the same in the living room of my own home."[32]

The most persistent association for Mercado of the image of *intemperie* [exposure] with the situation of her narrator is that having to do with her severe disassociation from what we might call the normative rituals of arrival. The narrator's immediate response to her homeland on her return to Argentina is to look for anchoring memories, to ritually seek out context in place; instead, she feels unmoored and adrift. She recognizes herself as a survivor of a nexus involving a fragmentation of identity that reaches into all aspects of her life, making her physically ill: "I was in a shipwreck" *[Estaba en un naufragio]*, says Mercado in an interview when asked about the genesis of this book, and *En estado de memoria* became her way of writing herself back home and to health.[33] Mercado is extremely eloquent in her descriptions of the disequilibrium and fragmentation figured through minute shifts in language and in semantics that totally change meaning. Her name provides one excellent example:

> I told him my name in turn, which, over the course of several weeks, he systematically distorted, changing the first *n* of my name to a *t*, and I never corrected the error. . . . A *t* in place of the *n*, an *i* substituted for a *u*, an *o* in place of the first *u*, etc., these things do not upset me as they used to; I now know that this is my name, there are no more doubts as to the identity that the name confers upon me, but this was not always so. . . . With Andrés, it did not seem appropriate to clarify that the second *u* in my name did not precede a *t*; I preferred to put my trust in the possibility that some illumination in another context would dissipate this particular flaw in our relations.[34]

While the narrator explains that Andrés' errors are not atypical of similar misunderstandings in the past, they nevertheless play an important role in the reconstruction of a state of memory that finds itself located a la intemperie, echoing the unsettling of identity and home in exile space.

The narrator is able to act upon her fascination with Andrés because he poses no threat, remaining docilely in his place, allowing her to come and go around him, and occupy unproblematically the safe ground of her home. His life is rapidly subordinated to her needs, just as his text becomes part of hers, and his challenges to her identity are discounted too quickly. Over and over again, he is described as "harmless" *[inofensivo]*. This from a woman who knows his background and who further informs her interlocutor that he was once a brilliant student who "had ended up that way due to a trauma."[35] This confidence, in turn, makes the narrator wonder about other traumas, about whether the gossipy woman sees her as also traumatized (the narrator knows that she has confused the woman by saying that she's from here, but not from here, that she's also from Mexico) and asking herself, "perhaps she thought that I was totally harmless" as well.[36] Those marked as "harmless"—the freak who points at the narrator while she's standing in line for the bus, Andrés the homeless man, the exiled writer— the flotsam and jetsam thrown up by the various traumas of the time and surviving "on the banks of the world"[37]—pose no threat, but equally have no input. Andrés especially does not compete with the narrator as a writer: "what he was willing to give did not constitute what could be called a narrative body."[38]

The gossipy woman on the bus seems to bear out Robbins' elucidation of an "assumption that to pass outside the borders of one's nation . . . is to wallow in a privileged and irresponsible detachment" (e.g., in this case, ignorance marginalizes the narrator who knows nothing about the area's harmless freaks and homeless people and who is totally uninformed about a human interest story saturating the Argentine media at that moment). Consequently, Robbins continues, the "cosmopolitan is held to be incapable of participating in the making of history, doomed to the mere aesthetic spectatorship that he or she is also secretly held to prefer."[39] The narrator's ignorance about Olmedo's suicide connects her once again with Andrés, who "preferred not to know what was going on in the world,"[40] and who consciously avoided news, rejected newspapers, and refused to speak to the narrator of current events.[41] Succinctly, such shifting alliances between, for example, the exile and the homeless man, the narrator and the gossipy woman, the exile and the reader, point to the uncertain ground creating and aligning "us" and "the others."

This assigned and necessary inoffensiveness of the outsider/marginalized person—the traumatized man who never left Argentina, the writer who is struggling to return—creates an absolute contrast with the general condition of the exile, who is, nevertheless and curiously, equally inoffensive while at the same time displaying utmost obnoxiousness. If the returned person seems out of touch with Argentine reality, the reality of the narrator and her companions in exile is constructed out of an obsessive reference to and reiteration of whatever scraps of Argentineness accompanied them to their host country of Mexico to an exclusion of interest in Mexican news, Mexican current events, and Mexican reality. As the narrator notes in an earlier text in the book, during the time of exile the monotopic of Argentina as the touchstone for conversation and contemplation created another kind of marginalization, one occurring within or at the borders of Mexican society. Argentine exiles remained blissfully ignorant of their host country, preferring instead to obsessively seek out any hint of a reference to their lost homeland: "Argentina, that wretched *[poca madre]* country that had expelled us and of whose situation we never stopped talking . . . filling the cracks and hollows of our reality, so to speak, with Argentine substance."[42] The exile community, in this manner, turned inward. To use a metaphor evoked earlier, the exiles folded back in upon themselves, becoming smaller and smaller like a repeatedly folded scrap of paper, and in this small and almost entirely irrelevant space, they created and projected a utopistic image that bypassed the memories of an ungrateful home country in favor of localized memories evoking a lost paradise:

> Our bond to the country we were forced to leave conditioned our lives; there were even some who were never able to bear the sum of their losses, who passed their days remembering their old neighborhoods and idealizing customs that, one might wonder why, were considered paradigmatic of a lost paradise; that substance of Argentina that they missed seemed to be embedded in mythologies of little interest . . . with neither intellectual nor imaginary value.[43]

The question here is not just one of belonging or of refusal to adapt into a predetermined foreign cultural context. More important, Mercado asks us to consider how we define what is one's own, what is foreign, how the choices one makes around such questions shape identity and reshape social reality. For Avelar, *En estado de memoria* "narrates the epochal crisis of the proper" and the "dissolution of dwelling" that in this work come to encompass the question of exile.[44] I would add that the intersection of "lo propio" (in the sense not only of what is proper, but what is one's own) and the exilic consciousness come to operate as a modality to explore the meaning of weighted terms such as *madre patria* [motherland] itself. Recall the felt inappropriateness of certain disjunctures grinding against each other: for example, the obsessive mythological construction of a mini-Argentina in Mexico while filling their Mexican dwellings with local indigenous artifacts of indifferent value. Or, on the other hand, the strange appropriateness of certain borrowings that destabilize ways of thinking connected to specific social structures: as in the subtle use of the Mexican-flavored insult "poca madre"[45] that overrides the more neutral Argentine phrase and intensifies the sense of cultural loss.

These grammatical and evaluative twists and turns of language and property accompany the trunks of memorabilia with the exiles' return to their homeland. On the one hand, Mercado dwells at length on the decoration of exile homes, both in Mexico and after the return to Argentina, noting the identical interior decorating schemes based on Mexican handicrafts that distinguish Argentine exile dwellings—furniture from Taxco, rugs from Chiapas, tablecloths from Michoacán—and on the other, the curious way that the obsession with Argentina during the exile years translates into a nostalgia for Mexico on their return: the endless "Argenmex" conversations in Argentina about chile, chipotle, and tomatillos and where to find cilantro. Avelar writes:

The text unveils the fundamental fallacy of all identitarian rhetoric by relating the predicament of a number of Argentine exiles who mystified an Argentine being and clung to national icons while away from home, only to complain after the return that those wonderful Mexican tortillas and chili [sic] could not be found in Buenos Aires. The most ideological facets of exile coalesced in these fetishes of an identity by definition alienated. These little objects, meaningless in themselves, appeared as substitutive, compensatory fictions for a political practice no longer available.[46]

I agree with Avelar that the fetish comes to occupy the place of lo propio when it has shifted its identitarian moorings, but would add the nuance that the concrete fetish objects are not the only things the Argenmex brings home; she also carries with her an unacknowledged body of constitutive metaphors, images that reshape thinking.

One of the ways that the narrator explores such issues is through reminders of cultural borrowings, both of objects and turns of thought; another is through a humorous exploration of the many misunderstandings that arise when native speakers of the same language discover a lack of cultural fit. For the newly arrived Argentine exiles in Mexico, one of these errors concerns microdifferences in courtesy formulas that shift their meaning and generate incomprehension. Argentine exiles had to learn to express hospitality with the courtesy form that consisted of saying: *We'll be expecting you in your house*, which Mexicans used when inviting to their home an Argentine, who at first believed that the Mexicans were announcing a visit to the Argentines' home; the misunderstanding could go on for quite some time, repeating the phrase *your house*, or with the attempted clarification, *your own house* ["su casa de usted"], with which phrase the Mexican wished to reaffirm the generous offer of his home to the foreigner; this generosity was never quite understood by the Argentine, whose interpretation was that the Mexican was assuming ownership of the Argentines' home, and the phrase *here you have your home* was never quite recognized, nor responded to with corresponding courtesy, which left the Argentine in poor standing and confirmed his inability to listen to others unlike himself.[47]

The lesson Mercado's narrator brings home with her to Argentina has to do with this seemingly minor, and apparently merely formulaic, difference. The question of one's own home, imprinted with the individual personality of the home dweller, blurs in the equivocal "su casa de usted."[48] Ironically, of course, what looks like a polite superficiality rings all too true. The Argenmex homes described by the narrator are nearly interchangeable, so that one's own home and the home of the other are distinguished only by the names of their inhabitants. And, of course, it is precisely the equivocal metaphor of home and homelessness that most insistently underlies the narrator's appeal to some ordering principle, if only that of a fetish.

The narrator sees her hapless fellow returnees with irony, but at same time, in her case, with her admitted dependency on the homeless man as a substitute (local) object of obsession, she half-acknowledges her concern that in stripping herself of the other, easily exoticized Mexican fetish objects she risks falling into an analogous trap:

I did not want the man . . . to become a theme, a topic, or, much worse, an object. . . .
I do not know whether these exercises of control, of my writing over that man's writing and his exposed condition, were demands of purity, but I needed to know, through a selective chemistry.[49]

She begins by clearing away all the traditional motives and structures of the narrative, establishing the grounds defining what she emphatically calls her own/proper writing in counterdistinction to what she describes as his own writing (the writing appropriate to him), and by specifying the relationship of her writing over/about his. Then, almost imperceptibly, the demands of intellectual purity erode and she slips into the delirious urge to tell a story that blurs the distinction she has taken such pains to establish in an almost identical move to that which she earlier associated with her humorous account of the rhetorical blurring of distinctions between one's own house and another's. The homeless man becomes in fact what he always was for her, despite her denials, her "key to the theme," although the narrator has struggled to retain his individuality and her ambiguous complexity in her response to him:

after my first meetings with Andrés, I entered a kind of conversational delirium. I would tell the whole world how I had met him, I wanted at all costs to transfer the problem to others, and, grossly, I have to admit, I tried to exorcise him through the mere act of describing his circumstances.[50]

In this position, there is an echo of Elena Poniatowska's elaboration of her long and, from some perspectives, vexed relationship with Josefina Bórquez, the woman whose testimonial she fictionalized as that of Jesusa Palancares in her testimonial novel *Hasta no verte, Jesús mío*. Poniatowska has stated many times that her reconstruction/reinvention of the Mexico City woman's life was both an homage to the strength of the Mexican woman and a very personal quest to understand and come to terms with her own Mexicanness, after having spent most of her youth outside her mother's home country (see, for example, the articles on Jesusa in *Luz y luna, las lunitas*). In a similar vein, in the Argentine text, the marginal city dweller, the homeless former student, Andrés, comes to cipher for Mercado the longing for a situatedness with respect to the before and after of her own Argentine identity: "I take advantage of my circumstances," he tells the narrator in their first conversation, "to make progress toward the solution of certain theoretical problems."[51] Unsurprisingly, the figure that captures her attention is not only a displaced person, who has seemingly been caught in a set of transitory circumstances not dissimilar to that of exile, but also a writer: more, he is a theoretician. Here too, as is the case with Poniatowska, by virtue of the process of reinscription, a certifiably authentic local other is brought into alignment with an apparent opposite who comes from a position of great privilege. Andrés, like Jesusa, all too easily falls back into the role of generalization and representation that their respective authors initially rejected. Jesusa Palancares overrides and overwrites a protesting Josefina Bórquez, and Andrés, of course, despite or because of Mercado's efforts to puzzle out his significance to her, ends up precisely as an iconic image, or a fetish object, and a markedly Argenmex one at that. Her and our last image of him is of watching him sleep, "wrapped up like a tamale in his blankets, resting his head on Tomás Eloy Martínez's novel of Perón,"[52] combining one of the Mexican-derived food metaphors that she so elaborately deconstructs in the superficial chitchat of her fellow returned exiles, with the evocation of Tomás Eloy Martínez's journalistic novel about the crucial figure in mid-twentieth century Argentine history. Mercado, thus, at one and the same time enacts a recuperation of the sleeping past, a recognition of a traumatic present, a salute to the power of fictional narrative to shape historical memory, and a teasing evocation of an alien reality—the tamal—that serves as its indigestible wrapper. Avelar would call this reference untimely; it is also, in Homi Bhabha's sense, unhomely, marking yet another shift in signification between lo propio and su casa, with all the culturally specific and equivocal meanings Tununa Mercado has been so careful to trace out for us in the course of this text.

In an article focusing mostly on readings of Toni Morrison and Nadine
Gordimer, Homi Bhabha rethinks Freud's classic study of the "Unheimlich" (usually translated as the "uncanny") through a postcolonial critical position that allows him to rethink Freud's key concept in terms of the unhomely. For while the
uncanny carries with it some element of the supernatural, of something hidden
and mysterious that is ambiguously brought home, in Bhabha's account, the postcolonial critic/writer's experience of the unhomely follows from "the estranging
sense of the relocation of the home and the world in an unhallowed place," and
he describes it as a common feature in border culture, in exile literature, and in
Third World literature in general. Bhabha continues:

> In the stirrings of the unhomely, another world becomes visible. It has less to do with
> forcible eviction and more to do with the uncanny literary and social effects of en-
> forced social accommodation, or historical migrations and cultural relocations. The
> home does not remain the domain of domestic life, nor does the world simply be-
> come its social or historical counterpart. The unhomely is the shock of recognition
> of the world-in-the-home, the home-in-the-world.[53]

Mercado's final image of the homeless man, *a la intemperie* [exposed],
wrapped like a tamal, head propped on book, is a complex one. It is, first of all,
a cipher of the narrator's own admitted cowardice, for after having struck up an
acquaintanceship of sorts with Andrés, she reaches a point where she no longer
knows what to say to him. For this reason, she avoids discussion by going to the
plaza early and watching him sleep instead. Here the social exchange, or social
accommodation, breaks down as the committed writer who identifies with the
marginalized other reveals herself to herself as the self-indulgent consumer of
iconic images, not at all different in kind from the other exiles whose purchases
and obsessions she mildly satirizes in earlier chapters of the book. In this manner,
Mercado suggests that the shock of recognition between conditions associated
with a recovered home and with homelessness does not hold up to sustained
analysis. Here, rather than committing herself to the difficult work that would follow her initial meditation, the narrator leaves us with the ethically ambiguous
conjunctions among the marginalized street people, the narrator's appropriation
of their lives and works, and the reader's delight in the gorgeous (fetish) object
that results.

Tellingly, at the point in which she backs away from further knowledge, the narrator replaces the historical subject with an aestheticized fictional character. Her
gesture reminds me strongly of Rachel Bowlby's observation that was made in reference to Nabokov's *Lolita* but, I think, equally applicable to the consumer/lover
ethics intimated here. Bowlby writes: "The poetic speed of consumption also mu-
tates into its opposite, a state of tranquil suspension, underwater slow motion . . ., a
silently timeless still life." Also, in "Exposure," the vivid memories of travel and
purchase and production of written texts slow down on the written page into the

timeless still life of the sleeping man. The returned exile, a reluctant consumer, reinvents herself as a lyrical ethnographer. The final chapter of this book, "El muro" ["The Wall"] concerns the not insignificant task of confronting this textual dilemma and, as already noted, breaking down the seductive metaphors, worrying at the edges of institutional and personal certainties, and finally, deconstructing even "woman writing as a woman."[54]

The deliberate aestheticization of Andrés as a silent object opens onto one set of issues that drives to the heart of the common perception of intellectual labor as a distanced, "pure" product. The metaphor of the tamal evokes a second set of references peculiar to the exile condition and the unhomely contaminations that creep in to disrupt attempts at reaccommodation. The book under Andrés' head suggests still a third line of questioning. It is commonplace in critical circles to bemoan the fact that in these globalized, postmodern days, the literary marketplace is flourishing, but for popular rather than elitist art. Franco notes, for instance, that "everywhere in contemporary Latin America, there is a sense of the literary intelligentsia's diminishing importance and displacement from public discourse."[55] Crassly speaking, all books put ideas up for sale, but they also create a dilemma with respect to the position of a presumed reader—does the author intentionally limit her work to an informed elite body of readers, or does she attempt to reach a wider audience? What are the implications of these choices in style and subject matter? Avelar poses the dilemma forcefully, in an explicit linking of globalization, the writing subject, and national cultural formations: "The literature produced in the aftermath of the recent Latin American dictatorships . . . confronts not only the need to come to terms with the past but also to define its position in the new present ushered in by the military regimes: a global market in which every corner of social life has been commodified."[56] Mercado refers obliquely to this problem with her discussion of Andrés's two books. One is an unnamed novel by the early twentieth-century Spanish writer and self-identified "Jacobin" politician Vicente Blasco Ibáñez (his 1905 *El intruso* would be the obvious candidate, as his most well-known work) chosen from among a pile of books, mostly cookbooks, in a garbage can. Nothing much is said of this book, except to mark the unusual conditions of its retrieval, and its primary function in Mercado's text seems to be that of serving as a foil to the other more important book.

The second book is a condensed version of Tomás Eloy Martínez's bestselling *La novela de Perón,* which Andrés tells his interlocutor that he has received as a gift. The narrator informs us that Andrés knows this text almost by heart, and it is the book that not only serves as his primary reading material (the narrator makes sure her readers know that he pointedly refuses to look at the easily available newspapers around him) but also doubles as a pillow. In a cultural tradition (ours) in which the perusal of the protagonist's library is a literary commonplace for revealing important facets of an individual's character, Andrés's random library of exactly two books has an overdetermined quality, both too much and too little information at the same time. The already overdetermined quality of this exchange is reinforced even further when the narrator of this novel? autobiography? asks her interlocutor about the status of her own representation in Martínez's novel. In a scene that evokes the early chapters of the second part of the *Quijote,* the narrator asks whether her cameo appearance has been retained in the condensed version of the novel: "When I asked him if his edition contained a scene in which, by a pure coincidence of fiction, my husband, my son, and I appear on a balcony . . . he said no."[57] This curious exchange signals the beginning of the narrator's definitive withdrawal from further conversations with the individual in favor of an interaction with texts; it suggests as well a reconfiguration of literary social relations in terms of a more equivocal exchange between a fictionalized narrator and a fictionalized interlocutor about the former's wholly spurious appearance in a fictionalized account of the life of Perón. To answer the question posed at the outset of this study by García Canclini— "What does it mean to belong, to have an identity at the end of the [twentieth] century?"—Mercado suggests that, like official history, personal identity is tied up with a merely written reality, a fictional text that must be radically put into question and ultimately exploded.

The place of memory, its *"estado"* ("state," in both senses) stages a personal encounter with official history that also counterposes itself to, and signals the end of, the nation-building novel, broadly understood as the novel at the service of the state—while deeply mourning its necessary disappearance. The right to memory, the obligatory quality of remembrance in this country of the Mothers of the Plaza de Mayo, comes into conflict again and again with the struggle for the construction of a new state that wants only to turn its back on the past. In this book, Mercado takes up the untimely task (to use Avelar's term) of writing her way back home, writing herself back into a partially erased national history that has traditionally been based on what she now knows are fictions of stable territory, stable identity, known destiny, and fictions that she fundamentally rejects as dangerous illusions—and yet, she is paralyzed by their loss. There is, as Robbins says in an essay on cosmopolitanism, "no alternative to belonging. But the exercise becomes more complicated as soon as we ask what it *means* to belong, or how many different ways of belonging there may be."[58] Mercado's text makes an unflinching and clear-eyed examination of this vexed issue.

Martín Hopenhayn would concur, although on very different grounds. He says:

Modernization-in-globalization tends towards loss of identity *[des-identidad],* homelessness *[des-habitación],* and the desingularizing *[des-singularizar]* of its inhabitants. . . . The globalized city seems to be associated with an expressive explosion, but after a short while all expression seems to be born from the same combinatory mechanics.[59]

The hope that Mercado offers at the end of her book, with the absorption of the writerly text into the widening cracks in the wall, is that the constraints of discourse can be transcended through acts of imagination as an agent for ethico–political transformation. Theoretically, then, Mercado's *En estado de memoria* offers a useful test case for exploring new articulations in culture analysis that allow for the linkage of a Latin American feminine consciousness to the concerns of globalized national identity constructions. It is also a deeply personal book about the cost of going home, when both the going, and the encounter with, home encode deeply painful processes of loss and recovery.

## NOTES

1. Frederick Jameson, "Preface," in *The Cultures of Globalization,* ed. Frederick Jameson and Masao Miyoshi (Durham, N.C.: Duke University Press, 1999), xii.

2. Jameson, "Notes on Globalization as a Philosophical Issue," in *The Cultures of Globalization,* 55.

3. Jameson, "Preface," xiii, xv.

4. Martín Hopenhayn, "Tribu y metrópoli en la postmodernidad latinoamericana," in *Enfoques sobre la posmodernidad en América Latina,* ed. Roberto Follari and Rigoberto Lanz (Caracas: Editorial Sentido, 1998), 32–33.

5. Santiago Castro-Gómez, "La filosofía latinoamericana como ontología crítica del presente: Temas y motivas para una 'Crítica de la razón latinoamericana'" (unpublished ms, 2000), 3–4.

6. Caren Kaplan and Inderpal Grewal, "Transnational Feminist Cultural Studies: Beyond the Marxism/Poststructuralism/Feminism Divides," in *Between Woman and Nation: Nationalisms, Transnational Feminisms, and the State,* ed. Caren Kaplan, Norma Alarcón, and Minoo Maoallem (Durham, N.C.: Duke University Press, 1999), 354.

7. Raquel Olea, "Feminism: Modern or Postmodern?" in *The Postmodernism Debate in Latin America,* ed. John Beverley, José Oviedo, and Michael Aronna (Durham, N.C.: Duke University Press, 1995), 197.

8. Jean Franco, *Critical Passions: Selected Essays,* ed. and intro. Mary Louise Pratt and Kathleen Newman (Durham, N.C.: Duke University Press, 1999), 52.

9. Amy Parry, "In Place of a Conclusion," 376.

10. Tununa Mercado, *En estado de memoria* (Buenos Aires: Ada Korn Editora, 1990). *In a State of Memory,* English trans. Peter Kahn (Lincoln: University of Nebraska Press).

11. Gabriela Mora, "Tununa Mercado" (Interview), *Hispamérica* 21, no. 62 (1992): 77–81, 78.

12. Néstor García Canclini, "Comunidades de consumidores: Nuevos escenarios de lo público y la ciudadanía," in *Cultura y tercer mundo 2: Nuevas identidades y ciudadanías,* ed. Beatriz González Stephan (Caracas: Nueva Sociedad, 1996), 10.

13. Idelber Avelar, *The Untimely Present: Postdictatorial Latin American Fiction and the Task of Mourning* (Durham, N.C.: Duke University Press, 1999), 20.

14. Avelar, *The Untimely Present,* 211.

15. Avelar, *The Untimely Present,* 2–3.

16. Avelar, *The Untimely Present,* 9.

17. Avelar, *The Untimely Present,* 211.

18. Patrick O'Connell, "Individual and Collective Identity through Memory in Three Novels of Argentina's 'El Proceso,'" *Hispania*, 81 (1998): 31, 31–41.

19. O'Connell, "Individual and Collective Identity through Memory," 35.

20. O'Connell, "Individual and Collective Identity through Memory," 37.

21. Mary Louise Pratt, "'Don't Interrupt Me': The Gender Essay as Conversation and Countercanon," in *Reinterpreting the Spanish American Essay: Women Writers of the 19th and 20th Centuries,* ed. Doris Meyer (Austin: University of Texas Press, 1995), 13, 17.

22. Franco, *Critical Passions: Selected Essays,* 10–11.

23. Jesús Martín-Barbero, "Hegemonía comunicacional y des-centramiento cultural," in *Enfoques sobre la posmodernidad en América Latina,* ed. Roberto Follari and Rigoberto Lanz (Caracas: Editorial Sentido, 1998), 50.

24. Franco, *Critical Passions: Selected Essays,* 60–61.

25. Diamela Eltit, "Cultura, poder y frontera," *La época* 3, no. 113 (10 June 1990): 1–2.

26. Mercado, *In a State of Memory,* 117; *En estado de memoria,* 148–49.

27. Mercado, *In a State of Memory,* 121–22; *En estado de memoria,* 155: "Hacer cosas es una manera de vivir; esto puede parecer obvio pero no lo es tanto para gente que pliega y despliega la existencia como si fuera de papel, y va plegando cada vez más chiquito, hasta no dejar más que un listón delgado donde pararse. . . . Si no hay labores, si los plegamentos se hacen sobre el puro ser y el ausente hacer, el contacto con el universo ha de ser descarnado y quemante."

28. Mercado, *In a State of Memory,* 126; *En estado de memoria,* 160: "El interés por el hombre de la plaza me ponía, sin yo quererlo, en un estado de excepción o, por lo menos, de emergencia . . . la que se siente cuando en un texto uno se tropieza con una revelación contundente acerca del ser."

29. Mercado, *In a State of Memory,* 121; *En estado de memoria,* 154: "En ese estado de intemperie no hay los pequeños cierres que clausuran, en tareas concretas o prácticas, períodos de tiempo . . . y sería infinito enumerar lo que no se acaba, no se cumple, ni tiene lugar en el lugar de la intemperie." An alternative to Kahn's translation of the first sentence could be: "In that state of exposure, there are no small closures that close off, in concrete or practical tasks, periods of time [Ed.]."

30. Mercado, *In a State of Memory,* 19; *En estado de memoria,* 29: "El tiempo del exilio tiene el trayecto de un gran trazo . . . pero se lo aparta, no se lo quiere percibir porque se supone que el destierro va a terminar, que se trata de un paréntesis que no cuenta en ningún devenir. Provisorio, el tiempo va de semana en semana."

31. Mercado, *In a State of Memory,* 126; *En estado de memoria,* 161: "No sabía cuál era mi intemperie y no podía saber por lo tanto cuál era la suya."

32. Mercado, *In a State of Memory,* 130; *En estado de memoria,* 165: "Si podía hablar con él en la intemperie no se veía muy bien que no pudiera hacerlo en la sala de mi casa."

33. Mora, "Tununa Mercado," 78.

34. Mercado, *In a State of Memory,* 134–35; *En estado de memoria,* 170–71: "Le dije también mi nombre que de manera sistemática él tergiversó a lo largo de las semanas, cambiando la primera *ene* de mi nombre por una *te*, sin que yo corrigiera el error. . . . La *te* por la *ene*, una *i* sustituyendo a una *u*, una *o* en lugar de la primera *u*, etcétera, no me hacen mella como antes; ahora sé que ése es mi nombre, no hay dudas sobre la identidad que me confiere, pero no siempre fue así. . . . A Andrés no me pareció conveniente aclararle que a la segunda *u* de mi nombre no le antecede una *te* y preferí confiar en que alguna iluminación fuera de contexto habría de disipar el equívoco sobre ese aspecto de nuestras relaciones."

35. Mercado, *In a State of Memory*, 132; *En estado de memoria*, 168: "Que se había quedado así como consecuencia de una trauma."
36. Mercado, *In a State of Memory*, 133; *En estado de memoria*, 169: "Quizás pensaba que yo era totalmente inofensiva."
37. Mercado, *In a State of Memory*, 134; *En estado de memoria*, 169: "A las orillas del mundo."
38. Mercado, *In a State of Memory*, 136; *En estado de memoria*, 172: "Lo que él suelta no constituye lo que podría llamarse cuerpo narrativo."
39. Bruce Robbins, "Introduction Part I: Actually Existing Cosmopolitanism," in *Cosmopolitics: Thinking and Feeling Beyond the Nation*, ed. Pheng Cheah and Bruce Robbins (Minneapolis: University of Minnesota Press, 1998), 4.
40. Mercado, *In a State of Memory*, 140; *En estado de memoria*, 178: "Prefería no saber los que pasaba en el mundo."
41. Mercado, *In a State of Memory*, 140; *En estado de memoria*, 178.
42. Mercado, *In a State of Memory*, 20; *En estado de memoria*, 30: "La Argentina, ese país poca madre que nos había expulsado y sobre cuya situación se hablaba sin parar . . . llenando por así decir con la materia argentina todo hueco de la realidad."
43. Mercado, *In a State of Memory*, 22; *En estado de memoria*, 33: "El apego al país que habíamos dejado condicionó la vida de todos nosotros; hubo incluso gente que no pudo sobrellevar la suma de pérdidas; que se pasaba el día pensando en su barrio, idealizando prácticas que no se veía muy bien por qué habrían de ser consideradas paradigmáticas de un paraíso perdido; la sustancia argentina que se extrañaba aparecía encarnada en mitologías de escaso interés . . . sin valor intelectual o imaginario."
44. Avelar, *The Untimely Present*, 221–22.
45. Literally "not much of a mother." Peter Kahn has translated *poca madre* as "wretched" in Mercado, *In a State of Memory*, 20 [Ed.].
46. Avelar, *The Untimely Present*, 216.
47. Mercado, *In a State of Memory*, 23–24; *En estado de memoria*, 35: "Tuvieron que aprender a ofrecer hospitalidad usando la norma de cortesía local que consiste en decir 'Lo esperamos en *su casa*,' para invitar al interlocutor argentino, quien creía que el mexicano se refería a *su* casa, anunciándole una visita; el equívoco solía perdurar largo rato, reiterándose el '*su* casa' con un refuerzo aclaratorio: '*su* casa *de usted*,' frase con la cual el mexicano afirmaba la donación generosa de su casa, la de él, al extranjero; este desprendimiento nunca era entendido y los argentinos interpretaban que el mexicano se adueñaba de sus casas, y el 'ahí tiene usted su casa de usted' no era captado ni correspondido con análoga cortesía, quedando el argentino mal parado y demostrando su incapacidad para oír a sus diferentes."
48. The reflexive pronoun "su" may mean the second or the third person singular [Ed.].
49. Mercado, *In a State of Memory*, 127; *En estado de memoria*, 162: "No quería . . . dejar que el hombre fuera tema, o tópico, y menos objeto. . . . No sé si estos ejercicios de control de mi propia escritura sobre la escritura propia del hombre y su condición de intemperie eran exigencias de pureza, pero yo necesitaba de una química selectiva."
50. Mercado, *In a State of Memory*, 138; *En estado de memoria*, 175: "Después de mis primeros encuentros con Andrés, entré en una especie de delirio de contar. Le decía a todo el mundo cómo lo había conocido, quería a toda costa pasarle el problema a otros, decomedidamente, lo confieso con pena, trataba de conjurarlo por el solo hecho de relatar su circunstancia."

51. Mercado, *In a State of Memory*, 129; *En estado de memoria*, 164: "Aprovecho mi circunstancia . . . para avanzar en la solución de ciertos problemas teóricos."

52. Mercado, *In a State of Memory*, 141; *En estado de memoria*, 179: "Envuelto como un tamal en sus cobijas, apoyada la cabeza en la novela de Perón."

53. Homi Bhabha, "The World and the Home," *Social Text* 10 (1992): 141, 141–53.

54. Franco, *Critical Passions: Selected Essays*, 62.

55. Franco, *Critical Passions: Selected Essays*, 197.

56. Avelar, *The Untimely Present*, 1.

57. Mercado, *In a State of Memory*, 139; *En estado de memoria*, 176: "Cuando le pregunté si en esa edición figuraba una escena en la que por pura obra de ficción estamos mi marido, mi hijo y yo en un balcón . . . me dijo que no."

58. Robbins, "Comparative Cosmopolitanisms." in *Cosmopolitics,* 249–50.

59. Hopenhayn, "Tribu y metrópoli en la postmodernidad latinoamericana," 27.

# 6

## Globalization, Philosophy, and Latin America

*Jorge J. E. Gracia*

The part of the world known as Latin America, that motley of countries located south of the Río Grande, has been, since 1492, regarded as a backwater place, subordinated to the interests of other places on the globe. During the more than three hundred years of Spanish and Portuguese domination, it was a colony, and like all colonies, subservient to the whims and needs of colonial powers. Political independence in the nineteenth century did not essentially change the situation, although new economic masters took the place of colonial ones. The United States, England, and France, in particular, displaced Spain and Portugal as centers of hegemony for the region.

The subordination of Latin America has permeated every aspect and dimension of the lives of Latin Americans. Economically, it has meant unchecked exploitation; politically, it has resulted in manipulation and interference; and ethnically, it has been the source of cultural imperialism. Economic exploitation has taken many forms, including the unchecked exportation of natural resources. Political manipulation and interference have ranged from the imposition of political structures alien to the region, and even the creation of countries for the benefit of foreign powers, to the repeated invasion of sovereign territories. Cultural imperialism has involved the imposition of foreign values, products, and ideas and the suppression of local ones.

The subordination of Latin America in philosophy, in particular, is as evident as in those other dimensions mentioned and has been repeatedly noted by Latin Americans themselves.[1] During the colonial period, Spain and Portugal often set the agenda of what was to be discussed and how. Because of the pervasive influence of scholasticism in the Iberian Peninsula, the language of philosophy in

Latin America continued to be Latin well after it had been abandoned in the rest of Europe. And Spain, in particular, exercised considerable control over the books and educational materials that were allowed to circulate in Latin America.[2] Groundbreaking treatises of modern philosophy were often forbidden and, therefore, difficult to get. Moreover, the Iberian powers tightly controlled the educational institutions in the colonies, the curriculum, and pedagogy, through a system of regulations. Finally, the overwhelming power of the Iberian Roman Catholic Church, which saw itself as the defender of Catholic theology as formulated by thirteenth-century scholastics and sanctioned by the Council of Trent, made sure that the topics of discussion of concern to scholastics remained areas of continued attention.[3] Thus, we find a concern with such issues as the problems of universals and individuation to which substantial effort had been devoted on the part of medieval scholastics. Thirteenth- and fourteenth-century figures, long regarded as out of fashion in Europe at the time, were still being discussed with great interest in Latin America. Instead of Descartes and Newton, who had captured the fancy of Europeans, Latin American intellectuals were encouraged to study and discuss Thomas Aquinas (1225–1274), John Duns Scotus (1265–1308), and Francisco Suárez (1548–1617), to mention just three of the most prominent ones. (Suárez flourished at the end of the sixteenth century, but his thoughts are rooted in medieval scholasticism). Whole schools of Thomists, Scotists, and Suarecians thrived south of the Río Grande well into the eighteenth century, when only relatively few scholars, primarily working in seminaries and ecclesiastical circles, paid any attention to them in Europe.

In this century, the situation does not change substantially. Even a cursory look at the history of Latin American philosophy in the first quarter of the twentieth century shows how dependent Latin American intellectuals and philosophers were on outside influences. José Ortega y Gasset's well-known visit to Buenos Aires in 1916 was, indeed, a major turning point for Latin American thought at the time. He became an instant success, and the ideas he introduced created a focus of philosophical attention for the next fifty years.[4] But even before Ortega, the influence of French and English authors dominated the philosophical landscape in Latin America.[5] This phenomenon received a particularly significant push in the 1930s, with the immigration of thousands of intellectuals fleeing the Spanish Civil War.[6]

In the context of this history, one has to wonder if the process of globalization that is taking place everywhere today is going to make any difference for Latin America in general and Latin American philosophy in particular. Will Latin America continue to be a subordinated, backward place where world powers and leaders can play their usual economic and political games, or will globalization give some room to Latin America and help it free itself from these forces of oppression? In the case of philosophy in particular, how will globalization change the pattern of subordination that has characterized it for the past five hundred years? To be sure, only history will answer these questions, but nonetheless, we can point to some elements that will play a role in the outcome.

## GLOBALIZATION

We need to begin by saying something about globalization, a much-mentioned but seldom discussed concept. What is globalization?

As the etymology of the word suggests, globalization has to do with a process that involves the whole globe. To globalize means to make global, or to affect the globe. Of course, the globe has been around for a long time, so it cannot be the end product of globalization or the object under construction through the process of globalization. This process must involve something else, and here two possibilities suggest themselves: some aspect of human experience and the human impact on the nonhuman dimensions of the globe.

In many ways, globalization has been present since the first appearance of humans on the globe. The moment we walked on the Earth, we began "to populate" it, as religious scriptures usually refer to it, and this involved growing in numbers, migrating, coming into contact with other humans, altering our surroundings in ways that are not different from many other processes that have taken place in human history, and developing a consciousness of a growing world.

The process of globalization has had its ups and downs. There have been some periods in human history in which attempts at globalization have been more effective than at others. Recall Alexander the Great's campaign to conquer all the world known to him. This man was a visionary who wanted to bring under his power, and probably Greek culture, all of humanity as he knew it. Another quite successful effort, as far as it went, was the Roman experiment. Surely this process, unleashed by the military power of Rome, has to be considered an attempt at globalization, even if its results were limited and restricted primarily to the Mediterranean basin.

The most successful process of globalization before our century, however, happened during the age of European world exploration in the fifteenth and sixteenth centuries. The encounters with America and Equatorial and Southern Africa, as well as the East, the colonization of many of these territories, and the attempt to bring peoples from all over the world under a few political and cultural umbrellas, were without a doubt processes of globalization.

Still, in all these cases, the process of globalization encountered serious limitations. Some of these were conceptual. People did not quite think of all the Earth as one and of all human inhabitants of the Earth as members of the same family. Tribalism, among many other factors, stood in the way of true and effective globalization. In addition, technology was rudimentary, so that the globe still turned out to be too large to make it possible for events in one part of it to affect quickly and effectively other parts. When it took three months to go from Madrid to Havana, the lives of the people who lived in these places were largely, and only occasionally, affected by what happened in the other place. It took three months to know in Madrid that Havana had suffered a devastating hurricane, and it took an additional three months for Havana to learn the response of the Spanish king. The encounters between Europe and America made the globe smaller, but technology was still such that people in different parts were allowed considerable independence and anonymity.

Today, matters are quite different, owing to the extraordinary technological advances of the last century and, particularly, this century. First came the industrial revolution and the development of the steam engine. This made possible both more efficient and quicker shipping and the development of the railroads. In this century, the revolution in transportation has been even more drastic, with the invention of the automobile and the airplane. Then came the explosion of the means of communication: the telephone, the radio, and television. Finally, we have computers and the Internet. These technological advances make it possible for an increasing number in the United States to know what is happening everywhere at all times. And this in turn has made it possible to influence people who are located at a distance from each other. Isolation is becoming a thing of the past. Indeed, the old view that the fluttering of a butterfly's wing in one place can automatically change the course of human history in another place is finally becoming true. A sneeze in Hong Kong causes the flu in New York City. The world is becoming a *barrio*, because we now know what is happening everywhere at all times, or at least we can find out. Gossip has gone global.

Globalization appears to have two sides to it, a negative and a positive. On the negative side, much could be said. Let me first mention homogenization. Increased globalization appears to lead to increased homogenization. Cultural variety is threatened and promises to give way to a uniform culture throughout the globe. Variety and diversity are being replaced by sameness. Wal-Mart, Coca Cola, and other cultural products of the industrialized world, and particularly the current dominant economic power, that is, the United States, are quickly replacing local cultural products.

The negative dimensions of homogenization may be gathered under three headings: epistemology, metaphysics, and aesthetics. With respect to the first, homogenization would seem to lead to a diminished number of epistemic possibilities. If culture becomes homogeneous and uniform, it would appear that humans would have less cognizance of the different possibilities. With respect to metaphysics, homogeneity would seem to discourage flexibility and change and to encourage rigidity and lack of creativity, which in turn can undermine adaptability to new challenges. Finally, aesthetically, a homogeneous world lacks the variety required for enjoyment. A world in which everyone eats the same foods, dresses in the same clothes, and reads the same books would be not just boring, but also uninteresting.

Homogenization is not the only undesirable consequence of globalization. Globalization also seems to promote dominance and abuse of the many by the few. If regionally, the control of technology can lead to domination, and this in turn can easily degenerate into the abuse of power and ideological control; there is no reason to think that things will be different in the larger world. As in the past, so likewise in the future: whoever controls the technology will control the world.

One clear effect of globalization is that the more advanced and richer will have increasing advantages over the less advanced and less rich. Economic influence, political power, and cultural impact will go one way. Coca Cola will become the drink of the world, if it is not already, and Wal-Mart will become the shop of the world. Naturally, these developments stifle local initiatives. The small shop may disappear, and the local drink may go the way of the dinosaurs.

This situation is exacerbated in cases where there are tightly connected groups that have access to technology and can use it to impose their views, tastes, and power on others. This is nothing new. We all know how totalitarian regimes of the right and left have been able to use technology, from weapons to the media, to control populations. And we also know how international corporations are increasingly determining the economic fate of peoples all over the world. Motivated by the insatiable greed of stockholders, corporations are propelled into mergers and consolidations in order to increase profits and are becoming economic mammoths with enormous power.

But there is another side to this story. There is also a positive side to globalization, for this process can improve the standard of living for parts of the human family deprived of the material goods enjoyed in developed countries. Moreover, the very ease with which knowledge can be disseminated and technology can be made available to many seems certainly to have advantages. Still, these advantages do not undermine the negative consequences of globalization that we have pointed out. The positive dimensions of globalization do not eliminate its very serious negative effects, nor does it make it clear that the positive and negative consequences of globalization, taken together, will yield a positive rather than a negative tally. A positive view of globalization requires more than this.

One thing that could be said in favor of it is that globalization can, in fact, work against the abuses of local power mentioned earlier, for it diminishes the power of nations and accordingly of oppressive national regimes. For oppressed segments of the population, in particular nations, such as women and ethnic minorities, globalization could be a way of eliminating or diminishing the oppression in which they live. Genocide, abuse, and discrimination cannot be kept secret in the global *barrio*. And once the existence of these is known, it is difficult for nations to ignore them. Consider how easy it was a few years ago for the superpowers to do as they wished when it came to segments of their own populations or of entire nations that were under their influence. Think of the Soviet Union and the invasion of Czechoslovakia or the situation of the Jews within that same country. In this hemisphere, we can easily think of unwarranted American interference in the internal affairs of Latin American nations. Likewise, the knowledge of how the United States treats some of its very citizens who belong to races and ethnicities other than the one, or ones, that are considered mainstream, creates embarrassment for the country and forces it to act in order to remedy these problems. There is also the concern for the influence that events in one place may have on events in other places. Chernobyl is not a local problem today. Globalization promotes

*Jorge J. E. Gracia*

the drift toward a world society in which nations lose some of their sovereignty to make way for the requirements of living together.

Knowledge is power, and knowledge of abuses may generate action. Likewise, knowledge of greener pastures elsewhere motivates those who have this knowledge and makes it possible for them to oppose and to resist those who prevent them from living as they think they should. This surely is a healthy consequence of globalization. The curtailment of nationalism is seen by many as a bad result of globalization, but in fact, it can be one of the best means to stop local and regional oppression. And there is still another side to this phenomenon. Technology has the capacity to empower the underdog. A shortwave radio has kept many who live under totalitarian and repressive regimes abreast of the truth. Technology makes it more difficult to control and manipulate information.

In short, establishing the value of globalization is not an easy matter. Globalization appears to be a mixed blessing, like most other things, in spite of the simplistic views that see it as either wholly good or wholly evil.


## PHILOSOPHY

The philosophical community is, like any other community, a social group, and social groups are united in various ways. For example, races appear to be united biologically; ethnic groups are united through cultural and social ties, which reflect historical relations; nations are united through territory and constitutions; religious communities are united by beliefs; and so on. So we may ask: What is it that unites philosophical communities?

One would think the answer to this question is easy: the search for love of truth. This Greek response has become the motto of the discipline. Yet the situation is not this clear. First, because some philosophers do not believe that there is truth, or that, if there were, philosophers would be able to get at it. Second, because even if we were to accept that philosophers search for truth, many nonphilosophers do so as well. I do not think we can easily disqualify from the search for truth such people as physicists, biologists, or even religious believers. Philosophical communities must be united, then, by something else.

One possible candidate that seems rather obvious is tradition. By this I do not necessarily mean a set of unchanging views concerning the world or methods of procedure, for philosophical views and methods within philosophical traditions do not remain stationary. Even within the most conservative philosophical schools, there is evolution, change, variety of interpretations, and disagreement. One is hard put to find complete agreement among all members of a particular philosophical tradition, even if we can easily find disagreement between them and members of other traditions. Therefore, the traditions that unite philosophical groups cannot be conceived as common views or even methods.

Looking more closely at philosophical groups, it appears as if they function very much like families united neither through biology nor common views, but rather through intellectual lineage. Intellectual lineage ties schools of Thomists, Marxists, Heideggerians, or analysts. In this context, it is more important who your mentor is than what you hold, for your mentor is the tie to your family. A student of Quine belongs to a certain group no matter what that student comes to hold, even if it involves views that are quite antithetical to those of Quine. Indeed, one often finds that certain views can be, and are in fact, shared by different traditions, yet the members of these traditions do not find them to be elements of unity. I am often surprised about the common elements between certain members of the analytic tradition and the continental one, and yet members of these traditions regard each other with suspicion and even hostility.[7]

The persons who initiate them and who function as their leaders frequently dominate philosophical families.[8] They function as gatekeepers whose task is to keep out those who do not belong and to promote the well being of the family. Sometimes these families are national, but at other times they transcend national boundaries. Philosophical families generate societies and organizations; they dominate institutions, journals, and professional meetings; and they exclude from participation those who do not have the proper lineage. This is very much the situation in Europe and the United States. In the latter, the most general split among families is between analysts and continentals. But there are also other divisions within the philosophical community. There are Thomists, Heideggerians, Marxists, Derridians, Quineans, Rawlseans, Habermasians, and so on.

Clearly this structure, both at the local and international levels, can lead to the kind of abuse mentioned earlier. Individuals who lack proper lineage are left out, regardless of their philosophical merit. And mediocre philosophers who have the right lineage and defer to family leaders are helped, encouraged, and supported.

## LATIN AMERICAN PHILOSOPHY

In Latin America, the prevailing situation of philosophy is similar to that in the United States and Europe, except that it is worse. The reason it is worse is that there are less resources to be shared. Under these conditions, loyalty to the philosophical family to which one belongs becomes even more important than in the United States or Europe. With less goods to go around, less jobs, places to publish, money for research, and so on, it is crucial to keep out those who do not belong to one's group.

As in the United States, the larger division among Latin American philosophers is between analysts and continentals, but within these, there are all sorts of subdivisions, some of which are homegrown, as is the case with philosophers of liberation. Apart from having separate associations, journals, research institutes, and venues for their publications and thought, each of these groups often depends on a leader or small group of leaders. In Latin America, these tend to behave as *caudillos*. Their egos are large, and their function is fundamentally to keep the group united. Most of them accomplish this task by controlling resources, such as positions, journals, publishing houses, and so on. In exchange for protection and patronage, they often require unconditional allegiance and loyalty to themselves. Some exploit their positions for personal goals and exercise unquestioned intellectual control. They are dictators on a small scale, and more often than not, they promote a cult for their persons and ideas.

Naturally, these petty tyrants are aware of their insignificance in mainstream Western philosophy, so much of their effort is geared toward receiving recognition outside of Latin America. Traveling in the United States and Europe is an essential component of this strategy. Having their works translated into one of the languages widely read, such as English or German, is another. Still another is trying to connect themselves with well-known philosophers in Europe and the United States. They do the last by inviting these philosophers to Latin America, where their egos are stroked carefully, by arranging meetings in which their work is discussed, by writing about them, by offering to translate their works, and so on. These strategies are pursued with enormous zeal and determination. But more important still, Latin American philosophers flatter these philosophers by becoming their followers. In doing this, of course, they contribute quite effectively by keeping Latin American philosophy in the place where it has always been: subordinated to the interests of philosophers from elsewhere. This result is particularly paradoxical in philosophical groups that promote their efforts as a way of breaking the hegemony of European and American philosophy.

## GLOBALIZATION AND LATIN AMERICAN PHILOSOPHY

The process of globalization, I am afraid, should have the same consequences in Latin American philosophy as it has in other areas of Latin American experience. On the one hand, it should facilitate rather than hinder the hegemony of those philosophical groups that have power and dominate the use of technology. Today it is possible to be completely up-to-date in Latin America about what is happening in Europe or the United States. If you emulate the analytic group in the United States, it is possible to have, almost upon publication, and sometimes even before publication, the latest thoughts of the leaders of this group. The Internet has made it possible for someone in Argentina or Mexico to be in direct touch with someone at New York University, Rutgers, or Princeton. And the same goes for Europe, although Europeans are still behind in the use of technology. Still, soon they will catch up, and then Latin American philosophers, who chronically feel left out, will be content to enter in a constant process of catching up that will never be completed. Many of these foreign philosophers are production machines whose philosophical dribble never seems to be interrupted nor come to an end.

Will Latin Americans be able to enter into dialogue with them? This is unlikely, because either they belong to different families or they belong to the same families but are regarded as poor relations.

But there is another side to the story, of course. The picture of philosophy elsewhere might make Latin American philosophers change their attitude and see that they can do as well as philosophers from the hegemonic world. After all, what is the difference between them? At the very least, the most important one is attitude. Will it happen? It is hard to tell. Globalization can go either way, and it depends very much on Latin Americans themselves and what they do with what they get.

One last point: It is in the nature of power to increase. Power calls for more power, and the powerful naturally want to become more powerful. This means that hegemonic philosophy cannot ultimately be blamed for what it attempts to do. Power cannot deny its nature. It makes no sense for Latin Americans, then, to complain about their philosophical subordination. If they want to be significant players in the philosophical field, they need to resist the inroads of hegemonic philosophical families. But does this mean that they must themselves establish families and dynasties? Perhaps there is no other way. If this is so, it is indeed a very sad commentary on the practice of philosophy today.

## NOTES

1. See Augusto Salazar Bondy, *Sentido y problema del pensamiento hispano-americano*, English trans. Donald L. Schmidt (Kansas City: University of Kansas, 1969).

2. See Vicente G. Quesada, *La vida intelectual de la América española durante los siglos XVI, XVII y XVIII*, cap. 1 (Buenos Aires: Arnoldo Moen y Hermano, 1910), but also Ismael Quiles, "La libertad de investigación en la época colonial," *Estudios* (1940), 511–24; and Guillermo Furlong, *Bibliotecas argentinas durante la dominación hispánica* (Buenos Aires: Editorial Huarpes, 1944).

3. See Jorge J. E. Gracia, "El escolasticismo ibérico: Puente entre la antigüedad clásica y el pensamiento colonial iberoamericano," in *Filosofía hispánica: Concepto, origen y foco historiográfico* (Pamplona: Universidad de Navarra, 1998), 45–81.

4. See José Luis Gómez-Martínez, *Pensamiento de la liberación: Proyección de Ortega en América* (Mexico: Ediciones EGE, 1995).

5. See Jorge J. E. Gracia, "Latin American Philosophy Today," *Philosophical Forum* 20, nos. 1–2 (1988–1989), 4–32.

6. For a study of this group, see José Luis Abellán, *Filosofía española en América (1936–1966)* (Madrid: Ediciones Guadarrama, 1967).

7. See the introduction to Jorge J. E. Gracia, *Philosophy and Its History: Issues in Philosophical Historiography* (Albany, N.Y.: State University of New York Press, 1992).

8. See Jorge J. E. Gracia, *Hispanic/Latino Identity: A Philosophical Perspective*, chap. 6 (Oxford: Blackwell, 2000).

# III

## ALTERNATIVE VISIONS OF GLOBALIZATION

# Humanity and Globalization

*Leopoldo Zea*
*(Translated by Mario Sáenz)*

## IDENTITY AND INTEGRATION: COMPETING WHILE SHARING

The great Latin American teacher and thinker from Colombia, the late Germán Arciniegas (1900–1999), when he was almost one hundred years old, and extraordinarily lucid despite a body that refused to serve him, wrote shortly before his death:

> The New World is the world with the new history. Never perfect, never free, it is threatened in ways never endured by the European nations. Everything here is different. We must defend ourselves with different weapons. . . . Everything in the New World compels us to original defenses and to the concerns that suit us best, as well as to a more profound knowledge of Europe and the Americas. . . . Inequalities in the economic development of the different parts of the hemisphere require a more refined care of our economic interests, and the moral and material defenses needed to resist the complexities of international life.[1]

Arciniegas is referring to that New World that entered history on October 12, 1492, and gave birth to the process of globalization that ended in 1989, thus setting in motion a new, hitherto unheard of globalization. Columbus's blunder, as he was looking for Asia in an unknown and, thus, new world, transformed a regional history of the world into a universal history, which integrated peoples and cultures under the imperial hegemony of Europe in its dual expression: a Mediterranean Europe of which Spain was an expression, and a Baltic and North Atlantic Europe of which Great Britain will become its best example. The former was an inclusive Greco-Latin and Catholic Europe, which integrated the peoples and cultures bathed by the Mediterranean; the latter was a German and Saxon Europe, which excluded others by its Puritanism.

Those were two expressions of Europe; they settled their differences with wars of religion for the sake of domination. Their hegemony overtakes the New World found by Columbus and baptized with the name "America." The America under Iberian hegemony was Latin; Saxon and so-called Western was the America conquered and colonized by Anglo-Saxon and Puritan Europe. From the Americas and the ease of their conquest, does Europe globalize or integrate the whole of the earth? The disputes will have to do only with different expressions of Europe itself.

It was marked in the twentieth century by two big world wars and two great revolutions: One, the Russian Revolution of 1917, was a social revolution; the other was a decolonizing revolution that began in Mexico in 1910, according to Toynbee. This all culminated at the end of World War II with the Cold War between capitalism and socialism, the United States and the Soviet Union. An exit from this Cold War by the second world power in 1989 set in motion the fall of walls and ramparts that separated peoples under the hegemony of one or the other of the two world powers.

A new globalization was then announced, a new form of universal integration, which was expressed in the bicentennial celebration of the French Revolution. It brought to mind the words of Victor Hugo when he said: "In the twentieth century there will be an extraordinary nation. It will not be called France, but rather Europe; and, in the century that follows it, it will be called Humanity." This prophecy was hindered by the disarticulation of the Soviet Union as it tried to integrate the capitalist way of life with socialism's spirit of solidarity. Instead, in the former Soviet Union, a competitive capitalism was encouraged, but this resulted instead in the formation of *mafias.*

The United States declared themselves absolute winners of the Cold War, with the moral and material right to direct and protect the planet from new threats that now come from the "envious" peoples of the Third World such as Iraq, which began the Gulf War.

Western Europe, under the supposedly protective hegemony of the United States, has rejected this new protection. Instead, it looks for its own autarchic integration. It became independent from the United States, from Eastern Europe, and from the colonies that the development of science and technology made dispensable to the extent that it can recycle raw materials or replace labor with the robotization of production. It set in motion a market economy of domestic products for those who can buy them. Left outside this economy was the old Soviet Union, the peoples of the Third World, and a United States burdened by the high cost of an anachronistic armament.

The emergence of Asia in this world market improves, popularizes, and lowers the prices of the products of this economy. This compels the European Community to abandon its autarchic project and to incorporate itself into an economy that is generating markets with millions of consumers. This is the other face of an economy that, in order to grow, needs a well-developed consumer class. To this one may add the announcement by the former president of the United States, William Clinton, of the vigorous incorporation of his country into the global market economy, based on the integration into the North American economy of those North Americans still marginalized because of race, sex, age, habits, and customs.

Europeans today create problems for themselves regarding identity and integration along the lines used in Latin America in the past. Victor Hugo's prophecy, remembered in the bicentennial of the French Revolution, is an old Latin American utopia that, at the dawn of the new century and millennium, becomes a prophecy. It is Simón Bolívar's nation of nations that will encompass the entire globe; it is also the Bolivarian José Vasconcelos's "cosmic race," the race of races. These are anticipations of a universal integration, starting from an equally universal identity. They are forms of identity and integration that contrast with past historical expressions of a nation *over* other nations or a race *over* other races.

Europe had made its own identity an unattainable model of the human *par excellence;* however, now it confronts problems of identity that would seem alien to it and that are the result of the globalization to which it gave itself origin. In its expansion, Europe disseminated, as exclusive to its own identity, values that it could recognize or negate in other persons and peoples. But these are values that other nations demand as their own, and they insist on their recognition. In this way, a new form of globalization and integration arises, in which all peoples and nations want to be understood in ways other than servile dependence for the benefit of a few.

The region of America that calls itself Latin was faithful to the spirit of integration of the Greece and Rome of antiquity and of the Spain of modernity, with the various peoples and cultures around the Mediterranean Sea: Europe to the north, Africa to the south, and Asia to the east. It was there where the integrative spirit projected and universalized itself throughout the continent. It was in what was to become the Latin region of the New World where the Old World found and integrated itself with the New, giving rise to the great problems of identity formulated in the region: Who are we? Indians or Spaniards? Americans or Europeans? Americans or Africans? Americans or Asians? We are all of them! A *mestizo* [mixed] race, richer than any that has ever existed on the face of the earth. Precisely because of being all of them, we have faced problems in the past and will face them in the future. Bolívar says, "All of us are born from the womb of the same mother; our fathers are different in origin and blood, and they all differ visibly in the color of their skin; this dissimilitude presents a challenge of the greatest significance."

Spain brings this challenge with it. It is the challenge of positing a diverse identity that, because it is diverse, is not possible to define. It is a challenge that became apparent in 1898 when Spain lost its last overseas colonies, ceasing to be

an empire. Then a type of questioning that had already begun in the eighteenth
century arises again: What are we? Goths or Moors? Mediterranean or Germanic?
Africans or Europeans? We are all of these, answers José Gaos from his
*transtierro:*[2] We are a peculiar *mestizo* race: Hispano American on both sides of
the Atlantic.

"We are," says Bolívar, "a small part of humanity and are in possession of a
world surrounded by wide oceans, new in all the arts and sciences, although old
in terms of the customs and traditions of civil society." It is a small and inclusive
world that will begin to grow from its own regional identity. "It is a grand idea,"
adds Bolívar, "to attempt to make only one nation out of the whole of the New
World, with only one bond to link all the parts with each other and the whole."
This integration will begin in Panama, situated at the "center" of the earth, integrated with the peoples of Europe and Africa by the Atlantic Ocean and with the
peoples of Asia, Australia, and eastern Africa by the Pacific Ocean. "In the course
of centuries," he prophesies, "perhaps one will find only one nation, a federal nation, covering the world."

What seemed in Bolívar's time a mere utopia is now a prophecy to be realized
in the future. When at the beginning of his first term as president of the United
States, William Clinton made a call to arms, not to impose his country's hegemony over people outside its frontiers, but rather to extend the "American
Dream" to all North Americans who had been marginalized from it because of
racial origin or because of sex, culture, religion, and social situation, and when at
the end of his first term he spoke of making the United States the first great multiracial and multicultural nation on Earth, the Latin American integrationist
dream began to be realized. This is a realization that puts an end to the two Americas, which are being transformed into only one America, because of their multiracial and multicultural composition. Parallel to this we see the preoccupation
over the meaning of European identity that originates in the unavoidable presence
of other races and cultures demanding a place in that conception of identity.

This multiracial and multicultural world gives rise to a new conception of
equality. We are equal because of our differences, but not so different from each
other that some could regard themselves as more human than others; rather, we
are different because of our unavoidable concreteness and our individuality and
personality. We are linked to each other by our capacity to recognize in each other
a fellow human, precisely because of our inescapable diversity.

This movement toward integration encounters strong resistance from those
who attempt to preserve an identity that refuses to share values and rights and that
they consider exclusively their own. This resistance gives rise to perverse interpretations that seek to justify exclusionary policies: Everybody is equal in his or
her difference, but everybody must keep to his or her place; there may be multiracial and multicultural nations as long as they do not mix with each other—
Blacks to their jungles and plains, Indians to their huts and communities, and
Whites and *Criollos* to their factories and centers of productions. White people

would respect the laws, habits and customs of the indigenous people of color; however, at the same time, they would respect (and the indigenous must also respect) the labor rules imposed by Whites, as inhuman as they may be. This had a name in South Africa—apartheid.

Some speak of globalization as if it were a fashion or an illness from which the innocent people of the Third World, for example, our mestiza America, must be protected. There are attempts to disarticulate and annul our mestizaje by imposing laws supposedly in defense of the so-called Indians. The international community is mobilized to demand respect for the supposed identity of these peoples as well as their supposed right to keep to a past that is not really their own, to keep anachronistic habits and customs, as well as languages that impede communication with other indigenous people or other nations. These are habits and customs used to delight the tourists so that ecologists can demand the preservation of these peoples just the way some animal species are preserved to avoid extinction.

But these are closed and anachronistic conceptualizations of identity applied equally to men and peoples and demanding their preservation. This has been the case with Mexico when it integrated its economy into those of the United States and Canada through the North American Free Trade Agreement (NAFTA). In the southern cone of our America, where Mercosur has been formed, the Mexican intelligentsia is cautioned about it and is asked to explain this supposed alienation of Mexico from the family of Latin American nations of which it is a part. It has been said that "when two culturally heterogeneous spaces compenetrate each other, one of them inevitably homogenizes the other." Some base themselves on what Samuel Huntington said, when asked what will happen to cultures with this heterogeneous interpenetration. He answered that "for the United States there is no problem at all; but Mexico will become transformed culturally into an appendage of North America."

The answer to that criticism was a simple one. The former president of the United States, George H. Bush, made a visit to South America and offered the same treaty to the southern cone as the one agreed to by Mexico in NAFTA. He went with the purpose of creating the markets that his country needed to transform its war industry into an industry that could compete in a market economy. It was then a market that could not easily enter Europe or Asia. No one rejected the offer then. In any case, I do not think that such a treaty would endanger the southern cone's cultural identity.

When Bush was defeated in his reelection attempt by the Democratic candidate William Clinton, Clinton made the treaty his own because he thought that it benefited his country. First, the House of Representatives opposed it, adducing the inequality of the economies the treaty tried to integrate. With great effort, the U.S. Congress approved the treaty already set in motion with Mexico. But it did not want to consider the incorporation into the same treaty of other countries in Latin America. For their own part, the countries that established Mercosur sought an economic integration with the European Community.

Beginning with the assumption of the supposed impossibility of integrating different cultural and economic spaces, liberalism is at a loss with forms of co-existence more in agreement with the idea of an identity that considers diverse human expressions as a factor in shared development. Liberalism makes of competition a source for a development that cannot be shared. In its Darwinian expression, the fittest impose their identity and interests.

However, under globalization, competition acquires a meaning different from traditional liberalism and its struggle for self-preservation. No one is superior or dispensable: everyone is necessary precisely because of his or her own concrete and special mode of being.

"Competing while sharing" would be the formula for a development that would benefit all: To compete from one's own concrete mode of being to attain higher goals for a development that will be shared. Those who arrive first should help those who fall behind because, when some fall behind, the development of all may be affected. The whole is a spiral, which may be an infinite spiral of production that generates employment and with it consumption that, in turn, creates more employment and consumption.

In a conference he gave recently in Mexico, José Borrell referred to a talk he had with King Hassan of Morocco: the king told him that if the West did not help them to develop themselves, they would again invade it as Tarik did, not with armies, but with immigrants infiltrating themselves gradually. This is the story of all great migrations, and today we are witnessing the massive presence of peoples of different ethnicities and cultures at the heart of the Western world—Europe and the United States. These represent changes that will give rise to problems of identity, which had not been the concern of the West until now. By contrast, "competing while sharing" is the new form of development during globalization.

How was the European Community, communitarian Europe, achieved? Helmut Schmidt, former Chancellor of Germany, has talked about it. It was not due to a dictator or tyrant of any kind. Instead, it was the result of a free decision made by the European nations as they faced the characteristic problematic of the Cold War. They decided freely to integrate their interests and put an end to differences that had given rise to wars that had then become world conflicts. Their decision was made with the same spirit that has animated the integration of Latin America from the time of Bolívar until today—integration *in* liberty. They have not ceded sovereignty; on the contrary, they have widened it. This integration was not imposed by globalization but is instead a response to it.

In that context of freedom in globalization, the meddling by people of that community—in the name of the globalization of justice—into the problems of our region of the continent, and considering that we have sovereignty, has negative consequences.

In the name of a supposedly globalized justice, European judges denounce crimes against humanity, demand the extradition of criminals, and get ready to judge and condemn them. This was the case with Augusto Pinochet. He is certainly a criminal, and he should be punished for crimes he committed against his people for the benefit of interests foreign to the Chileans. Those foreign interests justified Pinochet's crimes, representing them as necessary to save humanity from the communist danger.

The United States never hid the role that Pinochet played in the brutalities of the Cold War. Also, in Europe he was extolled as the champion of the Free World, the defender of Western and Christian civilization. No one in Europe condemned him then for the crimes he was committing. Now they condemn him, not for crimes committed against his own people, but rather, because of crimes committed against the citizens of the same Western nations that did not condemn those crimes at the time. This is similar to the "good old days" of Western imperialism when they would bomb or invade peoples who in some way harmed their interests. This is what happened to the people of Chile who had to suffer the brutality of repression because of interests foreign to them; now they have to suffer for the punishment of Pinochet who was an instrument of that repression, in a presumed, yet not widely accepted, globalization of justice.

Laws and supposedly legal actions have been generated and continue to be generated in the United States; these are, for instance, the embargo against Cuba and policies on narcotics trafficking. Both Europeans and Latin Americans reject those policies because they impose policies to which no one has freely consented.

Also, European judges, making use of a right no one gave them, threaten to prosecute anyone suspected of human rights violations who is so denounced, even though the accusers themselves provoked those crimes. This interference takes us back to times that seemed part of the past already, back to the old imperialist interference by the West over the rest of the world.

## DEMOCRACY AND NEOLIBERALISM

"The day when all Chinese eat and dress well, have good housing and education, travel, have leisure time to enjoy freely the highest expression of culture, and know that they are responsible for all of that, democracy will then begin. . . . On no one but the Chinese will the realization of that possibility depend," said Jiang Zemin.

With these words, China's leader Jiang Zemin answered questions at the UN that were asked by the media regarding the future of his people. The government that began with the Chinese Revolution thus prepared the people for such a future.

China's problem, and the problem of all peoples who entered modernity under the sign of dependency, is to change the situation that was imposed over the whole earth by Europe after 1492 and that gave rise to modernity as if it belonged exclusively to Europe. That is also our problem, the problem of the America of which we are a part, which was the first region of the earth that entered modernity by conquest and colonization.

That history has ended, writes the North American political scientist Francis Fukuyama: "End of history in itself, that is, as the last step in the ideological evolution of humanity and in the universalization of western liberal democracy as the last form of human government." Last and final step of humanity? Not so. It is, rather, the last and final step of humanity *par excellence,* a humanity hardly embodied in peoples such as ours.

"[T]he vast bulk of the Third World remains very much mired in history, and will be a terrain of conflict for many years to come," writes Fukuyama in "The End of History?" Regarding the socialist countries, such as the former Soviet Union and China, he says that they were "not likely to join the developed nations of the West as liberal societies any time in the foreseeable future."[3] In those places, fundamentalisms and nationalisms will hinder their transition to posthistory; they are peoples condemned to a history without end. Ten years after *The End of History and the Last Man,*[4] Fukuyama continues to insist on his vision. Recent events in the Balkans, the Middle East, and attempts by politicians in our America to prevent our emergence from "history," prove him right, thinks Fukuyama.

How does Fukuyama characterize that exclusive Western world? He represents it as "a homogeneous state, with a liberal democracy in the political sphere combined with easy access to VCRs and stereo equipment in the economic sphere." The source of income in this situation comes from the market economy for which neither former communists nor the disposable peoples colonized by the West, and whose raw materials and labor force are already anachronistic because of the development of Western science and technology, are prepared.

This is a scientific and technical, not a moral, superiority. It made it possible for Europe to expand over the rest of the world. But Europe also took care in limiting or blocking it from the people under its dependency. It did so by excluding, separating, setting apart, and maintaining the underdevelopment of the dependent nations, as well as stimulating ancestral habits and customs; in this way, they became museum pieces that go from the caveman to the television viewer, for the glory of man *par excellence.*

North Atlantic and Baltic Europe will stand out in terms of scientific and technological superiority, thus surpassing Mediterranean Europe of which the Iberian Peninsula is a part. This superiority becomes obvious in the Canal de la Mancha [The English Channel] with the defeat of the Spanish Armada.

Columbus set in motion the European expansion over the earth, looking for the shortest route to reach the riches of the world of Marco Polo's stories. He stumbles upon beautiful but naked people, terrified by the discharges of the harquebuses. Was this Paradise? And those people, are they angels or beasts? No, it was simply a land and people without someone to lord over them, who could be redeemed by Christianity. The other Europe will see those same people as part of the flora and fauna to exploit.

The Spanish empire, with another historical experience and mentality, kept separate the found populations, with their uses and customs, in communities that the Church would be in charge of caring for. But equally separate were the enslaved and uprooted Africans, brought in because it was thought that they could take more abuse than the indigenous Americans and the fruits of the conqueror's lust—the mestizo. The whole was thus organized in a complex arrangement of castes of marginalized and excluded people.

In the America under Spanish dominion, the Church was put in charge because of its hegemony of maintaining the mental dependence of the conquered, while the missioners would be in charge of protecting them from the conqueror's greed. Paradoxically, in the royal and pontifical universities created to those ends, the seeds of rebellion against colonization were planted. The Spanish Empire had to confront, moreover, the harassment of the empires that arose in Europe east of the Pyrenees and on the Atlantic. During the eighteenth century, it had to defend itself from the false accusations by Buffon and De Pauw who portrayed the Spanish colonies in the Americas and its peoples as inferior to the Old World; the corollary was the possibility of incorporating them into the march of "progress" under the dominion of western Europe.

Enlightened Bourbon Spain in the eighteenth century had to prove the opposite, namely, that this region of America was extraordinarily rich and its peoples well prepared to exploit its wealth. From different places in this region, scientific expeditions were organized to determine the extent of that wealth and the capacity of its inhabitants. The Prussian sage Alexander von Humboldt was invited to attest this reality; he contradicted Buffon's and De Pauw's false accusations, and he encouraged the inhabitants of Spanish America to exploit its wealth for their own benefit and not for the sake of any external power, Spain included. This was the essence of the idea of emancipation of the America under Iberian dominion.

While the Spanish Empire consolidated its hegemony over continental Europe, Anglo-Saxon and Puritan Europe extended itself throughout the north of America and the rest of the world. It was able to do by sea what it had not been able to do on land, thanks to its scientific and technological superiority. In North America, it exterminated and enclosed the Indians in reservations. In Asia and Africa, it allowed the continuation of the uses and customs of the natives as long as they did not impede its control over them; at the same time, it blocked their access to the science and technology that had made that dominion possible.

In the United States, Anglo-Saxon and Puritan America had emancipated itself from European colonialism. But it would do something more besides: it would dispute Europe's hegemony in the American continent and the rest of the world.

The United States began its expansion over the continent in 1847, in the war with Mexico. In 1898 they began their expansion over the world, displacing Spain from the Caribbean and the Philippines. In 1917 they intervened in the First World War started by the Europeans. The United States came out of it as creditors and hegemonic. They intervened in World War II against the German-Japanese Axis and defeated it, thus imposing themselves on Europe and the world that was under Europe's domination. But they would have to share in the fruits of victory with the other winner, the Soviet Union.

The European expansion that had been imposed on Asia stumbled, when faced with Japan's resistance, as had happened before to the Chinese, the Spaniards, and the Portuguese. In 1853, the North American commander Matthew Perry forced the Japanese to open up their ports. Had he known the consequences of this, he might not have done it; Japan then appropriated Western science and technology for its own use, contesting Western colonialism in Asia. In 1941, Japan attacked the United States in Pearl Harbor, extending the war in Europe to Asia.

With the end of World War II, the United States and the Soviet Union disputed between themselves world hegemony, giving origin to the Cold War. Science and technology on both sides built deterrent weapons of planetary annihilation. In 1984, Mikhail Gorbachev announced that the Soviet Union was getting out of the Cold War and armed competition; thus, he set in motion a series of changes so that his people and those in Europe under Soviet hegemony were to use science and technology to make instruments for self-reliance, without depending on the state. "The capitalist mode of life is not at odds with socialism, but rather simply expands it," he said. The Soviets opposed this abandonment by the state, and the disintegration of the Soviet Union was set in motion.

In 1989, at the end of the Cold War and with the fall of the walls that kept the world separate, Fukuyama published "The End of History?"[5] In that essay, he anticipated this situation. What he did not see at the time, nor does he comment on ten years later, is that, together with the socialists and the "Third Worldists," the United States also gets stuck in the history without end, bearing the burden of its already anachronistic armamentism, done for the sake of scaring off an enemy that no longer exists.

The vanquished of World War II, Germany and Japan, unable to build weapons, produced domestic wares for the happiness of people. In that way, they set in motion the market economy of which Fukuyama spoke. Western Europe emerged with Germany, making its integration possible, and it projected its economy as an autarchy, leaving out ex-communist Europe; its already dispensable overseas colonies; and the United States, the military protection of which no longer being necessary.

Japan, by contrast, developed its economy incorporating and sharing with the former colonies of the Western world in Asia. Its technology surpassed Western technology and made it cheaper. A new conception of liberalism became evident, in which in order to grow one must share and compete while sharing.

When he assumed his second mandate, William Clinton announced that his country had to incorporate itself into the global market economy, within a neoliberal system, by bringing into the mode of life and economy of the United States all those who were marginalized because of their race, culture, customs, and mores. Furthermore, regarding international affairs, he said that the development and security of the United States depended on the development and security of its neighbors and its neighbors' neighbors.

We arrive at the world conceived by Fukuyama in 1989; nevertheless, we do so by ways not contemplated in his essay. It is not with the absolute victory of the United States and the system it heads. Instead, what is emerging is being brought about by the people that seemed destined to have a history without an end to underdevelopment. What does Fukuyama think ten years later? In terms of politics and economics, the same as he did before, he responds; it is true, he says, that several of these peoples have taken up the technical science that allowed the Western world to arrive at the end of history, but it has not been used as it should.[6]

The recent crisis in Kosovo demonstrates that the communists have not overcome the obstacles that would leave them outside the glorious end of history. "The current crisis in Kosovo, tragic as it is, is not a world-historical event that will shape fundamental institutions forever after."[7] The failures in this economy are peoples' failures, not the system's. "But for all the hardship and setbacks suffered by Mexico, Thailand, Indonesia, South Korea, and Russia as a result of their integration into the global economy, there is not, as George Soros contends, a 'global crisis of capitalism.'"[8]

Fukuyama also tells us that it is not the market economy's fault that Mexicans, instead of integrating themselves, demand discriminatory laws so that so-called indigenous Mexicans can stay as they are, nor, he goes on, is it the system's fault if Mexicans ask for the opposite of what set the Chinese system in motion, to have Mexicans study to become self-sufficient and not depend on the state.

In addition, Fukuyama speaks of the Asian failure, the economic crisis that put an end to the supposed economic miracle of that region. About that region, he says, "The economic crisis that hit Asia has demonstrated the hollowness of Asian soft authoritarianism, because it sought to base their legitimacy on economic performance, making them vulnerable to downturns."[9] It is not a systemic evil, but rather it is due to the wrong use of the instruments of the system. It is purely and simply a human problem that those who are reaching the end of history are overcoming.

Fukuyama stops being Hegel's epigone and adopts Nietzsche. The failure is that man cannot overcome his humanity, that he is human, all too human. This is something that seems to be within reach only of nineteenth-century liberalism and the ideology of survival of the fittest. In his own words: "Those who attempted to find the End of History's key flaw in political and economic events of the past decade were barking up the wrong tree." The problem lies, for Fukuyama, on "the limits of human nature." To overcome them is the highest goal of the science and technology of the future:

> The open-ended character of modern natural science suggests that within the next couple of generations, biotechnology will give us the tools that will allow us to accomplish what social engineers of the past failed to do. At that point, we will have

definitively finished human history because we will have abolished human beings as such. And then a new human posthistory will begin.[10]

The end of history is not within the reach of all men but only of the supermen that Western science and technology will make possible. Before them, people like us will be crushed, or at least marginalized. Will the science fiction of Star Wars become reality? It seems that only the fiction will be within our reach, waiting for those who will realize it to make it possible. But is not *the end of the human* perhaps one more of Fukuyama's fictions that seeks to conjure away the stubborn presence of a multiracial and multicultural China? Is it a version of Clinton's multiracism and with it the way the United States makes its entrance into the global market economy? Does his prejudiced gaze, however, justify the resistance by some people to assume their responsibility to do for themselves what cannot be done by others?

## NATIONALISM IN A GLOBAL WORLD

We must look at nationalism, identity, and culture as they appear within the process of globalization that became apparent at the end of the last century and millennium. In this context, one must examine the role of engineering and of engineers in the development of nations under the new conditions of globalization.

Nationalism, which integrates diverse interests and identities for the achievement of common ends, expresses itself in culture. Nationalism manifests itself as imperialism when those ends transcend their appropriate and natural origin—its motto being variously: Great Britain above all! France above all! Germany above all!

The peoples and nations that suffer the impact of imperialism also confront it and resist against it. Various European nations since 1492 have expanded far and wide over the earth, beginning the process of globalization that now concerns us and that represents a new perspective of the nation.

Simón Bolívar already expressed this in the nineteenth century when he said: "In the course of the centuries, we may perhaps find a nation covering the universe—the federal nation." This proposal seemed perhaps at the time a utopia; however, with the end of the Cold War in 1989, it became the project set in motion by Europe itself, because of the military supremacy that the United States imposed on it for its own security when confronting the Soviet Union. Another utopia seemed to be on the way to realization, which had been expressed by Victor Hugo when he said: "Today we speak of France, tomorrow of Europe, and later still of Humanity."

With the disarticulation of the Soviet Union and the return home of the United States bearing the weight of its now useless armaments, there followed a Dirty War, with crimes of hatred and violence in the confrontation between blocs of nations.

Imperial globalization was set in motion by Spain, followed by Portugal, and then England, France, and Holland, each one of them looking for its own and concrete hegemony, while confronting the others. Was this a hegemony over the world? No, but rather over Europe. The colonies created by these nations throughout the world were in the service of imperial predominance in Europe; Spain, England, or France confronted each other in the exercise of this predominance. Their dominions in America, Asia, and Africa were used to pay the expenses of these intra-European conflicts.

This type of relation originated from the two great world wars of the twentieth century, the Cold War that followed World War II, and the Dirty War in which we are now living. In these wars, the peoples who gave their raw materials and cheap labor to the colonizers and offered their lives, also witnessed the destruction of their homes and saw how the right that they now demanded to share the fruits of that violence was denied to them. This is the world that emerged from the end of the Cold War, in 1989; now it is looking out for a nation of nations, in which the formerly colonized would be an equal part and not simply an instrument anymore.

What happens to sovereignty? Sovereignty is a European concept that each nation demands for itself, so that each nation can thus exercise its proper and concrete dominion, while denying it to others. But that is a concept of sovereignty that justifies the nullification of the sovereignty of others, if the latter affects the interests of the former. What would happen to this concept in a nation of nations? In it, each nation would become integrated into the others and would integrate the others within itself. It grows without annulling the others, making others grow while it itself grows. Sovereignty widens without negating the diversity of its origins, identity, and culture.

Bolívar's utopia developed from the ancient history of the Mediterranean Sea where there was an encounter of diverse expressions of the human and their cultures, namely, those that gave rise to Europe, Africa, and Asia. It was a diversity that Greece and Rome integrated into themselves. Greece did so by means of the *logos* that comprehends and makes comprehension possible; Rome did so by means of the law, by means of Right *(el derecho)*, which integrates others without denying their ethnic and cultural diversity. Greece hellenized, while Rome latinized others, making barbarian peoples the forces that one day would take their place.

In America—the new continent—as in the Mediterranean, there has been an encounter of the diversity of peoples and cultures that constitute the totality of the world of which America is also part: a continent surrounded by oceans, the waters of which bathe Europe and Africa on one side and Asia and Oceania on the other. From this continent, the nation of nations would develop and cover the entire globe; that is what is happening in our days all over the world, including Europe and the United States.

By contrast, it is asserted that globalization, expressed in free trade treaties with peoples of other races and cultures, will of necessity negatively affect so-called inferior cultures and ethnic groups, since it will compel them to subordinate themselves to those that are "superior." Samuel Huntington, of the United States, when asked about the free trade agreement [NAFTA] of his country with Mexico and Canada, responded: "For the United States there is no problem; it will be Mexico that will be transformed culturally into a North American appendix."

Alain Touraine of France, when asked whether it would be possible for Mexico to get a free trade agreement with the European Community similar to the one the latter has with Mercosur, answers that "it will be difficult for nations such as Mexico, Colombia, Peru, or Venezuela, because of the indigenous, African, and mestizo burden they bear; that is not the case with Mercosur. These multiracial and multicultural peoples will be able to have [a free trade agreement] only with the United States, subjecting themselves fully to U.S. domination." Alberto Methol Ferré of Uruguay says that "when two heterogeneous cultural spaces penetrate each other, one will inevitably assume hegemony over the other."

José Enrique Rodó, also Uruguayan, asserted that, on the contrary, "nordomania"—that is, the excessive admiration toward the United States that people in the South had during his time—was a form of freely subordinating ourselves to the United States. It resulted from the eagerness to make our identity a copy of that nation. Rodó showed how identity is being confused with the capacity to make use of the scientific and technical instruments that accounted for the material greatness of the United States and Europe. He also showed it was a mistake to think it was because of their special mode of being or characteristic identity that the United States and Europe achieved that greatness. That belief has given rise in peoples like us to the useless desire to be other than we are.

In this issue, it becomes apparent how important engineering and engineers are for Mexico and Latin America. The end of the Cold War made possible the emergence of Western Europe in the face of the armed supremacy of the United States, in defense of its security. This also gave rise to the emergence of the other loser of World War II, Japan. And like Germany, unable to produce weapons, Japan would then make domestic products, the production and consumption of which would give rise to the market economy of this turn of the century and millennium. Without renouncing its identity, Japan appropriated Western science and technology, improved upon them, lowered their costs, and made economic partners of the old European colonies in Asia, thus beginning the emergence of the Asian economy.

Europeans and North Americans recognize that fact. Nevertheless, North Americans like Huntington and his disciple Fukuyama say: "We recognize that Asians have overcome us scientifically and technically, but they will never overcome us in our morality. We would never make a man work twenty-four hours a day, as the Asians do." The leader of Singapore asks them: "We used to work twenty-four hours a day for you. Was that moral? Now we work twenty-four hours a day for ourselves. Is that immoral?"

An aberrant interpretation of identity is thus made as a way of separating peoples who are in relation to each other: Identity is viewed as something closed and ossified in a deceitful condition of superiority for some and inferiority for others. By being put in a condition of inferiority, the latter are left out of the enjoyment of their own achievements, which are rather for the benefit of the former. All men are equal by reason or genius, Descartes attested, and different only in their accidental qualities. But circumstance, ethnicity, and culture are accidental qualities in the Cartesian perspective.

According to that perspective, Descartes is, by virtue of reason, similar to all other men and, because of that, he is equal to an African, and Asian, or a mestizo. But it is implicit in that interpretation that he is different because of being White, a Westerner, or because his cranium allows him to use his reason well, which is not supposed to be the case with other races who have other somatic constitutions: equal but different and, because of that, each one in his or her place—some in their jungles, cattle tracks, and deserts; others in their factories and modes of production, which their identity has allowed them to create.

Confronting that discriminatory point of view, we respond: we are all equal because of being distinct from each other. Each one has his or her ethnicity and culture, but we are not so distinct from each other that some may be more human than others. Identity is not something closed, but rather, it feeds on its relation with others as others on it. Every expression of identity, independently of its origin, grows and furthers the growth of the identities of others. Obviously, identities change, but that should happen freely. It should not happen by means of the violence of conquest, nor by servile imitation in which one negates oneself in order to be. Technological and scientific development is not the patrimony of a few to the exclusion of others. Instead, it belongs to all peoples in the unique terms of their special identity. When Arnold Toynbee, the British philosopher of history, visited Mexico in 1953, he marveled at how Mexicans used what were then new technologies in the Papaloapan Basin, in terms of their particular identity, improvising answers to the problems they were confronting.

José Vasconcelos, inspired by Bolívar's idea of a nation of nations, speaks of a race of races and a culture of cultures, which he expresses in the utopian concept of the *cosmic race*. This is not a "race" per se, but rather, a *capacity* to recognize other fellow men and women and, through that recognition, an understanding of them as extensions of one's own self. Thus, the *cosmic race* is more than a race; it is a culture of integration of cultures and identities: it is a culture open to the diversity of expressions of the human.

A nation of nations, a race of races, and a culture of cultures are today preoccupations in the centers of power and in the culture regarded to be *the* culture *par excellence,* namely, the culture of Europe and the United States, because of the presence of *other* races and cultures. This presence places into question the universality of any concrete expression of humanity and culture that is simultaneously negating the universality of all other races and cultures.

Preoccupations about identity, which seemed to be peculiar to marginal peoples such as ours, are now problems that are posited in the centers of European culture, as they face the active presence of other races and cultures. These preoccupations put in crisis the pretension to believe that one's culture is the culture *par excellence.*

The scientific and technological superiority that made it possible for the West to expand far and wide over the planet is now being disputed and overtaken by peoples who, because of their especial identity and culture, were thought to be foreign to science and technology. Nevertheless, science and technology are simply instruments to the service of whoever makes them possible, without any cultural or racial exclusion. It is a kind of globalization that now becomes apparent as the opposite to the globalization that was based on the supremacy of one nation over other nations, a mode of being over other modes of being, one culture over other cultures, and an exclusive instrument of science and technology.

The central problem of the type of globalization that speaks of a nation among nations, an identity among identities, and a culture among cultures is how to live in it: how to live with others without negating them or negating oneself, sharing the fruits that give rise to the diversity of the human, and rejecting all forms of apartheid—an apartheid that asserts "all are equal by being different, but everyone in their places," such as this or that race to their jungles, deserts, dialects, and folklore; that other one to its factories, industries, and mines. On the contrary, one must assert that all are equal because they are different, but not so different that some are more human than others.

All peoples without discrimination shall be instrumental in accomplishing common goals, without subordinations, sharing the fruits of common efforts. Thence, it is necessary that the instruments of development be available to everybody. The same elements that throughout the course of history made the emergence and development of the so-called Western world possible must also be within reach of those peoples who have not yet attained that development but who made it possible by their work. For the sake of maintaining development for all, this must be done.

We are witnesses to a new competitive relationship, namely, to compete while sharing, and not by eliminating, for the sake of a common goal. Globalization is making it apparent that the weakness of some negatively affects the strength of others. That is what is meant when terms such as the "tequila effect," or the "samba," "tango," or "dragon" effects are used to speak of economic crises that spread over the earth, over wealthy and poor alike. The extraordinary advances in science and technology today make many types of raw materials and cheap manual labor unnecessary. However, to keep those advances, we need markets with the capacity to consume; this creates the imperative to search for consumers, but consumers cannot be found among people sunk in poverty. Today's poor may be, because of their numbers, the new required markets for an increase in production, thus making it possible to take them out of poverty, offering them employment, and opening up for them the possibility of becoming consumers. With consumption, the demand for more production will increase and development will become more shared, in a chain that will encompass the whole world.

Engineering, for instance, is more sophisticated each time, and there need to be more sophisticated means for generating easy production and mass consumption. There is a need for people to train others to act and live under conditions of globalization in a relationship, not of servitude, but rather, of solidarious dependence in the achievement of common goals. Engineering must thus prepare our peoples to live in these times of globalization, without damaging their own and concrete expression of humanity.

Bill Gates amassed one of the largest fortunes today with the mass production of computers. This has placed ever more sophisticated instruments of information within reach of an increasing number of people and through supply and demand placed them within the reach of all without having to subject themselves to the producers. People thus become freer and, therefore, more capable of acting in the community of communities, the new expression of globalization.

Owners of large fortunes are also the engineers of "our America" [i.e., Iberoamerica—*Ed.*], who, through various routes, prepare our people for living in and taking advantage of globalization. One of them is a Mexican, Carlos Slim, who, in a recent seminar organized by the Fondo de Cultura Económica, spoke about the origin of his extraordinary fortune: scrap metal discarded every year by the centers of power in their search for something more perfect each time. This is the case with computers that by being discarded are then within reach of our people who, in that way, become part of the extraordinary world of computers, however sophisticated it may be.

Another engineer is the Chilean, Fernando Flores, who teaches and prepares persons and enterprises to live in and use globalization to their advantage. About nations he says, following the old adage that one must not give them fish, but rather teach them how to fish, for whoever gives also sets the terms. The president of China, Jiang Zemin, when asked about the democratization of his nation, said: "The day when every Chinese eats well, and has good housing, a secure job, better education, adequate leisure time, and also knows that he owes all that to himself or herself and not to the State; that day democracy will begin in China and with it, absolute respect for human rights. Nobody will be able to put conditions on what others know is due to themselves and, least of all, will he be able to take it away from them."

The Argentinian, Enrique Menotti Pescarmona, is another engineer. He is one of the owners of the communications networks in our region, which makes entry into globalization possible by integrating the image and the word.

These are all noteworthy engineers, preoccupied by the society to which they belong and mindful of the challenges that the world offers. This can be our great opportunity to rise up as other nations, which for centuries were marginalized and used by an imperial and colonial globalization, have done. This emergence will not be easy because of the resistance from those who want to preserve conditions of marginalization and refuse to share what was achieved by marginalizers and marginalized together.

Fukuyama, who affirms the moral superiority of a marginalizing system and its people, says that peoples like ours will never be able to overcome them morally, scientifically, or technically, because we are human, too human, that is, corrupt, selfish, and envious.

What are the morality and the superiority, of which Fukuyama makes a show, that he says is impossible to overcome? What is the challenge that is impossible to meet by our people? The problem, for Fukuyama, seems to be to overcome the human, and this is being attained by the science and technology of the World *par excellence*.

As we saw above, Fukuyama ends his reexamination of "The End of History?" by raising the possibility that science will abolish "human beings as such. And then, a new posthuman history will begin."[11] But that is the overman. We, the humans, all too human, will have to content ourselves with going to the movies to watch the exploits of this superman in the stars. That is the challenge.

## NOTES

1. See Germán Arciniegas, *Arciniegas Polémico* (Bogota: ESPASA, 2001).

2. José Gaos (1900–1969) left for Mexico with the rise of fascism in Spain, his native country. But rather than calling himself an exile (*desterrado*, literally someone banished or moved *from his earth or roots*) in Mexico, he called himself *transterrado* (literally, someone whose earth or roots have moved across). Gaos became one of the germinal figures of twentieth-century Mexican philosophy. His reflections formed the foundation of both a rethinking of the history of Mexican philosophy as a tradition of its own and a rethinking of the meaning of philosophy through a methodical questioning of cultural identity as a philosophical question.—*Ed.*

3. Francis Fukuyama, "The End of History?" *The National Interest* 15 (summer 1989), 3–18.

4. See Francis Fukuyama, *The End of History and the Last Man* (New York: Avon Books, 1992).

5. See Francis Fukuyama, "The End of History?" 3–18.

6. Francis Fukuyama, "Second Thoughts: The End of History 10 Years Later," *New Perspectives Quarterly* 16, no. 4 (summer 1999): 40–43, 40. Francis Fukuyama, "Second Thoughts: The Last Man in a Bottle," *The National Interest* 56 (summer 1999), 16–33, 16.

7. Fukuyama, "The End of History 10 Years Later," 41. [See also Fukuyama, "The Last Man in a Bottle," 24. —*Ed.*]

8. Fukuyama, "The End of History 10 Years Later," 41. [See also Fukuyama, "The Last Man in a Bottle," 24. —*Ed.*]

9. Fukuyama, "The End of History 10 Years Later," 41. [See also Fukuyama, "The Last Man in a Bottle," 21. —*Ed.*]

10. Fukuyama, "The End of History 10 Years Later," 41; Fukuyama, "The Last Man in a Bottle," 33.

11. Fukuyama, "The End of History 10 Years Later," 41; Fukuyama, "The Last Man in a Bottle," 33.

# 8

## A Global Democratic Order: A Normative Proposal

### María Pía Lara-Zavala

Until now, it has been mostly the sociologists who have made use of the term "globalization" to describe and theorize different phenomena of world economy and trading markets, ecology, communication and mass media, and politics. This horizon of different problems conceived as problems related to globalization processes is in urgent need of thematization by philosophers, in order to find out if we can offer new perspectives with normative features that allow the term "globalization" to become a key concept for understanding our *Zeitgeist*, and to evaluate international political problems in relation to world democratization and respect for human rights. In this chapter, I want to rescue the term "globalization" from its common understanding among "globaliphobics,"[1] and "globaliphilics,"[2] and propose a "normative framework" for such a concept to highlight the possible practical paths that we need to consider in order to find a normative link between processes of globalizing democratic institutions of law and human rights and a growing trend toward a democratic culture of cosmopolitanism. Contrary to what many theorists from underdeveloped countries think, I want to propose that certain processes of globalization can be used to bring to light the necessity of worldwide cooperation in helping poor countries to build up democratic institutions and defend the basic rights of all the people that live in those countries. In my view, only by using globalization in a normative way can we rescue Kant's insight about the possibility of an age based on a peaceful coexistence that flows from the correlation between human rights with justice and solidarity in concrete ways through specific actions taken by worldwide institutions.

Two hundred years ago, Kant had the idea of conceiving a second foundational moment for democratic politics. He thought of "perpetual peace" and its pacifying effects as a second "social contract," which establishes a new political agreement between individuals to live in peaceful coexistence under conditions of a growing cosmopolitan culture and a strong defense of human rights. When Kant envisaged a "world public sphere" and a "world civil society," he was already pointing out the need for an internationalization of democracy by using the concept of international law—cosmopolitan law—to create what he called "a peaceful global order." Following his proposal in this century, Habermas and other theorists[3] have tried to further develop Kant's concept of world peace in relation to globalization processes. There are some important elements that these theorists have addressed in relation to Kant's ideas in order to recover them and to build a contemporary normative view. This new conceptualization of democratic expansion in our times should be an important new trend to consider in focusing on globalization. Thus, this chapter will deal first with a historical and critical recovery of Kant's important legacy; second, it will deal with the normative categories that we need to make the concept of globalization central for the development and radicalization of democracy; and, third, it will examine some concrete examples of historical consequences of globalization that are already pointing to the possibility of understanding a connection between a radical democratization of human rights and processes of democratic globalization.

## RECOVERING KANT'S NORMATIVE GROUNDS FOR A "COSMOPOLITAN ORDER"

There are important reasons why we need a normative framework to reconceive globalization processes. One reason is that the economy alone cannot produce social benefits for all, and the laws of the free market and trade cannot provide for better ways of living in a more humane order, for this order presupposes measures to cope with inequalities, such as poverty, hunger, and injustice. The idea that countries could overcome their social, economic, and political problems just by entering into the international competitiveness of the free market is proved wrong when we turn our attention to what happened in the Asian countries during the 1980s and 1990s. These countries' governments claimed that their economies improved by an aggressive economic effort to become competitive in terms of international market standards. By pursuing this very narrow path of economic growth and international competitiveness, they argued, their countries were involved in the collective effort of finding better ways to live a good life without transforming their political institutions. It is very clear now that not only did their lives remain unimproved in terms of wealth distribution and living standards, but their political institutions gave evidence of corruption, lack of respect for human rights, and a very restricted sense of freedom. Recently, those Asian regimes failed to maintain their economic standards while their authoritarianism seemed to be heading toward a critical point of political crisis.

Following the Asian path, some Latin American countries, such as Brazil and Mexico, developed strong policies to enter into the world market and improve their living standards through world trade agreements, but their efforts have made us aware that the market alone is an insufficient step in the path toward democratic modernization and development. Thus, the global trend toward recognition that privatizing state enterprises is a healthy measure for the development of the economy of underdeveloped countries and for the pursuit of aggressive policies to compete at the international level cannot be the only measures taken for a meaningful overcoming of the basic inequalities and low living standards that tie these countries to a very unfair distribution of wealth.

Overthrowing authoritarianism and building up democratic institutions can supply the needed measures to accomplish sufficient economic stability and better opportunities for all. These democratic institutions can provide for ways to bring about a healthy redistribution of wealth and a fairer social order that will much improve not only living standards but also the quality of life.[4] Thus, there are no real possibilities of integral development without democracy. Only democratic institutions and their goals to counterbalance the rigid rule of the markets can provide a healthy equilibrium toward a fairer society, a much-needed procedure that would allow those countries to fight against their own unjust traditions of corruption, clientelism, and daily practices of disrespect for human rights.

A democratic understanding of the law should begin by considering that individuals are bearers of basic rights. If this is true, then we need to consider a global space that could now take the lead on the path toward protecting rights by means of the different types of protection that were first offered by the nation-states.

Thus, one important aspect of Third World countries and their need to build democratic institutions is their ties with First World countries and their specific solidarity in achieving democratic transformations. However, in today's stratified world, there are irreconcilable interests that arise out of the asymmetrical interdependency between countries that are developed, others that are growing rapidly, and some others that are underdeveloped. The only way to make possible the connection among internal democratic demands, external procedures that can help and foster the building of democratic institutions, and an agreed-upon coordination with other countries that would be supported by an institutional space of global politics and governance will be through a world public sphere and a world civil society.

There is another good reason why we can reconsider that globalization needs to be framed on normative grounds. Just as various economic experiments have helped us see the need to pursue the democratization of countries and the need to spread global democratic measures and institutions to counterbalance the rigid blindness of the market's logic, we need democratic institutions to stop the civil, ethnic, and nationalistic wars that have produced the horrors of genocide, ethnic cleansing, and all kinds of crimes against humanity perpetrated in the last one hundred years. Our experience has built an important foundation of moral learning from the tragic wars that have proliferated as civil and ethnic wars in our century.

However, if moral learning is pointing in the direction of new institutions in which cosmopolitan law is possible, there is also an evident need to help those countries that have suffered traumatic events. These tragedies can be overcome by reeducating their societies in democratic ways and by developing important legal procedures for the accountability of crimes committed against their own fellow humans. The burden of the past is something that countries which have suffered civil, political, or ethnic wars do not know how to solve, and there is growing evidence that the more a country learns from its past mistakes, the greater is the possibility of building a conscious understanding of democratic duties and responsibilities. Countries that have recovered from traumatic events are now facing a basic social challenge about what to do with the people who committed such crimes and their victims. Two important things are at stake here. One has to do with the legal procedures that democratic institutions grant for accountability and individual responsibility in committing crimes against humanity or in any violation of human rights. A second element concerns the significant moral effect on society of the disclosure of the "truth" when the murderers are subject to public trials. It is important here to recover the important precedents of the Nuremberg and Tokyo Tribunals.

The creation of a collective moral consciousness of past deeds and the fostering of a collective space where moral learning produces a collective consciousness are important ways of linking nondemocratic countries with those that possess historically democratic traditions. Furthermore, international tribunals are needed, and a process must be set up for the determination and evaluation of what happened, for these represent the only hope for those countries in which their constitutions and political agreements impede the prosecution of their criminals because of the significant power and support that they still have.[5] Thus, the internationalization of human rights, along with the creation of a New Human Rights Court, would allow for accountability of crimes against humanity and war crimes beyond the nation-state's sovereignty.

It is for this reason that Axel Honneth has called our attention toward this historical moment as an important political stage of a new type—a new social contract following Kant's idea of "international relations [applied] to the situation in world politics: states ought to be able to emerge 'from the state of lawlessness, which consists solely of war' by giving up 'their savage (lawless) liberty,' just as individual persons do, and, by accommodating themselves to public coercive law, form a polity of all peoples *(civitas gentium)* that would necessarily continue to grow until it embraced all the peoples of the earth."[6] The normative framework of globalization should start by recognizing this as the historical framework of a new social contract to pursue peaceful coexistence among societies.

## NORMATIVE CATEGORIES TO THEMATIZE GLOBALIZATION

With this new social contract establishing a horizon for democracy based on human rights, some important new conceptualizations should be considered here. The first is our conceptual development of the idea of human rights as basic for a democratic order and how this idea has shifted from the initial conception for which human rights were protected by nation-states to the more actual revised idea that human rights can only be protected by the existence of international law and international courts that warrant accountability to individuals independently of their nation-states. Jürgen Habermas has addressed this issue fully in his essay "Kant's Idea of Perpetual Peace, with the Benefit of Two Hundred Years' Hindsight."[7] In it, Habermas argues about the need to conceive the idea of human rights on different levels: a moral level, that is, the moral content and validity of the idea of human rights; a political level, that is, the policies that allow the idea of human rights to pursue some concrete political goals; and a legal level, that is, the positivization of the idea of human rights attributed to each person as a human being into laws that bind individuals to respect them on the grounds of international laws. However, Habermas argues that "the conception of human rights does not have its origins in morality," but rather, he points out that "it bears the imprint of the modern concept of individual liberties and is therefore distinctly juridical in character." Habermas rightly suggests that "what gives human rights the appearance of being moral rights is neither their content nor even their structure but rather their form of validity, which points beyond the legal order of the nation state."[8] Thus, the connection between human rights and globalization must come from this link between, on the one hand, the validity of the idea of human rights expanding their scope beyond the political framework of the nation-state and, on the other, the globalization of democratic institutions.

The second element that will allow us to fully grasp the normative framework of globalization in connection to human rights and democracy concerns the moral learning processes that have taken place since 1945. Let me address this historical issue with a reconstruction of the idea of human rights.

One can trace the idea of human rights back to the Virginia Bill of Rights and to the 1776 American Declaration of Independence, as well as to the 1789 *Declaration des droits de l'homme et du citoyen* in the French Republic. Both kinds of declarations were inspired by the political philosophies of John Locke and Jean Jacques Rousseau. The idea of human rights was immediately linked to the democratic concept of the nation-state and, thus, they depended on how concretely constitutions regarded their protection and their sanctions.[9] However, the conception of human rights lays bare a peculiar feature that needs to be examined here. The most important feature of human rights is that they are "constructions" that conceive of individuals as the bearers of rights. Because of their universal scope, independently of whether these rights are defined and protected by a specific constitution of a nation-state, their validity refers to the fact that they can be applied to every human being as such; therefore, the concept of human rights shares the kind of universal validity that moral norms possess.[10] This historical reconstruction, however, only serves us here to highlight that the creation of a conception of human rights having universal validity was not fully understood until the catastrophic event of the Holocaust and the important measures that were taken to revise the idea of human rights after the end of the Second World War.[11] The year 1945 became a turning point that led to new alternatives and strategies to pursue the positivization of human rights with a broader scope than the one offered originally in the creation of the nation-state. As Arieh Neier has said:

> [A]n international system of rights protection grew out of World War II in direct re-lation to the crimes of the Nazis. Its main provisions included the United Nations Charter, the statutes of the Nuremberg and Tokyo Tribunals, the Genocide Conven-tion of December 9, 1948, and the following day, the Universal Declaration of Hu-man Rights. Next came the four Geneva Conventions of August 12, 1949, with their provisions spelling out war crimes.[12]

The aftermath of the Second World War became a public arena where new crimes were typified and some practical and important measures were taken in re-sponse to the morally significant experiences of this century. The events that are now called the Holocaust, or the Shoa, and the totalitarian regimes that ignored the basic understandings of our normative ideas about humanity have become the symbols of our moral learning paths toward an understanding of the legal nature of positive human rights.

The moral lessons of these traumatic events opened up a space for a global public debate about the real meaning of categories such as "humanity." It is wor-thy of note that the most insightful recovery of the conception of humanity comes from Hannah Arendt's study of totalitarianism, which focuses on the techniques perpetrated by the Nazis to dehumanize human beings. With an explicit method of "deconstructing" the concept of humanity, Arendt is able to define "humanity" in a rather interesting way. She claims that humanity means plurality, spontane-ity, the capacity for initiating action, and an enlarged mentality. In her section called "The Perplexities of the Rights of Man," Arendt claims that

> the declaration of the Rights of Man at the end of the eighteenth century was a turn-ing point in history. It meant nothing more nor less than that from then on Man, and not God's command or the customs of history, should be the source of Law. Inde-pendent of the privileges which history had bestowed upon certain strata of society, certain nations, the declaration indicated man's emancipation from all tutelage and announced that he had now come of age. Beyond this, there was another implication of which the framers of the declaration were only half aware. The proclamation of human rights was also meant to be a much-needed protection in the new era where individuals were no longer secure in the estates to which they were born or sure of

their equality before God as Christians. . . . Therefore throughout the nineteenth century, the consensus of opinion was that human rights had to be invoked whenever individuals needed protection against the new sovereignty of the state and the new arbitrariness of society.[13]

In the chapter titled, "Ideology and Terror: A Novel Form of Government," Arendt focuses on the techniques that may lead to the historical disappearance of humanity (i.e., its becoming superfluous) when living under totalitarian terror.[14] By describing one by one the steps when terror begins to erode the capacity to react, to move, and to act, Arendt finds that "dignity" is erased, and with it, all traces of our common humanity.

In relation to Arendt's intentions, Dana Villa concludes that Arendt "wants us to take in—slowly, painfully, miserably—not merely man's inhumanity to man, but the fact that psyche, character, and the moral life were all largely destroyed by the camps. She wants us to realize that human power can, in fact, transform human beings into animals—indeed, into 'perverted animals'."[15] Thus, Arendt's legacy of defending "humanity" as a normative term can help us appreciate her as an important theorist who gave us a new sense of the relation of the concept of humanity to human rights.

While Arendt offers a useful insight about the meaning of humanity in its political and moral dimensions, she does not do the same regarding the legal dimension. Nevertheless, she had an important intuition about it in her discussion of human rights connected to the experience of totalitarianism, and her account described the puzzlement generated when people factually became "stateless" in a specific and unprecedented historical turning point. Arendt claimed that the element that was missing from our normative views in the first declarations of the rights of man was the idea that one needs further protection beyond the protection of a nation-state, because we—humans—can easily slip and become the destroyers of our own compatriots. However, she did not see that what was needed between the idea of humanity and our defense of human rights was the mediation of the law, that is, the positivization of human rights as a basic legal concept.

We saw in the preceding that the concept of human rights has been associated with the normative idea of humanity and, as such, it has been the object of many criticisms that have focused on the moral content of the idea of humanity, which, for some theorists has only been used as an excuse for people to wage war on others as the impersonation or embodiment of evil. Carl Schmitt developed the strongest criticism through his own concept of the political. He began by claiming that the politics of human rights was set up to represent the natural struggles between nations as struggles against evil, and thus, the idea of humanity was a cloak for "bestiality."

Habermas has addressed Schmitt's criticisms against the idea of humanity by introducing important distinctions among morality, politics, and legality. Habermas correctly pointed out that the concept of human rights cannot be confused with morality, but rather, that violations of human rights can only be condemned and fought from the moral point of view in a mediated way, that is, within the framework of a legal order and according to institutionalized legal procedures that protect us from a moral dedifferentiation of law and guarantee full legal protection even to those accused of committing crimes against humanity. Thus, according to Habermas, positions like the one taken by Carl Schmitt against the politics of human rights only extend as far as a criticism of the use of "civilizing" war through international law to protect, above all, the sovereignty of states to conduct wars without any legal restrictions.

Even though Arendt was capable of giving new meaning to the concept of humanity, and her illustrative phrase "the right to have rights" was an important insight that pointed out our insufficient understanding of the problem of defending individuals who cannot be protected by nation-states, we are only now aware of the contradictions at the heart of the positivization of human rights. Arendt's answer to this problem was not only wrong, as Jean Cohen has rightfully argued,[16] but it led her to discredit the only politics that could defend stateless persons, a positive globalization and enforcement of human rights policies and agreements. For, as Jean Cohen suggests, "by institutionalizing new connections and relations, by articulating international codes, especially if these are protected by independent supranational courts to whom individuals could appeal, international law has a key role to play in a wide range of domains."[17] In short, law at an international level would play a role parallel to the one that the nation-state played when rights were first part of the constitutions of democratic nations. Nevertheless, to have this possibility open in realistic terms, one must focus first on the idea of how world subjects would see their involvement in the positivization of a democratic rule of law protecting human rights. To successfully take a step like this, we, the subjects of a global order, who obey and create the laws needed for a world constitution, would need to see ourselves in our very creation. We are still far away from such a realization, however. If this is too long a step to reasonably take in the international order, then we need now to bring into focus the need to exert pressure on "the changing consciousness of citizens," so that they see globalization as an important process for democratizing the world, as it has an impact on all the fields of domestic and international affairs. Today's citizens of the world must realize that by perceiving themselves as global subjects, they will become members of a global community that leaves them no choice but cooperation and compromise.

## A WORLD PUBLIC SPHERE AND A WORLD CIVIL SOCIETY

The traumatic experiences of our century, especially after 1945, have clarified some of the problems related to our initial understanding of human rights and the political institutions needed to support such policies. One of our first lessons has been to learn that only those countries with no democratic institutions have immersed themselves in fratricidal crimes.

Thus, two things seem to be important mechanisms in helping those in need of protection. First, we need a form of international law that can deal with the political aims of nations and limit their state power with some kind of coercive force of a higher authority when those countries are violating human rights. Until now, even our strongest world institutions have revealed their limitations when dealing with those issues. Second, a needed public forum of nations would help to publicize such violations and open new forums for discussions in which the claims of the dispossessed could be recognized and defended. These forums are not only a normative condition, but also today they seem to be empirically possible, judging from some recent events. I will consider here different kinds of examples and evaluate their possible contradictions with the aim of showing that publicity, although effective, can also distort and produce unwanted consequences. Thus, the consciousness of individuals must create a counterbalance to publicity's unwanted effects by looking for ways of globalizing strategies for the institutionalization of democratic measures and pressures on those countries in much need of help.

The first interesting example is the Zapatistas' struggle in Mexico. The Zapatistas group from Chiapas had addressed public opinion and international institutions, seeking protection from the Mexican state after they "declared" war on the state of Mexico. International public opinion indeed put a limit on the power of the state of Mexico against repressing the Zapatista movement, even though there had been military occupation in the Chiapas state because of the formal declaration of war that the Zapatistas made. Mexican civil society and a larger community of world civil society became active subjects who sought the protection of Indians' rights, as well as the creation of an open forum to discuss Zapatista demands. A world public sphere opened its space for the acknowledgment of the demands of the Zapatistas, and publicity provided the needed information for nongovernmental organizations that later came to offer all kinds of help. This pressure on the government of Mexico led to the initial peace talks that were called *Los acuerdos de San Andrés* (the San Andrés Agreements).[18] However, world publicity did not offer enough information after the president of Mexico presented the Zapatistas with a new document in which their claims were translated within the framework of Mexico's constitution. Two important things happened: On one hand, many leftist groups from all over the world saw the Zapatistas in a very positive light; they themselves recovered, through the Zapatista struggle, a utopian ideal and saw the Zapatistas as embodying a new kind of "revolution" (see, for example, written statements by Alain Touraine on this). On the other hand, world civil society did not focus on the importance of discussing legal documents that could be analyzed by international experts to see if the changes that former President Zedillo was proposing respected the legality of the constitution, and at the same time, the San Andrés agreements were already signed. Instead, the groups that came to Mexico were mainly interested in seeing themselves reflected in the Zapatistas' mythical recovery of leftist ideals. The role played by many of the NGOs [nongovernmental organizations] that came to Mexico was mostly financial and technical, but they also offered poor advice on the necessity of learning to negotiate their demands in a more public way that involved a prior discussion with other organizations also fighting in defense of Indian rights. Thus, the legal framework of the discussion was lost and so were the first agreements that were signed with the Mexican government. As a result, the important first steps that led to the initial agreement were undone, and the political struggles among the different groups in the state of Chiapas broke openly into a civil war.

In my opinion, what should have happened was something slightly different. Because Mexican democracy is still in transition, many legal and practical problems are still at stake. The lack of political ability to negotiate in a country that is used to corruption, clientelism, and oppression seemed to play a major role in the Zapatistas' lack of skill at political negotiation. Many leftist groups and Marcos himself—the most important leader of the Zapatistas and a non-Indian—proved intolerant. This made negotiations impossible.

The international publicity of the documents and the legal assistance from world institutions, like the United Nations, could have played a different role and helped redirect the discussion strictly in legal terms to see if the changes meant something different from the agreements already signed. The government of Mexico felt that the sovereignty of the country was at stake, but what is really important to notice here is that the efforts made by all those humanitarian groups helped maintain the absence of any important initiative to help reopen the political space for negotiations. Meanwhile, many different groups (mainly NGOs) had already offered much help. Many communities, and the Zapatistas themselves, regarded the outside world as a much more promising stage for help than that offered by internal negotiations. Thus, the aim of publicity being a special forum, not only for information but also for stimulating further discussions of those issues, did not occur. On the other hand, a world civil society, acting with only short-term goals in mind, helped with concrete, finite actions but failed to insist on the need to revive the forums for the purpose of negotiation. Zedillo's government did not pursue any further effort to restart the discussion with the aim of solving this problem; instead, it believed that simply letting time pass would eventually make the Chiapas problem a less interesting and pressing issue for the international community. Actually, public interest has faded, and public opinion has turned its focus onto other matters.[19]

Mexicans are very aware now of the importance of how world institutions see their country and that the international community is well aware of the many violations of rights that seem to persist in our daily life. When Mary Robinson, the High Commissioner for the defense of human rights from the United Nations, came to report what was happening in Chiapas, the whole attention of Mexico's civil society was focused on her and the results of her report to the international community. She was seen as a possible mediator between the world and our country, and all energies were directed at making her see the difficult situation that prevailed in the state of Chiapas. Robinson acknowledged that too many expectations were put on her role as the person in charge of watching that human rights were respected in Mexico. However, she acknowledged that her role was very limited and offered to look for further assistance from her organization but left feeling overwhelmed by the high expectations of Mexican civil society. Mexicans expected her report to influence world opinion and put pressure on the Mexican government's disinterest. Again, what was needed here was an organized world civil society that could strongly publicize her visit and her opinions, as well as feedback from outside groups pressing for more open measures, to insist the Mexican government recognize that negotiations are the only way to solve the problems in Chiapas.

The lesson from this story is that we need an international public sphere that provides an arena for influencing the resumption of negotiations in Mexico and pressures both parties—Mexico's government and the Zapatistas—to use negotiations as an important part of a democratic process that defends the right of the integration of Indian communities. But we also need a more democratically organized process in which the institutions of civil society become aware of the dangers of allowing all kinds of interests to be mixed with the fate of those oppressed. A helpful participation from these groups should be to insist in raising awareness among public international bodies so that they help to sponsor Mexico's project of democratization by first fostering the legal inclusion of Indians' rights in the Mexican constitution. Moreover, we also need to see that the communication exercised by those groups that clamor against some injustice, or for the recognition of their rights, needs to pass through the filter of "world" publicity, to make their reasons publicly accessible and answerable to others, particularly to those who do not share their opinions and judgments. However complicated this process might be, it would be only the first step; a further step should be to learn to take criticism, to learn to negotiate beyond one's particular interests, and to seek to transform one's utopian ideals into formulations that highlight "the civic impartiality" that best describes the jointly shared *[solidaria]* integrative strength of civil society.

The second example I will mention here has to do with the role played by nongovernmental organizations to help raise awareness of the role that "world citizens" can play as they exercise pressure against purely one-dimensional economic goals. Greenpeace, for example, has played an important role in generating such awareness. One of their organized actions was to warn against the policy of former British Prime Minister John Major's government of throwing the contents of an oil platform into the ocean in 1995. In Germany, for example, the whole community of civil society organized itself not to use or buy any products coming from the British firm Shell. After boycotting Shell gas stations for several weeks, Major was forced to issue a public statement saying that his government had withdrawn from the decision to spill the contents of the platform into the ocean. In this case, the success of the German boycott in generating subjects of a world civil society was crucial in being able to completely redirect the interests of the British state toward a reconsideration of the issues of waste disposal.

Greenpeace has led other important battles with less success, but their range of activities throughout the world makes us aware that organizations such as this could influence the policies of powerful states so that they take into account the fate of other, less powerful states.

The third and last example I will use is of a very different kind. Carlos Niño, an Argentinian legal scholar, claims in his book, *Radical Evil on Trial*,[20] that there are different problems concerning "retroactive justice," which are mostly related to the sovereignty of states. The possible transition of a country from being governed by an authoritarian regime toward democracy entails conflicts of interest. First, the need to secure a peaceful transition to a democratic order is often done through political agreements with many different groups including, many times, those that represent the authoritarian rulers of dictatorships. But second, it is impossible to define democratic processes without the acknowledgement of crimes that violated the rights that should now be the basis of their constitutions. This is the case with many countries in Latin America; their democratic transitions entailed giving amnesties and pardons to murderers who still felt they were right in doing what they did. A third issue that concerns the legal and the moral spheres is related to the "diffusion of responsibility"; massive human rights violations cannot be committed without the acquiescence of many people; how, then, can countries that are negotiating a transition to democracy judge their past rulers and those people who helped them commit their crimes? Furthermore, how can a legal system prosecute criminals when those criminals are covered by their own authoritarian laws and have pressed for further amnesties?

The answers to these questions are not easy. As I have claimed before, there is a positive view of past experiences that can help us clarify some possible answers. An important consideration is that such crimes only occurred in authoritarian or totalitarian regimes. This is one of the reasons why Carlos Niño thinks that it is important to develop a theory of "retroactive justice" for massive human rights violations because these violations are possible whenever there is no democracy. By implementing a political process of retroactive justice, argues Niño, "we help societies to protect democratic values and stress the moral learning process of disclosing the accountability of a crime." "An aggressive use of the criminal laws," claims Niño, "will counteract a tendency toward unlawfulness, negate the impression that some groups are above the law, and consolidate the rule of law." In order to restore democracy or to build one up, "some degree of investigation and prosecution of massive human rights violations is necessary for consolidating democratic regimes."[21]

However, during the twentieth century, silence and impunity were the norm rather than the exception. The tendency to forget or forgive such crimes has always been related to the threat by former authoritarian rulers to interrupt the transition to democracy with a military coup. Those societies have to face a double-edged decision: They seek to become democratic and to be regulated by the rule of law, yet at the same time, they are compelled to issue legal pardons and amnesties and to throw a blanket of silence over the past; however, these foster impunity and oblivion. Thus, countries like Argentina, Chile, and Uruguay have been forced to create the most "bizarre" laws of forgiveness and impunity. A much-needed law for global citizens is needed in these cases, for only such a law can protect individuals from state arbitrariness. A rule of international law will be successful only when it can penetrate the sovereignty of states and prosecute individuals (i.e., former government functionaries) for crimes committed by them as part of their political and military service.

Thus, the example of Spanish judge Baltasar Garzón filing a demand for the extradition from England of Augusto Pinochet, a former dictator of Chile (who was protected from legal accountability in Chile because of his chair in the Senate), so that Pinochet could be prosecuted in Spain for committing several crimes (torture being the only one accepted in the legal terms of England), is the first important precedent toward the goal of globalizing citizenship. The evident collisions of state interests and juridical initiatives are one important element to consider here. The state's sovereignty will hardly allow for the further development of individual accountability beyond the nation's scope. Thus, it is important to search for ways in which accountability could be coordinated with the strengthening of legality in all countries. It is obvious that the only way to have criminals like Pinochet prosecuted is through the help of the international legal system and of public figures like Judge Baltazar Garzón, who has played such an important role as a member of world civil society. Other countries, such as Belgium, France, and Switzerland, had also asked for Pinochet's extradition from England to face other crimes. As we know, Pinochet's case was not solved through this legal course of action, contrary to Judge Garzón's wishes; nevertheless, Garzón has successfully opened the symbolic prosecutions of others who, like Pinochet, live as if they deserved to be honored for committing the most despicable crimes against humanity.[22]

Garzón is the leading figure of a successfully launched debate about the next steps we must take, if we are to agree with the democratic defense of human rights and the needed global support to make respect for human rights possible. As the debate has now been opened and the mass media have shown a growing interest in these issues over the last few years, it is not impossible for us to see that Kant's global order is not merely a utopian ideal, but rather a new normative framework for the globalization of democracy.

## NOTES

1. A recent term publicly used by the former Mexican President Ernesto Zedillo to name those who oppose globalization as imperialist forces of domination.

2. The Leftist Mexican newspapers immediately responded to Zedillo's term by using its opposite to describe those who see globalization as the center of neoliberalism.

3. See, for example, David Held, *Democracy and the Global Order: From the Modern State to Cosmopolitan Governance* (Stanford, Calif.: Stanford University Press, 1995).

4. See Amartya Sen, *Inequality Re-examined* (Cambridge, Mass.: Harvard University Press, 1992).

5. The case of former Chilean dictator Augusto Pinochet is but one example of this problem.

6. Axel Honneth, "Is Universalism a Moral Trap? The Presuppositions and Limits of a Politics of Human Rights," in *Perpetual Peace: Essays on Kant's Cosmopolitan Ideal*, ed. James Bohman and Matthias Lutz-Bachmann (Cambridge, Mass.: The MIT Press, 1997), 155–56.

7. Jürgen Habermas, "Kant's Idea of Perpetual Peace, with the Benefit of Two Hundred Years' Hindsight," in *Perpetual Peace: Essays on Kant's Cosmopolitan Ideal*, 113–54.

8. Habermas, "Kant's Idea of Perpetual Peace," 137.

9. Habermas clarifies this idea by explaining that "the model of constitution making is understood in such a way that human rights are not pre-given moral truths to be discovered but rather are constructions. Unlike moral rights, it is rather clear that legal rights must not remain politically non-binding. As individual, or 'subjective,' rights, human rights have an inherently juridical nature and are conceptually oriented toward positive enactment by legislative bodies" [Habermas, "Remarks on Legitimation through Human Rights," *Philosophy and Social Criticism* 24, no. 2–3: 157–71, 164].

10. Habermas clarifies that "it is constitutive to the meaning of human rights that, according to their status as basic rights, they belong within a framework of some existing legal order, whether it be national, international, or global, in which they can be protected. The mistake of conflating them with moral rights results from their peculiar nature: apart from their universal validity claims, these rights have had an unambiguosly positive form only within the national legal order of the democratic state. Moreover, they possess only weak validity in international law, and they await internationalization within the framework of a cosmopolitan order which is only now emerging" [Habermas, "Kant's Idea of Perpetual Peace," 140].

11. See Jeffrey C. Alexander, "From War Crime to Holocaust Trauma: Progressive and Tragic Narrations of the Nazis' Mass Murder of the Jews," in *Cultural Trauma*, ed. Jeffrey C. Alexander and Neil Smelser (Berkeley: University of California Press, forthcoming).

12. Aryeh Neier, *War Crimes: Brutality, Genocide, Terror, and the Struggles for Justice* (New York: Random House, 1998), xiii.

13. Hannah Arendt, *The Origins of Totalitarianism* (New York: Harcourt Brace Jovanovich Publishers, 1975), 291.

14. Dana Villa explains that "the horror of totalitarianism," its "radical evil," is the creation and treatment of masses of human beings as superfluous; it thus presents us with a new danger to the human condition, one that darkens our "moral horizon." See Dana R. Villa, *Politics, Philosophy, Terror: Essays on the Thought of Hannah Arendt* (Princeton, N.J.: Princeton University Press, 1999), 15.

15. Villa, *Essays on the Thought of Hannah Arendt*, 21.

16. See Jean L. Cohen, "Rights, Citizenhip, and the Modern Form of the Social: Dilemmas of Arendtian Republicanism," *Constellations* 3, no. 2 (1996): 164–89.

17. Cohen, "Dilemmas of Arendtian Republicanism," 177.

18. See John Womack Jr., *Rebellion in Chiapas: An Historical Reader* (New York: The New Press, 1999), 304–15.

19. For information about the historical documents of the Zapatistas as well as other important documents, see Womack, *Rebellion in Chiapas*.

20. Carlos Santiago Niño, *Radical Evil on Trial* (New Haven, Conn.: Yale University Press, 1996).

21. Niño, *Radical Evil on Trial*, x.

22. Garzón also issued orders of extradition for Roberto Eduardo Viola, Leopoldo Fortunato Galtieri, Antonio Domingo Bussi, Roberto Astiz y Emilio Massera, all high-ranking military officers during the cruelest years of military rule in Argentina during the 1970s. See *La Jornada* (Mexico City daily), Wednesday, 3 November 1999, 62.

# 9

# Latin American Feminism and the New Challenges of Globalization

*María Mercedes Jaramillo*
*(Translated by Mario Sáenz)*

In any review of the history of Latin American women during the twentieth century, the conquests that they have made are undeniable: citizenship, as well as access to higher education, salaried labor, property, maternal legal authority, divorce rights, and family planning. But these advances have had an uneven reach because many women neither have enjoyed nor now enjoy the same benefits. Ethnic, economic, geographic, and cultural barriers have prevented broad and similar access to all the conquests of women's struggles. Only women of the elite class have been able to enjoy the fruits of these achievements; moreover, they have also benefited from the poorly paid labor of women of the lower classes and of Black, indigenous, peasant, and immigrant women, who perform domestic tasks, many times under denigrating conditions.[1] Access to the public sphere has not necessarily meant a double shift for well-to-do women, since they can delegate domestic tasks and family care to others. By contrast, wage labor for working-class women has meant a doubling of their workday, as well as the neglect of their home responsibilities.[2] At the same time, their partners do not assume domestic work in an equitable way, and low-income families generally do not have subsidies, childcare centers, or teams of houseworkers to make domestic housework easier.[3]

During the last decade of the twentieth century, state support for families was weakened by processes of globalization,[4] and by neoliberal ideology, which disqualified the welfare state's social policies as in themselves antidemocratic, inefficient, and illegitimate.[5] These criticisms have been partly responsible for the reduction in the size of the state and the dismantling of social programs that eased the problems of the working classes and allowed some social mobility with programs that addressed schooling, housing, and health. The impact of policies of structural adjustment has been greater on women, since they usually care for the old and the very young. These facts, among others, have had repercussions on the feminist movement, since women's agendas vary depending on class, place of origin, age, education, religion, sexual orientation, and political affiliation.

Conditions such as the ones just mentioned had fostered the emergence of the first feminist and suffrage movements that appeared at the beginning of the twentieth century in those regions of the Americas in which there was an urban working class struggling for the improvement of their working conditions, social benefits, and wages. Female teachers and workers, workers' mothers and wives, as well as some women from the ruling elites, began to gather in charity societies, usually sponsored by governments or private enterprise, in a desperate attempt to alleviate the grave social problems affecting the working class. These paternalistic and benevolent associations did not remedy problems regarding health, nutrition, housing, and education, which most troubled workers; however, it was in these spaces that there took place the first encounters among women of diverse social, cultural, and political origin who had a common goal. It was in them that the opportunity arose to analyze everyday problems and share ideas and strategies to solve them.[6]

The first women's meetings were regional, and they were specifically attended by female teachers and educators; at these meetings problems regarding education, health, and citizenship rights were discussed.[7] These were matters of common interest, which affected the quality of life of women and the family. Women of the elite and wives of presidents and other politicians attended international congresses in which the problems of society in general and Latin America in particular were analyzed. Although the themes discussed at those congresses were often similar to those discussed at the traditional male political conferences, the gender perspective would become evident in the recommendations made and the projects proposed at the plenary sessions, as was the case in the First Interamerican Women's Congress (Guatemala, 1947), where it was proposed that national resources and incomes be invested in agricultural programs and health and education projects. Moreover, at that congress, there was a denunciation of the politicians and diplomats who had attended the Rio de Janeiro Conference, and a plan was recommended for defense and hemispheric armaments at great expense to the national budgets.[8]

The development programs designed for Latin America during the 1960s, as a result of the social crises and revolutionary movements challenging the ruling regimes and threatening the status quo, were unable to resolve the conflicts that became more acute with the presence of military governments. In this social, political, and economic environment, the United Nations declared The International Decade of Women (1975-1985), which started with The International Year of Women. This event had important repercussions for the whole continent, as women's congresses became more diverse and numerous, projects designed for and oriented toward women were created, and regional and local programs centered around specific themes were devised.[9] Today women of diverse social, cultural, ideological, and political strata attend these events.[10] The subjects discussed cover different aspects of modern life, for example, work, health, education, sexuality, violence, nutrition, and old age. The various areas of interest to women have become the subject of publications, seminars, and specialized organizations. These encounters express the new openings and changes in attitudes in societies, the histories of which have been eminently hierarchical and patriarchal. These events have served as models for subsequent meetings and international activities, for they create webs of communication and are helpful in the exchange of information and strategies that are used by communities and in women's personal lives.

It is evident that the feminist movements of the twentieth century managed to open spaces in the public sphere and to create representative democracies. For the first time in the history of the continent, the presence of women in the different programs and projects of the state was necessary for its legitimation. This fact has given visibility to women's problems, setting the stage where they can voice their demands and criticisms of the patriarchy's waste of natural, economic, and human resources.[11] The effectiveness of women's protests reached its climax with the Madres de la Plaza de Mayo (Mothers of May Square in Argentina) and with the awarding of the Nobel Peace Prize to Rigoberta Menchú in 1992.

Recent openings to women's representation and participation have generated conflict, as is to be expected when attitudes and policies undergo change. This conflict has arisen partly because of the implementation of quotas and partly because of the design of programs without previous field studies that would point to viable programs or without a prior consultation of the chosen communities regarding their needs and interests. Many times, the programs are designed and directed from outside the communities; this causes conflicts that must also be analyzed. The disagreements between, on the one hand, state policies and nongovernmental organizations (NGOs) and, on the other, the communities and women have arisen in areas in which the latter have not undergone a process of learning and adjustment so that they may act effectively in the public sphere in which their presence is now demanded. There is also resentment because of the loss of state support for, and subsidies of, programs that were effective or that were perceived as necessary by the communities themselves. Today some resources are simply earmarked for programs focused on women, since these have greater political visibility and may, therefore, obtain international or private support without, however, being necessarily the most suitable or urgent.

These facts have created diverse problems: (1) a merely nominal presence of women so that required quotas are filled, approval for policies is obtained, and business may go on as usual; (2) many international organizations only sponsor or implement programs for women, often to the detriment of social programs that would have a greater impact on the chosen community; and (3) the new responsibilities that women have in the politics of organization and participation triples their work, and family relations suffer.[12] Perhaps some of these facts may help explain some women's resistance to participate actively in grassroots organizations and in politics. I think that it is essential to undertake fieldwork and other studies to analyze this problematic more deeply to avoid negative reactions that may harm the weakest sectors in society. But the tension created between the interests of the community and women's rights should not be to the detriment of the changes already implemented in the laws that protect those rights; on the contrary, points of common interest and compromises must be sought to resolve conflicts between women's rights and the community.

Women's rights have followed a slow and long process of agreements and disagreements among women of diverse origin who have different interests and projects.[13] However, those policies that have favored women also benefited society as a whole with the development of effective and long-range programs such as family planning,[14] economic, social, and political empowerment, personal autonomy, and access to higher education; these have, as Nikki Craske attests, improved the lives of women:

> At the beginning of the century only the richest in most countries had open access to education. As economic conditions improved, girls were often ignored in favour of boys. Gradually the situation became equitable, with girls matching boys firstly at primary school, then at secondary school and finally in tertiary education. Women are currently outnumbering men in some university subjects. Education is not the panacea for all development problems, but the impact of improved educational attainment is significant. Influencing job opportunities, and consequently income, family size, and attitudes to marriage, it changes expectations about what life has to offer.[15]

Today's women's associations and NGOs have a long reach, and they can orient women toward multiple aspects of modern life in both the private and the public spheres. These groups benefited from developments in telecommunications and social programs directed toward the improvement of the standards of life of the community and the family. These women's groups exert political pressure for better economic conditions for women, struggle against social and domestic violence, create avenues of communication among diverse women's groups, promote grassroots organizations that search for solutions to the problems that affect communities, publish and distribute magazines and pamphlets dedicated to subjects of interest to the family and women, all while seeking to educate women and raise their consciousness about their rights and duties.[16]

The diversity of interests and goals among women's groups is an indication of the advances made, but also of the many different problems affecting Latin American women, for the processes of urbanization and modernization, which accelerated in the last decades of the twentieth century, affected women in different ways while transforming the dynamics of family and community life. Women began to share in the labor market in a way that was disadvantageous to them because of their lack of education and training: low wages and bad labor conditions were the pressures that compelled them to look for training and higher education and to demand a larger space for them in the public sphere.

However, despite the achievements attained in education,[17] the women's presence in the labor market does not correspond with their participation in politics[18] or their economic remuneration.[19] Furthermore, the working day of poor women is longer than and just as indispensable as men's. On the other hand, the processes of female socialization, still rooted in Marian stereotypes, make many women regard their work as secondary to man's work; this fact leads them to devalue their own participation in the labor force and undervalue their economic contribution to the family.[20] The idealization of women as mothers and their limitation to their biological reproductive capacity continues being determinant in the control of the imaginary of patriarchal ideology, which women themselves also reproduce in the family hearth and is later reinforced by other institutions (e.g., the church, the school, the media). For as Lola G. Luna says:

> The family is the key institution that channels patriarchal ideology and where the unequal sexual division of labor and the learning of gender hierarchization is produced. In it, an area of triple reproduction is organized—i.e., biological, social, and concerning labor power—that makes women responsible for duties and tasks, which until a short time ago were regarded even by women as "natural" because of sex. Today it is beginning to be accepted that, with the exception of biological reproduction, the remaining reproductive tasks are a question of gender, that is, assigned by ideology.[21]

The feminization of poverty has been linked to the feminization of some professions and the discrediting of other so-called women's jobs, the lack of remuneration for the care of the family or for domestic labor, a wage discrimination system grounded in the perception of man as head of the family and job insecurity. This situation has affected the welfare of women in general and also that of the less-favored classes, which depend on their subsistence from the active participation of all its members.

The feminist movement is not monolithic, and it has never been so, although many times alliances were created to obtain common benefits. During the Cold War period, when the policies of the "National Security State" were introduced,[22] Latin American countries faced dictatorships that imposed the "Dirty War" against dissidents that included disappearances and forced exile, and displacements and unemployment; these events had a negative effect on social welfare and the very survival of the family. During these times of crisis, women united to denounce the military's abuses and to demand democracy and an immediate solution to their problems. The movements organized by the relatives of the disappeared, such as Madres de la Plaza de Mayo; testimonial literature, such as the books by Domitilia Barrios and Rigoberta Menchú; community kitchens; and the stories about the tragedy of the Chilean people embroidered in the *arpilleras*[23] are examples of the Latin American women's agency that captured international attention and made visible the abuses committed by the dictatorial regimes.

Little by little, democracy began to take root in the continent, but women's groups that struggled for democracy began to lose ground and, oftentimes, national and international support. Following a wave of militancy and commitment, expectations were raised among the women's groups that were hoping for greater political participation in the new democratic governments; these expectations were not realized because of lack of political preparation among many women and real commitment by the political parties. Instead, the political spaces that are now shared with women are usually directly related to issues concerning the welfare of the family, as well as those subjects defined as feminine or projections from women's role as mothers.

Some women attained power because of the political influence of their families. In isolated cases, women have become presidents in governments of transition[24] and reconciliation.[25] That was the case of Violeta Chamorro in Nicaragua, and in her case one must recognize that her government was more transparent and democratic than Alemán's government. During the 1990s, some women ran in presidential elections and won, for example, Janet Jagan (1997) in Guyana and Mireya Moscoso (1999) in Panama. Others, by contrast, were not successful: Noemí Sanín in Colombia and Irene Sáenz in Venezuela. It is important to note, however, that Sanín and Sáenz have their own political careers and may have thus started a new period of political participation by Latin American women.

The conquests attained in the twentieth century allowed women to participate as never before in the public sphere, despite limitations and unequal access to the benefits of the modern world and technology. The creation of gender studies from varied perspectives, such as economic, historical, sociological, and literary perspectives, has allowed for reflections on how women have participated in Latin American cultural, economic, social, and political tasks. The success of many professional women in public administration, education, politics, and cultural life has created an intellectual and critical elite capable of analyzing theoretical models, governmental projects, and political processes that affect the region in general and particular communities. Women's direct participation in society has changed and widened cultural, political, and social spaces; ideas and styles have been introduced into the public arena that were not allowed there before because of their so-called feminine character. A good example of this change is the well-known slogan by the Chilean women who confronted the dictatorship without abandoning their feminist ideals: "We want democracy in the nation and at home."[26] This slogan pointed to the inseparable connection between the public and the private, for both spheres are directly related to each other.

The pretended depoliticization of the private sphere is a fallacy that has permitted the exploitation of women's and children's work, which contribute to the household economy and to the reproduction of labor. This fallacy has also permitted minimal salaries for the working class, since the contribution made by women and children to domestic labor and in the informal sector is an essential complement to family income and social welfare. They are "invisible adjustments," which are delegated to women and children and which deny them access to education, health, adequate housing, retirement, and recreation.

The Latin American women's movement has had a close connection with the social problems of the region, since it is impossible for the women of the urban working class or for peasant women to separate their welfare as women from that of the family. The class relations that determine their position in the social pyramid and their access to material goods are their priorities. The social movements of mothers, wives, and daughters of the disappeared, the displaced, the kidnapped, the recruited by the different armies from the right and the left, the political prisoners, and the marginalized have been linked to human rights groups and groups in opposition to the dictatorships.

By contrast, the feminism that has been linked to the academy and to women of the cultural and economic elites is closer to the theoretical and critical currents of European and U.S. origin. Its priority is to criticize women's asymmetrical position in their family and professional lives. This latter type of feminism has a different agenda: equality of rights and duties, equality in salaries, and equitable access to power. Professional women have access to information and technology, and they look for vindication in their jobs and personal lives. They demand changes in romantic and professional relationships, autonomy for their bodies and in their sexual life, and a greater commitment by their partners to share equally in domestic responsibilities.[27]

The access to information and to world events created by the information revolution has been able to destabilize ideologies, economies, political regimes, frontiers, and established values. The patriarchy, with metanarratives that legitimated privileges and the asymmetrical distribution of material goods, rights, and duties, has been brought into question by diverse philosophical, political, gender, and cultural perspectives. The goal is no longer assimilation to the dominant values. Instead, inclusion of the "other" is the objective because it is recognized that minorities have been able to survive in the spaces of the dominant cultures by means of hybridization processes. Also, today we know and can attest that what is acceptable, positive, or beneficial for a region, community, or individual may not have the same significance for others. Other actors have appeared on the stage and have questioned exclusion, denounced exploitation and repression, and demanded the inclusion of other types of agenda. Undeniable examples of this type of process are the Nobel Peace Prize to Rigoberta Menchú,[28] peace dialogues with armed groups, and the trials of military personnel involved in the Dirty War. All these events have not only raised doubts about dominant values on class, gender, and race, but they have also revealed the social and political implications of those values. Values regarded as "natural" or as the only way to be and act, while supported by an elite that enjoys privileges and an unequal distribution of wealth and power, are undermined by revolutionary movements, feminism, the gay movement, the theology of liberation, the green movement, NGOs, alternative medicine, and popular culture, to mention only a few counterdiscourses that give evidence of social malaise and confrontation of the status quo.

This last decade of accelerated changes, virtual connections, and cultural hybridization shows that the vitality of the human experience rests on the capacity to incorporate new elements that enrich the milieu, broaden expectations, and discard those elements that hinder individual and social development. We live during a time of sharp contradictions, for technological advances have not been paralleled by social advances, industrial development has been at odds with the preservation of the natural environment, and market rules impose themselves on ethical principles and state laws. As E. San Juan has said, there can be development without progress and growth without improvement.[29] For every time we are more connected through the information media, we are also more isolated as communities and as individuals. We have more machines that facilitate, speed up, and improve labor, but we find that there is less free time for creative leisure, reading, or gatherings of friends. The speed of production, information, and technological development have had a great impact on the different spheres of everyday life, but the reach of this revolution is unequal, not only on the planet as a whole but also within nations themselves. The negative effects of globalization can be seen in the various demands that sectors marginalized from progress and development make; these problems worsen because of the separation between the peripheral regions and the center, or between the countryside and the cities, and also because they are more acute among women than men.

However, the possibility of gaining access, even if only in virtual form, to other cultures, modes of organizing the human environment, and other worldviews has broadened the meaning of humanity and civilization, as well as the individual cultural horizon. We are now witnesses of different and diverse human behaviors and ways of acting, which used to be exotic because of their remoteness but are now part of our everyday experiences as media spectators *[teleespectadoras]*. The woman of today can see and recognize herself in others and confront her horizon of expectations to confirm, the majority of times, similarity in difference, for as human beings we confront similar challenges to which we respond with similar attitudes. Her life experiences as media spectator and cybernetic traveler have given the contemporary woman the possibility of sowing and reaping from someone else's experience and experimenting with new attitudes and solutions along with the necessities and conflicts of the present world.

Never before have human eyes and ears had such a long reach; this fact irrevocably changes the conduct of the human being and the community, which are not as isolated as in the past. The challenges that audiovisual media create for the educational system and for writers and political leaders are enormous and inevitable; they are not simply competing for time, since the malleability and accessibility of these media have transformed them into powerful rivals.[30]

The omnipresence of information and communication media made visible the possibilities that technology and consumer goods offer, fed the desire to gain access to them, and changed the traditional ways of assuming everydayness, study, work, and recreation. Women want, more than ever before, to participate in and to enjoy the goods that they see around them.

The resignation and submission with which exclusion was accepted in the past are each time more foreign to the women of today. Forms of indoctrination of a conservative and religious nature have been replaced by the imperatives of the here and now, which seek to create democratic spaces in the political, social, and ideological fields. We should, therefore, promulgate education, participatory and universalistic culture, and liberating ethics. That is why we think it is essential to support participatory democracy in Latin America and to include in the political, economic, cultural, and educational agenda the multiple women's voices that from remote corners of the world or from heterogeneous individual positions express their right to a full life.

## NOTES

1. Testimonial literature has denounced this aspect of the life of domestic employees. Rigoberta Menchú, Elvia Alvarado, Ana María Condori, Ramona Carvallo are some of the women who have developed narratives of some of their experiences as domestic workers.

2. Child abuse and negligence, low schooling, low academic performance, home accidents, child labor, and juvenile delinquency have a direct relation to wage labor by women who, when they go to work, have to delegate their obligations to older sons and daughters; these children have to assume from a very early age adult duties. Domestic tasks replace schoolwork; also, play and leisure are many times severely punished for being "unproductive."

3. The ideas in this essay are the product of classes that I have taught with my colleague Nan Wiegersma at Fitchburg State College. Also, many of the ideas come from *Las desobedientes: Mujeres de Nuestra América*, a text that I coedited with Betty Osorio: Maria Mercedes Jaramillo and Betty Osorio, eds., *Las desobedientes: Mujeres de Nuestra América* (Santafé de Bogotá: Editorial Panamericana, 1997).

4. Peter Marcuse in his essay "The Language of Globalization," distinguishes between the causes and the effects of globalization while defining this concept, which has been used to describe different aspects of modern life. The term has been used to refer to a series of diverse phenomena, which have multiple economic and political consequences, as well as different effects, such as "advances in information technology, widespread use of air freight, speculation in currencies, increased capital flows across borders, Disneyfication of culture, mass marketing, global warming, genetic engineering, multinational corporate power, new international division of labor, international mobility of labor, reduced power of nations-states, postmodernism, or post-Fordism." See Peter Marcuse, "The Language of Globalization," *Monthly Review Press: An Independent Socialist Magazine* 23 (July–August 2000): 3–52. Marcuse emphasizes that it is indispensable to separate advances in technology from increases in the concentration of power: "Separating *advances*

*in technology* from the *global concentration of economic power*, and seeing how their combination has changed *class relations*, is critical both for analysis and for political strategy." See Marcuse, "The Language of Globalization," 24.

5. Magdalena León, ed., *Mujeres y participación política. Avances y desafíos en América Latina* (Santafé de Bogotá: Tercer Mundo Editores, 1994), 10.

6. Jaramillo and Osorio, eds., *Las desobedientes,* xxxix.

7. Women in Latin America got the right to vote in a period of thirty years—between 1929 (Ecuador) and 1961 (Paraguay). Political parties from both the left and the right were afraid of giving women the vote, since they thought women were irrational and susceptible to the influence of confessors and husbands. When a party in power granted the vote to women, it was because they were hoping to gain advantage by channeling this new force. See Jaramillo and Osorio, eds., *Las desobedientes,* xxx–xxxii.

8. Francesca Miller, *Latin American Women and the Search for Social Justice* (Hanover, N.H.: University Press of New England, 1991), 126.

9. According to Nan Wiegersma, "United Nations development agencies have been working to try to promote women and create economic opportunities for women in the growing international market by opening up educational and political positions formerly closed to women and by promoting women's enterprises. The dominant view of the UN staff, as expressed in *Women in a Global Economy* (New York: United Nations, 1994), is that the negative effects of economic transformations are short-term and are caused by structural inequalities which limit women's access to resources. According to these agencies, legal and cultural restraints limit women's access to resources and their responses to new market incentives. Thus, while the International Monetary Fund and the World Bank continue to promote structural adjustment programs that affect women negatively, United Nations agencies have been working to open up markets to women by, for example, promoting credit programs for small women's enterprises."

10. Approximately 40,000 women attended The International Conference of Women in Beijing in 1995, and there were about 2,000 committee meetings and workshops. The large size and diversity of the conference made communication among the participating women difficult. However, despite the logistical and technical problems, alliances were formed among dissimilar groups with common objectives; also, new groups and fields of interest were created. The most controversial subjects were abortion, genital mutilation, abuse of women, and child prostitution. The areas of greater disparity between men and women were participation in politics, wages, responsibility for unpaid labor, land and home ownership, and unequal access to credit programs. Between 7 percent and 11 percent of women benefit from loans in Latin America and the Caribbean. See "The Revolution for Gender Equality," 4.

11. One may mention here, for instance, women's opposition to war budgets, army recruitment, inflation in the prices of household goods, as well as their demand for education and health services.

12. The political and community visibility of some women has created problems for them in their own family and community. Thus, for example, Domitila Barrios is accused by her community of profiting economically from her testimony on the life of Bolivian miners; Elvia Alvarado separated from her partner who could not accept her absence from home or her trips to other communities; and Rigoberta Menchú was blackmailed through the kidnapping of her nephew, who was kidnapped by the very parents of the child.

13. It is worth remembering, for example, Domitila Barrios's astonishment in 1975 when she learned about the priorities and denunciations made by the women of the developed countries, which were incomparable to the daily problems confronted by the women and communities of miners in Bolivia, whose workday began before dawn and ended at midnight, to mention only the basic reproduction of the vital cycle.

14. For example, what the Institute of Family Welfare in Colombia has achieved in its three decades of existence has reached far and wide, as far away as peripheral and remote regions, and it has made its various services accessible to women of the popular classes. Families not only have been able to plan the number of children, but they have also benefited from nutrition, disease prevention, and sexual education programs. For more information on this subject, see Silvia Galvis, *Se hace camino al andar. La otra historia de la planificación familiar* (Santafé de Bogotá: Gráficas Ambar, 1995). The average number of births in the continent went from 6 percent in the 1960s to fewer than 3 percent in the 1990s. Women's achievements are connected to women's education and family planning: "Latin America today is not markedly wealthier than in 1965. But its women have much higher levels of education, access to health care and employment. . . . Women in Latin America have gained substantially more rights and better treatment than women of the rest of the developing world. The region's experience shows that this is the most important key to limiting the population explosion" [*Women's International Network News*, 74].

15. Nikki Craske, *Women & Politics in Latin America* (New Brunswick, N.J.: Rutgers University Press, 1999), 42.

16. Jaramillo and Osorio, eds., *Las desobedientes*, xxx.

17. According to Peter Hakim's report, the Latin American educational system has deteriorated, and in some countries it is in crisis, in need of reform, or much greater support: "Except for three nations—out of 33—with large indigenous population, there's no difference in literacy rates of men and *women*. Boys and girls enroll and graduate in equal numbers from primary and secondary schools. More *women* than men go to college. In many places, they now are the majority of students in such traditionally male fields as law and medicine." See Peter Hakim, "Gender Equality in Latin Region," *Christian Science Monitor* 91, no. 127 (May 27, 1999): 11.

18. Women have fewer than 20 percent of the legislative positions around the world (see Craske, *Women & Politics in Latin America*, 209). The percentages of women's share of power shows great differences among Latin American and Caribbean countries in 1996:

| | |
|---|---|
| Antigua and Barbuda | 26.7 |
| Argentina | 5.2 |
| Bahamas | 30.3 |
| Belize | 6.0 |
| Bolivia | 7.3 |
| Brazil | 13.7 |
| Chile | 10.3 |
| Colombia | 20.5 |
| Costa Rica | 27.2 |
| Cuba | 9.1 |
| Dominican Republic | 9.8 |
| Dominica | 25.0 |

| | |
|---|---|
| Ecuador | 3.4 |
| El Salvador | 26.8 |
| Grenada | 22.5 |
| Guatemala | 16.7 |
| Guyana | 14.6 |
| Haiti | 22.2 |
| Honduras | 14.1 |
| Jamaica | 14.3 |
| Mexico | 7.5 |
| Nicaragua | 17.4 |
| Panama | 9.4 |
| Paraguay | 4.3 |
| Peru | 13.2 |
| Saint Kitts and Nevis | 16.7 |
| Saint Lucia | 5.0 |
| Saint Vincent and Grenadines | 19.2 |
| Suriname | 11.3 |
| Trinidad and Tobago | 13.8 |
| Uruguay | 13.7 |
| Venezuela | 14.5 |

[*Human Development Report* (New York: Oxford University Press, 1999), 238–41].

19. The average salary of women in Latin America is 71.6 percent the salary of men. [See Valdez and Gomariz in Craske, *Women & Politics in Latin America* (1995): 53.]

20. The following quotation from the Report of Human Development in 1995 analyzes the situation of women worldwide. It expresses concretely gender inequalities and women's burden at the end of the twentieth century. It is important to evaluate these disparities despite the remarkable advances made by women in the last two decades.

Women work longer hours than men in nearly every country. Of the total burden of work, women carry 53 percent in developing countries and 51 percent in industrial countries.

On average, about half of this time is spent in economic activities in the market or in the subsistence sector. The other half is normally devoted to unpaid household or community activities. . . . In developing countries, more than three-quarters of men's work is in market activities. So, men receive the lion's share of income recognition for their economic contribution—while most women's work remains unpaid, unrecognized and undervalued. . . . If women's unpaid work were properly valued, it is quite possible that women would emerge in most societies as the major breadwinners—or at least equal breadwinners—since they put longer hours of work than men.

The monetization of the non-market work of women is more than a question of justice. It concerns the economic status of women in society. If more human activities were seen as market transactions at the prevailing wages, they would yield gigantically large monetary valuations. A rough order of magnitude comes to staggering $16 trillion—or about 70 percent more than the officially estimated $23 trillion of global output. This estimate includes the value of the *unpaid* work performed by women and men as well as the value of the *underpayment* of women's work in the market at prevailing wages. Of this $16 trillion, $11 trillion is the non-monetized, invisible contribution of women.

Such a revaluation of women's work will thoroughly challenge the present conventions. For husbands to share income with their wives will become an act of entitlement rather than benevolence. The basis of property rights, divorce settlement, collateral for bank credit—to name only a few areas—will have to change completely. Men will also have to share more of the burden of household and community work.

If national statistics fully reflect the 'invisible' contribution of women, it will become impossible for policy-makers to ignore them in national decisions. Nor will women continue to be regarded as economic non-entities in market transactions." (See "The Revolution for Gender Equality," 6–7)

Spike Peterson and Anne Sisson Runyan also contrast the global inequalities between the situations of men and women: Women perform 65 percent of unpaid labor, receive less than 35 percent the value of rent, own less than 2 percent of the land, and represent more than 60 percent of the illiterate. Also, 70 percent of women live in poverty and, including children, constitute more than 70 percent of refugees. See V. Spike Peterson and Anne Sisson Runyan, *Global Gender Issues: Dilemmas in World Politics,* 2d ed. (Boulder, Colo.: Westview Press, 1999), 6. At the same time, their share in better-paid jobs or their presence in the halls of power is marginal. The occupations in which female labor is concentrated in Latin America are clerical work, nursing, sales, and domestic service [Craske, *Women & Politics in Latin America,* 50–51].

21. Lola G. Luna, *Mujeres y participación política. Avances y desafíos en América Latina* (Santafé de Bogotá: Tercer Mundo Editores, 1994), 30–31.

22. [The doctrine of the "national security state" was first applied in the southern cone of South America, in Chile, Argentina, and Brazil during the 1970s. It was characterized phenomenally by a marked increase in institutional violence through the wholesale kidnapping and killing of "subversives," and other leaders of unions and opposition parties. Structurally, it is characterized by the radical restructuring of capital-labor relations and the establishment of neoliberal economic systems. The political phenomena and the economic restructuring are intimately tied as made evident by the Augusto Pinochet-Milton Friedman political-economic axis.—*Ed.*]

23. [A Chilean *arpillera* is flour or sugar sackcloth on which cloth pieces are embroidered. The women who made these works are also called *arpilleras*. *Arpilleras* normally depicted landscapes, holidays, and everyday events. But with the overthrow of the democratically elected president Salvador Allende in 1973 by a U.S.-sponsored military coup, the content of the *arpilleras* changed. During the years of military dictatorship in Chile (1973–1989), women in groups or as individuals began to embroider *arpilleras* with artistic depictions of a political protest, the closing of a factory, or similar scenes of people's struggle for survival under fascist rule and terror.—*Ed.*]

24. Isabel Martínez de Perón became president (1974–1976) with the death of her husband (Juan Domingo Perón); a military junta overthrew her when she was no longer considered necessary as head of state. The following women have become presidents in Latin America and the Caribbean during periods of transition: Lidia Gueiler in Bolivia (1979–1980), Rosalía Artega in Ecuador in 1997, and Ertha Pascal-Trouillot in Haiti in 1991 (Pascal-Trouillot had already participated in the public sphere as a member of the Supreme Court in 1986, but his brother had been attacked for opposition to the Duvalier regime). In Panama, Mireya Moscoso won the presidential election in 1999; she is the widow of former president Arnulfo Arias. The following political figures have emerged

because of their able management of public administration and their government programs: Irene Sáenz in Venezuela, who was a candidate in the presidential elections of 1998; Noemí Sanín in Colombia, who was a presidential candidate in 1998, winning 27 percent of the votes, and who will possibly run in the 2002 elections; the Argentine congressperson Graciela Fernández Meijide (1995–1997); and the Brazilian congressperson Benedita da Silva, running for the Workers' Party, is the first black woman to win a congressional seat in Brazil.

25. In Nicaragua, the presidential campaign of UNO (*Unión Nacional de Oposición/* National Union of Opposition) skillfully managed the image of their candidate, Violeta Chamorro, as both the mother of a family divided politically, like the rest of the country, since her children were in opposing parties, and as a victim of the regime of Anastasio Somoza, since her husband, Pedro Joaquín Chamorro, was murdered by the dictatorship because of his work as a journalist; these facts made it possible for her to become president and defeat the discredited and weakened Sandinista government.

26. Miller, *Latin American Women and the Search for Social Justice*, 239.

27. In the last decades, Latin American women writers have created a literary corpus that explores sexuality and woman's eroticism in an open and direct manner. They have expressed their desires, fantasies, and fears with a rich verbal and metaphorical imagery, without fear of being marginalized by society as their predecessors were. Authors such as Isidora Aguirre, Albalucía Ángel, Pía Barros, Sabina Berman, Micheline Dusseck, Sara Levi Calderón, Andrea Maturana, Cristina Peri Rosi, Luisa Valenzuela, Rosario Ferré, and Lydia Vega defy the myth of feminine passivity and unveil the complexity of love relationships and the conflicts produced by patriarchal culture. Helena Araújo and Lucía Guerra are among the pioneers in the elaboration of a theoretical corpus on Latin American women's writing. Willy Muñoz's book, *Polifonía de la marginalidad. La narrativa de escritoras latinoamericanas*, analyzes the works of some of these authors and shows the alienating effects of the patriarchy, where in spite of other achievements, women still struggle against ignorance and poverty.

28. The denunciations made by Rigoberta Menchú and her work in favor of Guatemalan Indians would be comparable more or less to the denunciations and campaigns that in another period but with similar interests Manuel Quintín Lame Chantre carried out in Colombia. Both Menchú and Quintín Lame were persecuted and accused by their respective governments and ruling elites in an effort to discredit them. The Nobel Peace Prize that Menchú received shows, on the one hand, the rapidity with which information travels in the current age, and on the other hand, the sensitization of the international intellectual community and its undeniable support for social justice.

29. E. San Juan, *Beyond Postcolonial Theory* (New York: St. Martin's Press, 1998), 2.

30. We already know that whoever controls the media controls public opinion. On the other hand, the international reach of information and freedom of expression have been mechanisms of control used by dictators and absolutist governments. We also know that the notions of candidate or commodity that prevail in today's society are simply the ones that better used the media, without being necessarily the best or most rational.

# IV

## PROJECTS OF LIBERATION AND SOCIAL TRANSFORMATION

# 10

## Feminism and Globalization Processes in Latin America

*Ofelia Schutte*

The aim of this chapter is to describe contemporary processes of globalization as they take place in Latin America and to evaluate the effects of these processes especially on women, using a postcolonial feminist ethical perspective as a critical standpoint. Initially, I offer some reflections on the cultural location from which this chapter is written.[1] Intellectuals in the developed world occupy a position of privilege in relation to their counterparts in the developing world, regardless of one's personal desire for an equal reciprocal relationship. This historically determined inequality does not detract from the arguments or insights one may offer, but it does make me conscious of the fact that I do not write from a location experiencing the worst impact of globalization processes, a factor that may bias my outlook. Nevertheless, I offer a strong critique of globalization processes insofar as these are designed and implemented by neoliberal economic policy. In order to frame this critique, it is important to distinguish between economic and political development. There is an evident tension in the West in the interaction of these two concepts. Concepts of political development (if informed by progressive social views) will clash with concepts of economic development (if informed by neoliberal views). The reason is that concepts of political development informed by progressive social views place a high priority on social justice, political equality, and (more recently) on environmental justice, whereas concepts of neoliberal economic development have as their single goal the strengthening of a global capitalist market. In contrast to modern concepts of political equality, neoliberalism requires and thrives on inequality.

Despite the evident clash between an economics that promotes inequality in the constant play of maximizing its self-interest and a politics that demands equality in the name of some common good owed to all citizens, I believe there is empirical room for modifying (neoliberal) economic policy through (progressive) political action. By means of a postcolonial feminist ethical perspective, I point both to the negative effects on women resulting from neoliberal globalization policies and to the constructive effects of feminist critiques of globalization and feminist political action. The critiques of globalization serve to demystify its aura of legitimacy, inevitability, and success. They point to the ethical void at the core of neoliberal globalization initiatives by showing the failure of these initiatives to take into account globalization's impact on ordinary people in the developing world, including women and girls, or the social costs, both short term and long term, of policy focused on trade and maximizing profits. The critiques I shall review also point to the limits a market-oriented, positivistic concept of growth places on human creativity, on transgressive art, and on cultural creation in general. My objective is to reaffirm here, as I have argued elsewhere, that a feminist ethics of development is needed from which to evaluate the merits and limitations of political and economic development.[2] This orientation builds on my previous work regarding the construction of identity in terms of socially oriented emancipatory projects.[3]

## THE CRITIC'S LOCATION

A global feminist ethics (if there is to be such a thing) must first acknowledge the asymmetries of power between North and South marking women's lives.[4] For this reason, I prefer a use of the term "postcolonial" that acknowledges these asymmetries of power (not all uses of postcolonial do this) rather than "global" to situate such an ethical perspective. Indeed, global all too often connotes homogenization across places and cultures, which is the exact opposite of what a post-structuralist feminist perspective would want to invoke. The asymmetries of power marking North and South America have economic as well as historical components. The conquest and colonization of the Americas—with its array of racial, gendered, military, religious, and scientific hegemonies—is one such historical source; the advance of Western capitalism and its specific configuration of class society in developed and developing societies—as well as the relation between the two—is another. Cultural differences across the Americas point to incommeasurable worlds that may not be readily translatable to interlocutors from asymmetrically constituted sites. Surely, when such incommeasurables are at stake, the elements that risk exclusion from representation in mainstream cultural transactions are those pertaining to the lifeworld of the less empowered parties.

My position does not entail that people across very different societies and cultures will be unable to agree on a certain set of values or mutual interests. On the contrary, reaching agreements across cultures is a valuable and, indeed, necessary aspect of social and political relations, particularly in this age of global technologies in which values are easily communicated across national borders. What I hold is that, given the asymmetrical conditions of power between dominant and subaltern parties (regardless of the public rhetoric that all parties to agreements are equal), the terms of such agreements and/or the languages in which global mainstream values are represented, even when well intended, embody the ideological presuppositions of the dominant parties and cultures. Discourses are effects of power, just as they are instrumental in generating new relations of power. As it pertains to feminism, the voices of women from developing countries that are most likely to be heard in the North are those that already speak within the discursive framework of the North's expectations. This means that to ensure the most open arena for discourse across cultures holding asymmetrical relations of power, the North's speakers must engage in a conscious practice of decentering their habitual standpoints. They must be prepared to accept suggestions that are not readily or always expected. I am convinced that of all the questions having to do with globalization, perhaps the most troubling is how globalization processes affect those persons, activities, and nonhuman entities excluded from its benefits. The reason is simple: globalization involves a process of integration or mainstreaming into a competitive transnational market economy. The failure to become integrated—or, at the extreme, the failure to obtain sufficient conditions for survival and growth under the terms of the neoliberal global economy—therefore represents the ultimate penalty that globalization inflicts on its victims.

## FEMINIST CRITIQUES OF GLOBALIZATION

Feminist critiques of globalization derive elements from feminist economics, political theory, and activism.[5] A sharper critique, whose theoretical base is broader than feminist, appears in literary criticism and cultural studies.[6] Feminist critiques, whether reformist or radical, are directed at globalization understood as a process in Western capitalism that seeks to integrate as much of the world as possible into one giant market. This sense of globalization refers, according to the neoliberal doctrine it implements, to the liberalization of markets, the privatization by capital of previously nonprivatized (often public or state-supported) programs, and the so-called flexibilization of the labor force. It also refers to the exclusive valuing of the monetized domain of the economy, with the result that voluntary or unpaid work is undercounted and/or devalued.[7] Because women's activities are overrepresented in the category of voluntary work and unpaid care work, feminists have a justified interest in analyzing why such work by women is invisible or undervalued by neoliberal policy.

Neoliberal globalization processes are enhanced and supported by technological advances and by conservative political measures. On the technological front, the extraordinary growth in technology and information sciences allows communication to flow almost instantaneously around the world, enabling large volumes of highly profitable long-distance and transnational financial and commercial transactions. On the political front, governments have been persuaded to enter into international trade agreements that supersede the national regulation of financial flows, trade, and commerce. Such agreements promote the flow of financial transactions, capital, and goods across national borders in ways that especially benefit transnational businesses and corporations. Because global commerce is aimed at extracting the highest possible profit for investors, with respect to the cost of human labor, the goal is to drive its cost down to the lowest possible denominator. Private companies (as well as governments) are led to downsize their labor force. This action is justified to the public as intended to relieve the alleged burden on taxpayers (in the case of governments) or to make products more competitive in price (in the case of the sale of commodities). Jobs that used to employ full-time workers are outsourced to lower paid, part-time, temporary and/or foreign labor. With trade barriers down as a result of international trade agreements, products can be manufactured or partially assembled virtually anywhere in the world as long as the price of labor is cost-effective.

The displacement of jobs created by profit-intensive capital flows also leads to the displacement of populations. Another aspect of the global economy is the steady migration of populations to sites they associate with improved subsistence or income. All aspects of these globalization processes affect women, whose lives are destabilized by economic hard times and by the increasing gap between the wealthy and the poor. Globalization offers some possibilities of economic improvement to skilled women who either are not involved in caring activities toward their family members or are able to benefit from substitute caregiving assistance. However, in ignoring or devaluing unpaid care work that on the whole is done primarily by women, globalization fails to create equitable conditions for women to be fully integrated into the neoliberal economy. It may be observed that globalization destroys good full-time jobs with benefits, replacing many of them with part-time jobs. At first glance, this appears to benefit women over men, since it was men who held the better jobs (now discarded), while women appear to be the primary targets for part-time labor (insofar as the rest of the time they are often occupied with unpaid care work). Public relations campaigns in favor of neoliberal globalization therefore make it appear as if women as a group are among the main beneficiaries of the global economy. But this is misleading. Women in part-time jobs do not benefit when men lose full-time jobs. In cases in which they share a household with a male income earner, the loss of his job is a total loss for the household, regardless of whether the woman gains part-time employment. The benefit would be for both women and men to hold full-time, well-paying jobs. At present, more data are needed to track the actual effects on women and men of the "feminization of poverty."[8]

Other features of the neoliberal global economy lead to questionable results for women. For example, there are certain structural problems of trade liberalization as currently practiced that impact adversely on women's concerns for a decent quality of life. The World Trade Organization (WTO), founded in 1995, aims to reduce what it calls "obstacles to trade" on a worldwide basis. Among the things considered obstacles to trade are important elements of people's quality of life. For example, the WTO considers "regulations on foreign investment, environment protection, health and safety standards, laws on the ownership of natural resources and technology, and systems for placing government contracts and designing and operating social security systems" as barriers to trade.[9] The WTO acts on profit-oriented regulations that in turn suppress, delegitimate, or make obsolete various regulations a nation may have held regarding job security for workers, affirmative action for women and minorities, or environmental protection. These considerations and the laws based on them become invalidated by the WTO and its signatory countries whenever they are thought to interfere with the profit motive. The deregulation of quality-of-life issues occurs because short-term profit is placed ahead of long-term values. Against this view, there is a feminist consensus that "trade rules are . . . important but cannot take precedence over human rights and environmental sustainability."[10]

Feminist economists do not assume that globalization processes are inherently bad for women, but they point out that the effects on women's lives are uneven and that some women—particularly poor and rural women in developing countries—are hurt far more than others.[11] They argue, however, that even assuming that globalization offers uneven effects for women, "unless gender issues and concerns are widely understood, acknowledged, and addressed, globalization will only exacerbate the inequalities between men and women."[12] There are a number of structural reasons for this, although perhaps the easiest one to grasp is globalization's effect on maternity and women's work, which affects workingwomen of childbearing age. For example, recent studies in Argentina show that professional women are increasingly delaying their pregnancies—first from their twenties to their thirties, and now to a time closer to their forties—because of variable and insufficient labor rights regarding pregnancy and childbearing leave for working mothers.[13] With few reliable rights to protect them at work and in conditions of high unemployment and job scarcity, continued dependence on a wage-earning job takes precedence over personal lifestyle options. Moreover, neoliberal structural adjustment policies mandate state cuts for social assistance programs. As in the North, the burden of care shifts to the domestic sphere of the household, whose members must undertake the care of the young, the old, the sick, and the disabled.[14] Again, women are impacted disproportionately, since they are the principal caregivers. Seen from the angle of women's experiences and daily concerns to care for their loved ones, the profit drive of neoliberal globalization is blind to the concrete needs of ordinary people.

The term "social reproduction" is used by social scientists to refer to all the activities taking place in the home that guarantee the reproduction of the labor force from day to day and from generation to generation. Social reproduction includes caring for and raising children, cooking, cleaning, making sure the home environment

is safe and healthy, fetching and preparing the meal ingredients, washing and iron-
ing clothes, repairing torn clothes, caring for the sick and disabled, and providing
emotional support for household members so that their sense of integrity, humanity,
and dignity is promoted in the intimate home environment. The neoliberal economy
tends to ignore all the preceding as economically irrelevant activities insofar as they
are unpaid or do not register a cash flow in the monetized domain.[15] At the same
time, the neoliberal economy reduces or shuts down assistance to citizens in the areas of health, education, and social services, arguing that the system would function
better if part or all of these services were privatized. Unfortunately, privatizing
health, for example, limits the access of the poorest people to services because of
prohibitive costs. Alternatively, public facilities accessible to the poor are inade-
quately staffed because of the lack of public resources. Under neoliberal policies,
there is no public structure, such as the state, that can serve as a supplier of jobs.
Rather, the generation of new jobs and income must come from private enterprise or
investments in a highly competitive market. Because markets are now open to global
competition, affected companies that fail to cut down on costs, including labor costs,
can easily go bankrupt. The purported benefits of such policies—lower consumer
prices, lower inflation—only benefit a part of the public in the developing countries
as long as severe poverty persists and the system continues to generate increased
inequalities.

For those who lack accumulated capital or who may not have had sufficient access to education or training (categories in which many women and girls may be
disadvantaged), it is not possible to benefit from this economic order. The road is
difficult and uneven for many. It is not surprising that new forms of sex trade and
even child prostitution are on the rise.

Globalization is also shaping sex commerce. Some developing countries are
marketing sites for sex tourism, including interracial sex commerce.[16] A propor-
tion of women will sell sex because there is demand for sex and, comparatively
speaking, selling sex may be their best survival option. There is also a proliferation of women migrants or would-be migrants to the developed world who fill a
market demand for domestic help[17] and for Internet-mediated mail-order brides.
These are among the real effects of globalization and its impact on girls' and
women's lives, contrary to the ubiquitous "benefit to consumers" claim one constantly hears about in the globalized media.

## POLITICAL ORGANIZATION AND RESISTANCE
## TO GLOBAL EXPLOITATION

So far, I have mentioned some of the highlights of the neoliberal global economic
program along with its negative or limiting impact on women. Women's response
to facing the challenges of neoliberalism has been to insist that the gender impact
of global economic policies be understood (so that damaging policies are identi-

fied and changed, if possible). Women have also organized politically to ensure a larger voice for women's issues and concerns both before the state and in civil society at large. In addition to grassroots mobilizations at the local level, women have engaged in global organizing and transnational advocacy programs, including work conducted through, or in association with, the United Nations and with foreign-sponsored nongovernmental organizations (NGOs).

As is well known, in Latin America, the impact of neoliberal global economics coincided chronologically with a larger opening toward democracy in most of the region's countries. Politically, the democratic opening has provided a boon for the women's movement. It would not be farfetched to say that the women's movement has been one of the major players in the democratic transitions. The cause of modern democracy and the cause of women's equality are historically interrelated. As in North America, the arguments for universal suffrage in Latin America mobilized women in the first wave of the movement to demand the right to vote and the right to equal political participation. In the 1970s the United Nations sponsored a Decade for the Advancement of Women (1975–1985), coinciding with the second wave. With its opening conference in Mexico City in 1975, the feminist agenda acquired significant international (as well as local and regional) visibility. One of the things the United Nations' decade achieved was to create an international network of activists that would articulate local and national activities with an international project for women's rights.

The three initial goals the United Nations identified for the Women's Decade were equality, development, and peace. Sharp economic and political antagonisms divided the (male-dominated) planet. It must be recalled that those were still the days of the Cold War. The Soviet-sponsored socialist bloc mobilized women for socialism, while the capitalist bloc mobilized women for Western values. Then, after the dissolution of the Soviet Union and the Eastern European socialist bloc, the advancement of capitalist neoliberal economic programs gained an increased impetus. At the same time, the new global linkages strengthened activists committed to human rights and equality internationally. In the early 1990s, what had been an international women's movement mediated by the concept of nationality was shaped and transformed into a global movement for women's rights in the context of the United Nations' ethical concept of human development. The United Nations Development Programme has documented these goals in a series of yearly reports. In addition, the United Nations Development Fund for Women (UNIFEM) articulated a global vision of women's leadership and what a just society must offer women and girls: an end to violence against women, a respect for women's rights as human rights, and a demand that women and girls be fully included in plans for economic and social development throughout the world. While it is true that this vision of women's emancipation was advocated in a dialogue with the world's national governments (given the United Nations' structure as a forum for nations' representation) and this did not allow for radicalism, nonetheless, the integration of a pro-women's agenda into the rest of the work of the United Nations has had a number of positive effects. By the mid-1990s and, specifically, the Beijing conference of

1995, a global gathering of official and unofficial delegates was celebrated in China. It is interesting to see how the Beijing experience, including the planning for it and its aftermath, affected the feminist and the women's political movement in Latin America.

In an exceptionally well-informed essay, Sonia Alvarez has shown the complexity of both the symbolism and the reality of the Beijing conference on the Latin American feminist movement.[18] She notes that over 1,800 participants from Latin America attended the NGO-sponsored unofficial conference in the "backwater town of Huairou, China," that met parallel to the official United Nations Conference on Women in Beijing.[19] The large size of the group reveals, according to Alvarez, an immense internal diversity currently characterizing the Latin American women's movement.[20] To use the term "feminist" here, though, would be a little misleading. Since the mid-1980s in Latin America, the boundaries between women who identify themselves as feminist and women who are active in the women's movement without using this label are rather fluid. The fluidity resulted partly because of the region's democratic opening throughout the 1980s. As Alvarez explains, this opening allowed many feminists whose consciousness had been forged in opposition to public power (during repressive regimes) to embrace electoral politics openly and even run for office as candidates for the opposition.[21] When running for and being elected to office, they had to move on to a range of projects other than feminism. It should also be noted, as Alvarez does in another section of the paper, that eventually friction and tension arose between feminists who joined public office and those who mistrusted the power of institutional agencies (including the United Nations).[22] A class division cut through the feminist movement, with some women privileged in positions of power and others, claiming a more authentic connection to their feminist roots, radically questioning the legitimacy of such power.

Nonetheless, the result by the 1990s (and beyond) is the presence of a broad spectrum of women in various institutions and public roles who also championed the cause of women's rights. The breadth of their activities, however, signifies a "*decentering* of contemporary Latin American feminist practices."[23] In other words, the political action of women who hold progressive views on gender issues is not confined to the feminist movement as such. Instead, such women occupy posts all across professional and political fields, integrating gender issues into whatever work they are doing. Alvarez points out that, at the same time, many self-identified feminists have accepted an expanded conception of feminism's goals. In particular, they see the goals of feminism as not limited to women's issues *per se*, but as offering an approach to issues spanning public policy as a whole.[24] If Alvarez's analysis is correct—and I see no reason to doubt it—we are witnessing both a decentering of the feminist movement and a much more far reaching effect of feminist ideals, as women influenced by feminist ideas but not totally defined by them increasingly occupy influential roles in society. This phenomenon creates difficulties for a researcher if she wants to trace a tidy map regarding feminism's range of operations and boundaries. What in fact has happened is that there are no such distinct boundaries. Boundaries are crossed back and forth enabling new alliances to be formed at the activist and political levels: "With the expansion of black feminism, lesbian feminism, popular feminism, ecofeminism, Christian feminism, and so on, the mid-1980s and 1990s witnessed the proliferation of new actors whose political-personal trajectories often differed significantly from those of earlier feminists."[25] These data show that as women's experiences change, so does their appropriation of feminism.[26] To this I would add that some of the fundamental factors causing women's experiences to change are the globalization processes that redefine women's economic, social, and political participation in their respective communities.

Globalization processes have touched the lives of Latin American women in more than economic ways. For those who have access to the Internet, including activists for social and political change, it is now possible to link up with counterparts across the region or simply to learn of other groups' activities and successes. Examples of feminist organizations and collectives that have used the Web to disseminate views, to provide news or information about grassroots organizations and projects, or to post articles are Fempress,[27] La Morada,[28] and Creatividad Feminista.[29] An interesting feature of these grassroots women's collectives is that no overarching (masculine) entity controls them. In other words, no political party, no church, no nation, no global body, no economic conglomerate controls their multifaceted projects. Some of these Web sites offer information about female sexuality and women's life stages, as well as support groups for lesbian women, topics that move beyond the usual representations of gender found in the mainstream media. The dissemination of local activities and interests through information technologies not subject to the control of political parties and the proliferation of meanings with respect to feminism (so that only its plural form, "feminisms," makes sense anymore) are both structural features of postmodern times. Thus, the same global economy that displaces people, undermines their security, and generates unemployment by destroying large numbers of steady, long-term jobs, in so doing, creates discontent and mobilizes people to use the democratic instruments available to them in order to resist injustice and demand change. The significant amount of gender-related activism in Latin America demonstrates that women do not take the negative effects of globalization passively.

## ACADEMIC STUDIES ON DEMOCRACY

For their part, Latin American intellectuals, sometimes in association with their Spanish counterparts, have also shown their commitment to the strengthening of democratic processes by writing on democracy and evaluating whether the global economy's performance in the region has benefited democratic institutions. So far, economic studies of neoliberal economics tend to show that neoliberalism and structural adjustment have increased, not diminished, existing inequalities both across and within countries. In an analysis of the impact of neoliberal structural reforms on the implementation of human rights policy in Latin America, the Brazilian scholar José Eduardo Faria concludes that the simultaneous weakening of the state and the rise in inequalities pose grave questions regarding the future of human rights in the region. He notes that the utopian character of human rights (if they are truly to be universalized and realized) leads to "a paradoxical situation: the more they are affirmed, the more it turns out that they are denied."[30] Clearly, society has not achieved the social or economic order that would guarantee human rights universally. How can a representative democracy prevail, he asks, without a sufficiently strong state "to correct, or at least, attenuate" the economic, regional, and ethnic inequalities marking various segments of the citizenry?[31] Or what does it mean to have a right to property when there are nonexistent conditions for vast numbers of people to become property owners?[32] Faria points to conditions of "social fragmentation" in which the concept of justice "tends to disappear from the collective consciousness," replaced by a forced obedience to those in power and a sense that society splits into those who are included and those who remain excluded from present economic and political gains.[33] He argues that this fragmentation made visible by the poverty and misery of large sectors of the population represents a weakening of democracy (a democracy so many people fought so hard to obtain), since the poor have no effective representation in government. In such circumstances, appealing to human rights carries a utopian connotation and an implicit denunciation of the present state of affairs.[34] The ideal of human rights—extended to mean "the rights to life, to work, to health, to education, to nourishment and housing"—therefore becomes essential to the promise and implementation of a truly democratic agenda.[35] The sentiments and thoughts expressed by Faria are shared by many survivors of the repressive 1970s regimes in the southern cone, for whom the hope of the 1980s democratic opening was short lived, since it was accompanied on the economic front by the structural adjustment processes that left so many poor and disenfranchised people in the camp of the excluded.

The Argentine feminist philosopher María Luisa Femenías brings another voice to this debate by emphasizing informal channels of strengthening democracy at the popular level. She proposes the strengthening of social and political networks of solidarity as a way of reinforcing the effectiveness of an all-too-formal democracy. Femenías notes that even if the precepts of the law are formal and unpredictably implemented (as political observers concede), still "self-generated networks of solidarity constitute . . . a firm base from which to demand recognition [before the law]."[36] Femenías points to examples of women's political action taking unusual and nonhegemonic approaches, yet reaching some measure of political efficacy. A well-known example is the case of the Mothers of the Plaza de Mayo who defied the repressive government authority, and by the power of their moral appeal, they eventually brought down the legitimacy of authoritarian rule. But Femenías also mentions several other women's grassroots movements. These include women in farming, women in neighborhood associations, and women in community networks.[37] These groups used unconventional ways of mobilizing to achieve particular objectives and often dispersed once the objectives were achieved.[38] Nonetheless, these forms of association were empowering to those who participated in them and thereby helped to strengthen a participatory democratic agenda. Although it is a long struggle to change the system on behalf of full equality for women, Femenías points to the pervasive networking among women along different lines of the political process to promote progressive gender legislation reform.[39] In relation to grassroots efforts such as these, Alvarez pointed out that decentralizing the feminist movement has expanded its political effectiveness in helping women of different backgrounds and occupations unite for purposes of gender reform.[40] While it is true that the nation-state has been weakened significantly by neoliberal policies and that such economic policies have damaged labor rights, environmental protection, and many gender-related interests, the new political circumstances seem to offer women activists some opportunities to form influential coalitions on certain specific issues with respect to political development.

## CULTURAL STUDIES CRITIQUES

Another important counterhegemonic critical sector comes from progressive thinkers in South America who insist, against trade liberalization and the flexibilization of the labor force, that human rights are nonnegotiable. The insistence not just on human rights as conservatively understood but understood generously as a base for the protection of multiple human needs and of yet-to-be unspecified differences is foremost in the democratic left's discourse. For example, the Argentine cultural critic Beatriz Sarlo states in a recent article that "the Left should maintain several completely nonnegotiable [principles] . . . the question of human rights as a perennial open question is one of them. . . . This question is nonnegotiable and spills over onto the expansion of rights, the emergence of new needs, and the multiplication of differences."[41] Sarlo adds another very interesting point in the battle to unmask the dominant globalization ideology's claim of inevitability. She calls for a political left that is "antimimetic."[42] She characterizes the complacency of contemporary politics as incorporating a series of mimetic practices, among them: "surveys, the construction of a public opinion reflecting existing conditions, the conservative populist backing of all social fears, the automatic acquiescence before the established relations of power."[43] Sarlo's concerns are well taken. While the monitoring of public opinion is important in a democracy, the pressure on public opinion is to conform to the needs of the market. If public opinion, however, is shaped by the needs of the market, what is there left for democracy to do except to promote civil and political measures that continue to favor the market economy of liberalization, profit making, and the search for the cheapest labor and goods possible? The media's imparting of information to the public and its use of public opinion surveys constitute a vicious circle. Because large corporations often own the mainstream media, it stands to reason that they will promote the ideology of neoliberalism as the sure and reliable path to progress. Insofar as this is the case, we find ourselves in a revolving wheel where the needs of the market shape the popular mind, while everyone so (mis)informed will feel represented democratically the more that the government and public spheres are indeed controlled by the needs of the market. The global market's trajectory acts like a mirror before which the public checks to see if its political choices are satisfactory.

As evident in Sarlo's critique, the postmodern and post-structuralist critiques of representation are key avenues for a creative progressive approach to assessing the ideologies of globalization. Using a post-structuralist epistemology, the Chilean cultural critic Nelly Richard has called attention to the order of representation in the media and in human knowledge as a sociocultural construction—yet a construction so habitual that we consider it "natural."[44] More specifically, she considers the constructed order of the feminine and of the feminine writer as these images and meanings circulate in the literary market. "The 'gods of consumerism,'" Richard writes, "receive offerings as well from women writers whose works are successfully promoted by the international literary market that today converts the feminine and the Latin American into the double marginality illustrative of its offers of diversity, which translate center and margins into the same language of market pluralism."[45] Richard warns that "recognition and identification are the tranquilizing keys that link the reader to a matrix of meaning in which what is *legible* is born from the absolute and fixed identity between signifier and signified."[46] Richard is pointing here to the dangers of globalization as a technology that homogenizes meanings pretending at the same time to be an organ for maximizing pluralism as it incorporates those global others into the North's schemata of representations. It is sad to say that in the global market's reconceptualization of diversity, the truly diverse fails to qualify for representation because it is encoded differently from the signifying system that controls the global messages. Indeed, as anyone who has struggled with the meaning of "pluralism" and "diversity" in the United States will recognize, a certain canon of diversity that is extremely problematic is often constructed, framing the official meaning of "diversity." As this model attains popularity and becomes acceptable to the public, it acts as a cover-up for those transgressive alterities that social conventions find unmentionable.

This discussion leads us back to the problem many Latin American feminists have fought recurringly, namely, the suppression of *feminista* [feminist] by *femenina* [feminine][47] along with the latter references reassuring enactment of normative heterosexuality. Seen from this post-structuralist critical Latin American feminist perspective, the neoliberal market disciplines the conceptualization of the "global," the "plural," the "diverse," "the feminine," "the Latin American," and so on, as it includes some players among its economic, social, and political beneficiaries, while excluding others. By the same token, what counts as "Latin American philosophy" and "thought" (*pensamiento*) according to the criteria of neoliberal globalization is subject to the same hegemonizing dichotomy. For this reason, it is important to remain politically alert to the seductions of the market and to insist on the value of progressive political alternatives whether we take a feminist route to the analysis of globalization or we adopt some other line of approach or methodology.

In the end, I hope this analysis has shed some light on the complexity of globalization processes and the importance of bringing gender and cultural location into a discussion of the direction and effects of these economic processes. Although I have not brought in other variables such as race, ethnicity, or class to the discussion, I believe these are equally important in providing a picture of those who are most vulnerable to the impact of globalization. The analysis I have given is meant to include the needs of the most marginal—hence the critique of neoliberalism and its exacerbation of economic inequalities. Through intellectual critique and analysis as well as political action, an ethical vision of human development can shed light on those aspects of globalization that fall far short of long-standing ideals of political equality, fairness, and social justice. The Latin American context in which these processes are played out and the alternative political options and criticisms suggested in response to them are truly enlightening as we face common challenges in today's global economy despite our multiple, nonhomogeneous locations.

## NOTES

1. In this essay the English translations from Spanish language sources are my own.

2. Ofelia Schutte, "Political and Market Development: An Ethical Appraisal," *Journal of Social Philosophy* 31, no. 4 (2000): 453–64, 460–63.

3. Ofelia Schutte, *Cultural Identity and Social Liberation in Latin American Thought* (Albany: State University of New York Press, 1993), 1–8.

4. Ofelia Schutte, "Cultural Alterity: Cross-Cultural Communication and Feminist Thought in North-South Dialogue," *Hypatia: A Journal of Feminist Philosophy* (spec. issue on Global, Postcolonial, and Multicultural Feminisms, ed. Sandra Harding and Uma Narayan) 13, no. 2 (spring 1998): 53–72.

5. Lourdes Benería et al., "Introduction: Globalization and Gender," *Feminist Economics* (spec. issue on Globalization, ed. Lourdes Benería et al.) 6 (2000): vii–xviii; reviewed by Priti Ramamurthy, "Indexing Alternatives: Feminist Development Studies and Global Political Economy," *Feminist Theory* 1 (2000): 239–40, 240–56.

6. Gayatri Chakravorty Spivak, *A Critique of Postcolonial Reason: Toward a History of the Vanishing Present* (Cambridge, Mass.: Harvard University Press, 1999), 312–21; Nelly Richard, "Feminismo, Experiencia y Representación," *Crítica cultural y teoría literaria latinoamericanas* (spec. issue of *Revista Iberoamericana,* ed. Mabel Moraña) 62 (1996): 733–44.

7. Lorraine Corner, *Women, Men, and Economics: The Gender-Differentiated Impact of Macroeconomics* (New York: United Nations Development Fund for Women, 1996), 20–21.

8. UNIFEM Biennial Report, *Progress of the World's Women 2000* (New York: United Nations Development Fund for Women, 2000), 11–12.

9. UNIFEM Biennial Report, *Progress of the World's Women 2000*, 152.

10. UNIFEM Biennial Report, *Progress of the World's Women 2000*, 154.

11. Paloma de Villota, ed., *Globalización y género* (Madrid: Síntesis, 1999), 22–23.

12. Benería et al., "Introduction: Globalization and Gender," x.

13. Ana María Amado, "La Opción entre la Maternidad y el Trabajo,"*Fempress: Agencia de Prensa Latinoamericana de la Mujer* 149, no. 1 at www.fempress.cl, Santiago de Chile, 13 December 2000 (accessed May 2, 2002).

14. For a groundbreaking book on the topic of the work involved in caring for dependents and the need for justice for caregivers, who are predominantly female, see Eva Kittay (1999). In an essay in progress, "Women, Dependency, and the Global Economy," I analyze the impact of the gender division of labor on unpaid care workers in light of the cutbacks on social assistance implemented by the neoliberal global economy.

15. Corner, *Women, Men, and Economics*, 30–31.

16. Laurie Shrage, *Moral Dilemmas in Feminism: Adultery, Abortion, and Prostitution* (New York: Routledge, 1994), 142–45.

17. Grace Chang, *Disposable Domestics: Immigrant Women Workers in the Global Economy* (Cambridge, Mass.: South End, 2000), 125.

18. Sonia E. Alvarez, "Latin American Feminisms 'Go Global': Trends of the 1990s and Challenges for the New Millennium," in *Cultures of Politics, Politics of Cultures,* ed. Sonia E. Alvarez, Evalina Dagnino, and Arturo Escobar (Boulder, Colo.: Westview, 1998), 293–324.

19. Alvarez, "Latin American Feminisms 'Go Global,'" 293.

20. Alvarez, "Latin American Feminisms 'Go Global,'" 293 ff.

21. Alvarez, "Latin American Feminisms 'Go Global,'" 298.

22. Alvarez, "Latin American Feminisms 'Go Global,'" 311–17.

23. Alvarez, "Latin American Feminisms 'Go Global,'" 299.

24. Alvarez, "Latin American Feminisms 'Go Global,'" 299.

25. Alvarez, "Latin American Feminisms 'Go Global,'" 301.

26. Alvarez, "Latin American Feminisms 'Go Global,'" 302.

27. Fempress at www.fempress.cl (accessed 13 March 2002).

28. La Morada at www.la-morada.com (accessed 13 March 2002).

29. Creatividad Feminista at creatividadfeminista.org (accessed 13 March 2002).

30. José Eduardo Faria, "Democracia y Gobernabilidad: Los Derechos Humanos a la Luz de la Globalización Económica," *Mundialización económica y crisis político-jurídica* (spec. issue of *Anales de la Cátedra Francisco Suárez*) 32 (1995): 73–100, 100.

31. Faria, "Democracia y Gobernabilidad," 76.

32. Faria, "Democracia y Gobernabilidad," 89.

33. Faria, "Democracia y Gobernabilidad," 89.

34. Faria, "Democracia y Gobernabilidad," 94–100.

35. Faria, "Democracia y Gobernabilidad," 78.

36. María Luisa Femenías, "Igualdad y Diferencia en Democracia: Una Síntesis Posible," *La democracia en latinoamérica* (spec. issue of *Anales de la Cátedra Francisco*

*Suárez)* 33 (1999): 109–32, 127.
37. Femenías, "Igualdad y Diferencia en Democracia: Una Síntesis Posible," 126.
38. Femenías, "Igualdad y Diferencia en Democracia: Una Síntesis Posible," 126–27.
39. Femenías, "Igualdad y Diferencia en Democracia: Una Síntesis Posible," 131–32.
40. Alvarez, "Latin American Feminisms 'Go Global,'" 299–302.
41. Beatriz Sarlo, "Contra la Mímesis: Izquierda Cultural, Izquierda Política," *Revista de Crítica Cultural*, ed. Nelly Richard, 20 (June 2000): 22–23, 23.
42. Beatriz Sarlo, "Contra la Mímesis: Izquierda Cultural, Izquierda Política," 23.
43. Beatriz Sarlo, "Contra la Mímesis: Izquierda Cultural, Izquierda Política," 23.
44. Nelly Richard, "Feminismo, Experiencia y Representación," *Crítica cultural y teoría literaria latinoamericanas* (spec. issue of *Revista Iberoamericana*, ed. Mabel Moraña) 62 (1996): 733–44, 734.
45. Nelly Richard, "Feminismo, Experiencia y Representación," 742.
46. Nelly Richard, "Feminismo, Experiencia y Representación," 743.
47. Alvarez, "Latin American Feminisms 'Go Global,'" 297.

# 11

## Latin American Liberation Theology, Globalization, and Historical Projects: From Critique to Construction

### Iván Petrella

*A mi abuela Maruja y mis Viejos*

Globalization today is an obsession, celebrated by the political right, attacked by the left, ever present in the mass media, and the focus by now of myriad popular and scholarly books. There is still no agreement about how to define the concept; some even question whether such a thing as globalization is even taking place.[1] There is no way to deny, however, that our understanding of the world is shaped, for good or ill, by this concept. For the purpose of this chapter, I take globalization to mean the contemporary context in which devising alternatives to neoliberal market capitalism has become increasingly difficult.[2] At least critics and propagandists alike agree on this point. In this chapter I examine how Latin American liberation theology has responded, and how it may further respond, to globalization so understood.[3] The essay is thus expository and interpretative in relation to liberation theology in the present, as well as constructive in relation to its future. It develops in the following fashion: First, I provide a brief overview of liberation theology's development. Second, I present and assess liberation theology's three main responses to the rise of neoliberal capitalism in the 1990s. I will claim that despite their strengths, all three positions suffer from the inability to devise concrete alternatives to globalization. Third, I turn to liberation theology's foundational works to recover the notion of a historical project. I suggest that the lack of a notion of a historical project disables liberation theology from adequately meeting the challenges posed by globalization. Finally, I outline an alternative, yet complementary, approach that may open up a space for the development of a historical project to counter the increasing hegemony of neoliberal capitalism.

## INTRODUCTION: LIBERATION THEOLOGY'S DEVELOPMENT

Latin American liberation theology was born at the crossroads of a changing Catholic Church and the revolutionary political-economic ferment of the late 1960s and early 1970s.[4] In the first case, the Second Vatican Council (1963–1965) opened the door for a fundamental rethinking of the relation between Christian faith and the world by asserting the value of secular historical progress as part of God's work. Papal social encyclicals such as *Mater et Magistra*, *Pacem in Terris,* and *Populorum Progressio* focused not just on workers' socioeconomic rights but also on the rights of poor nations in relation to rich nations. In addition, Vatican II gave greater freedom to national episcopates in applying church teachings to their particular contexts. In the second case, the Cuban revolution, the failure of the decade of development, and Kennedy's "Alliance for Progress," as well as the exhaustion of import-substitution models of development, led to the rejection of reformist measures to ameliorate the massive poverty that plagued Latin America.[5] Political and economic views became increasingly radical as groups of priests, workers, and students organized in militant revolutionary groups that espoused socialism. At the same time, starting with Brazil in 1964, a succession of military coups led to the imposition of national security states. These two trends—religious and political—came together at the Second General Conference of Latin American Bishops (CELAM) at Medellín, Colombia, in 1968. Documents from this meeting analyzed Latin America's social situation.[6] They argued that the continent suffers from an internal and external colonialism caused by a foreign exploitation that creates structures of institutionalized violence. Mere development, the documents asserted, could not overcome this condition of dependency. The concept of liberation emerged as an alternative.[7]

Liberation theology's foundational texts, those of its inception and expansion, were written from within this world view.[8] As such, they share the following presuppositions: (1) a sharp dichotomy between revolution and reformist political action, the first seen as necessary, while the second deemed as ineffectual or as an ideological smokescreen that supported the status quo; (2) the poor were seen as the primary, and at times exclusive, agents of social change; (3) a sharp dichotomy between socialism and capitalism, with socialism as the social system that could remedy the injustice of the latter; and (4) a priority was given to politics in the narrow sense of struggle over state power, with little attention to issues of gender, ecology, race, and popular culture.

Liberation theology's historical context—that is, the sociopolitical and religious context within which liberation theologians work—has changed dramatically since the late 1960s and 1970s.[9] At the ecclesial level, the main changes lie in the rise of Pentecostal groups and the Vatican's clampdown on liberation theology by silencing theologians and replacing progressive bishops with conservative ones.[10] At the same time, Vatican documents have incorporated central liberationist concepts such as the preferential option for the poor and liberation. On the political front, the first change lies in the collapse of communism. In my mind, all the other changes need to be understood in relation to the demise of the socialist alternative. For liberation theology, the fall of the Berlin Wall represents the loss of a practical alternative to capitalism.[11] In fact, the prospect of an alternative seems to have disappeared from view. One has to go back to the beginning of industrial capitalism in the nineteenth century to find a similar period.[12] A second change lies in the perceived decline of the nation-state's ability to control economic activity within its own boundaries. A third change stems from the technological third wave. New technologies allow for the almost instantaneous transfer of information from one corner of the globe to the other and facilitate, among other things, speculative attacks on currency that have made controlling economic policy so difficult for Latin American states. The fourth change lies in the upsurge of culture and the subsequent downgrading of the traditional political sphere, the struggle for state power.[13] What all these changes boil down to, most importantly, is that alternatives to neoliberal market capitalism have vanished from the horizon.

## CURRENT RESPONSES TO LIBERATION THEOLOGY

Liberation theologians have developed three moves in response to the increasing dominance of neoliberal market capitalism. I call these moves "reasserting the core ideas," "reformulating or revising basic categories," and "critiquing idolatry," whether of the market or of modernity at large. While the same theologian may make more than one move in the same work, the differences in emphasis remain pertinent enough so that each position can be analytically separated as follows.

### Reasserting the Core Ideas

This first position disentangles liberation theology's core ideas—concepts such as the preferential option for the poor, the reign of God, and liberation—from Marxism as a social scientific mediation and socialism as a historical project.[14] It builds on a number of essays that sought to separate liberation theology from the death of socialism symbolized by the fall of the Berlin Wall.[15] The argument is simple and can be stated in three steps: (1) liberation theology was never intrinsically tied to any particular social-scientific mediation or historical project; (2) the discrediting of a particular mediation and/or historical project thus cannot affect liberation theology's core intuitions or ideas; and (3) the current worldwide situation of growing inequality between haves and have-nots makes liberation theology's central intuitions as necessary as ever.

This position admits a change in the context within which liberation theology is done. According to Gustavo Gutiérrez:

> In the past years we have witnessed a series of economic, political, cultural and religious events, on both the international and the Latin American plane, which make us think that important aspects of the period in which liberation theology was born and developed have come to an end. . . . Before the new situations many of the affirmations and discussions of that time do not respond to today's challenges. Everything seems to indicate that a new period is beginning.[16]

Gutiérrez then separates the essential from the inessential in liberation theology:

> Theologies necessarily carry the mark of the time and ecclesial context in which they are born. They live insofar as the conditions that gave them birth remain. Of course, great theologies overcome, to an extent, those chronological and cultural boundaries, those of lesser weight—no matter how significant they might have been for a time— remain more subject to time and circumstance. We are referring, certainly, to the particular modes of a theology (immediate stimuli, analytical instruments, philosophical notions, and others), not to the fundamental affirmations concerning revealed truths.[17]

For Gutiérrez, in the particular case of liberation theology, that essential revealed truth "revolves around the so-called preferential option for the poor. The option for the poor is radically evangelical and thus constitutes an important criterion to separate the wheat from the chaff in the urgent events and currents of thought in our days."[18] Notice that Gutiérrez distinguishes the revealed truths of theology from the vehicles that carry those truths. There is thus a distinction to be drawn between liberation theology's revealed content and the socioanalytical tools used to explicate that content. The discrediting of a particular mediation does not touch the preferential option for the poor as the core of liberation theology.

Jon Sobrino, like Gutiérrez, begins his reassertion of the paradigm by stressing the need to rethink liberation theology in the light of current events.[19] He then proceeds to make the notion of liberation the central element: "What is specific to liberation theology goes beyond particular contents and consists of a concrete way of exercising intelligence guided by the *liberation principle*."[20] For Sobrino "liberation is not just a theme, even if the most important, but a starting point: it ignites an intellectual process and offers a permanent pathos and particular light. This . . . is the fundamental aspect of liberation theology."[21] Sobrino too, therefore, separates essential from inessential elements in liberation theology. Liberation is not a "content" but a guiding light and principle. Liberation, therefore, cannot be tied down to any particular political program or philosophical analysis but precedes and guides them. They come afterwards; their failure does not disprove the guiding principle.[22]

To recapitulate the first position outlined: One strategy pursued by theologians in the face of the shift in their political, economic, and cultural context lies in the reassertion of liberation theology's core ideas. The theologian separates a central element—whether it is the preferential option for the poor, liberation, or the Reign of God—and asserts that despite all this, this element remains untouched.[23] The impulse behind this position is correct. It is true that liberation theology, despite what many critics claim, rarely fully identified with any mediation or historical project. Thus, the discrediting of such a mediation does not touch the heart of liberation theology with its focus on the poor, the construction of God's reign, and liberation. Liberation theologians are right to argue that in an increasingly divided world these elements remain as necessary as ever. The way these elements are defended, however, exacts too high a price. What allows this position to work is the emptying of the idea defended. It is no longer clear what the preferential option for the poor, the Reign of God, and liberation mean in practice without the incorporation of some sort of social scientific mediation, whether Marxist or not; without such mediation, it remains impossible to provide an alternative to the shape globalization is currently taking. All three tacitly acknowledge the need for new mediations but make no headway in their incorporation. Sobrino writes that "liberation theology makes of God's Reign its central content and conceives itself as the adequate theory for its construction."[24] Construction, however, requires more than the reactive and rearguard defense of a set of theological concepts. Gutiérrez, drawing from the indigenous cultures' focus on solidarity and reciprocity, calls for an ethic of solidarity that can inspire a popular economics.[25] The vagueness of the proposal, however, does little to advance the claimed necessary refashioning of liberation theology for this millennium.[26] Here no alternative to globalization can be found. While necessary and presupposed by the other positions to be reviewed, this move remains incomplete.

## Revising Basic Categories

Position two, the revision of some of liberation theology's basic categories, takes the first move reviewed a step further. It accepts the thesis that liberation theology's central ideas—the preferential option for the poor, liberation, and the Reign of God—remain essential in today's context. Unlike position one, however, position two begins to reformulate aspects of early liberation theology—the focus on revolution, the understanding of the poor as history's driving force, and the emphasis on capturing state power—in order to open a space for the implementation of new sociopolitical, economic, and cultural mediations.

Pedro Trigo is the most influential exponent of this position.[27] The centerpiece of his reformulation lies in staking out an alternative to both early liberation theology's revolutionary world view and the contemporary market-oriented neoliberal world view. For Trigo, liberation theology made "the people" (*el pueblo*) the revolutionary subject of the underside of history.[28] This people was conceived as the engine of revolutionary change and historical salvation, a unified subject whose interests were those of humanity at large. This understanding of a historical subject, according to Trigo, lies discredited. The contemporary social imaginary, however, is that of a marketplace where each individual buys and sells different products from appliances to eschatological and political salvation. Every alternative to this marketplace—whether political, economic, or cultural—already falls within it. For this social imaginary, therefore, there is no underside of history.[29] In principle everyone is included, although some have more clout than others. While the first option dangerously exaggerates the role of the poor in history, creating a monolithic subject with a blank check to refashion society in a totalitarian fashion, the second option is a model based on the exchange of goods and services the poor do not possess. Tacitly excluded from the market, the poor are in fact excluded from society. For Trigo, if these are the only two social imaginaries available—the people as revolutionary subject and engine of history or a market model in which the poor are apparently included but in reality excluded—then "liberation theology has no future."[30]

Trigo's proposal begins by rejecting the market model of society and basing a new social imaginary on the concept of "humanity."[31] The market model is "based on the image of an athletic track, in which each athlete runs on his own."[32] In this model, relationships are secondary and derivative of individuals. As the absolute standpoint, the individual voluntarily chooses whether to enter into a social contract with others. Instead, Trigo argues that humanity, as a collective, is primary and that "each human being, from the very beginning of his or her life, is found in a fundamental unity with everyone else. . . . Society is a bodily reality, a social body."[33] For Trigo, the notion of humanity as a social body means that human life possesses an unavoidable social dimension.[34] By "the underside of history," Trigo thus means the perspective of those who have been marginalized. Since relation is primary, marginalization requires having been actively excluded from society, while in the market model, marginalization, in which the individual is primary and stands up and against society, stems from the refusal to establish social bonds. The underside of history, therefore, is the standpoint of those excluded from the social body, witnesses to the violation of a common humanity.

While the concept of humanity is the centerpiece of Trigo's rejection of the market imaginary, the concept of "everyday life" is the cornerstone of his reformulation of liberation theology. As seen, Trigo rejects the notion of the poor as a revolutionary subject. Such a notion implies that the poor live only at extraordinary moments in history, and they discount the everyday processes of survival, resistance, and creation present in marginalized communities. Such a notion also ignores the role of popular culture in sustaining community. Instead, Trigo insists that everyday life is the preferred venue through which the poor act: "As we have been describing the historical strength of the poor, it becomes clear that its privileged sphere is everyday life and its densest result is to recreate, heal, and strengthen the social fabric."[35] Resistance, in this case, is "not an ideological declaration of principles nor can be reduced to a political program. Resistance occurs in everyday life, it is found in the cyclical rituals of community life."[36] While liberation theology has traditionally privileged the political sphere, Trigo's reformulation widens the area of possible resistance and change:[37] "We insist that the historical strength of the poor is not exercised in politics as a privileged realm but in the sphere of everyday life recreating, healing, and strengthening the social fabric."[38] The flourishing of civil society—through the creation of myriad social organizations independent of the state but coordinated among themselves—is more important than the conquest of governmental power.[39] The poor are no longer the exclusive privileged subjects of liberation; they are, however, an integral part of a subject that must be wider in scope, including the world's poor communities as well as professionals from both the poor and rich nations, "the international of life."[40]

To recapitulate position two: This position accepts the thesis that liberation theology's central intuitions—the preferential option for the poor, liberation, and the Reign of God—remain relevant in the current historical context. Position two goes beyond position one, however, in reformulating other aspects of liberation theology. To date, that reformulation focuses on the rejection of a unified revolutionary subject of history, the refusal to accept the dichotomy of reform and revolution, and an espousal of popular culture and civil society as the privileged arena for liberation. Each point is important. The rejection of the poor or the people as a unified revolutionary subject avoids an idealization of the poor as a class as well as the temptation toward revolutionary violence. No class fully embodies history. Rejecting an understanding of the poor as a unified subject also forces the recognition that social progress requires an alliance across different social groups both within the nation and worldwide, thus Trigo's "international of life." The rejection of the dichotomy between revolution and reform makes piecemeal change—often belittled by liberation theologians—as valid as it is necessary. Revolution is also usually understood as requiring an intellectual vanguard that will lead the people and thus suffers from an ingrained elitist bias. This too is rejected, placing change in the hands of communities on the ground.[41] Finally, the turn toward civil society stems from the previous two points. It is in civil society that different groups come together—women, indigenous peoples, the underclass, and ecological activists—to demand rights. Here wider social alliances can take place.[42]

While position two's intent to revise and construct is valid, current attempts suffer from a number of problems. First, the exaltation of civil society as the new venue for radical politics may well be the product of misplaced hope. Trigo, for example, claims that "this network of communities and groups constitutes the creation of the historical power of the poor, fed by faith and popular religion. As it becomes denser, it diversifies until it covers educational, formative, recreational, productive, and health aspects, as well as religious ones. And this diversity is kept connected by a deepening of the fraternal relations that are cultivated starting from the community."[43] Scannone too claims that "the universal phenomenon of the rise of civil society is also found in our Latin America,"[44] but social science literature on Latin America, however, documents the increasing political apathy of the majority of the population.[45] The disarticulation of social groups rather than their growth seems to be the trend. Second, the exclusive focus on civil society downplays the continued importance of structural political and economic change. For Trigo, the solidarity of inhabitants of the rich countries

> with the poor of the world must reach and transform their own cultural being. It is not a matter of their giving their free time or their economic surplus but that they be different citizens within their own nations, their political communities, and culture. They have to rediscover in their histories an alternative tradition and recreate it to become what they are (political and cultural beings) in a different manner, that is, to put forth in those communities potentialities left aside or untried, so that those political and cultural communities can transform themselves.[46]

While it is true that fundamental change requires a conversion in outlook, the focus on civil society exhibits a puzzling lack of the political and economic analysis required for devising alternatives to globalization. Position two also goes too far in downplaying the importance of state power. The ability of civil society to flourish is tied to the legal regulatory framework of the state.[47] Reform needs to occur from the top down as well as bottom up. Finally, it remains an open question whether the focus on civil society and the fostering of myriad social organizations are not, in reality, the expression of liberation theology's political defeat.[48] Today, at a time when no wide-ranging alternatives to capitalism appear on the horizon, there seems to be no other choice than to call for conversion and concertation at the community level. The exaltation of civil society and corresponding demotion of liberation theology's political ambition, therefore, comes dangerously close to making a virtue out of necessity.

## Critiquing Idolatry

Position three develops a critique of the idolatrous nature of capitalism and modernity more generally. Like the first position reviewed, this position's argument can be stated in three steps: (1) for liberation theology, God is a God of life, (2) an idol is a God to whom lives are sacrificed, and (3) capitalism and modernity are examples of idols since they take priority over human life. Franz Hinkelammert is the most influential exponent of this strand of liberation theology.

In his essay "Liberation Theology in the Economic and Social Context of Latin America: Economy and Theology, or the Irrationality of the Rationalized," Hinkelammert examines the different ways liberation theology has been combated throughout its development. He then identifies a recent shift in the strategy through which liberation theology is opposed.[49] Today, he argues, opposition no longer takes the form of denouncing liberation theology for its attempts to begin to realize

God's kingdom materially but instead takes the form of co-opting its understanding
of the relation between God's kingdom and history as well as its basic terminology.
Hinkelammert takes as his example a speech delivered by Michael Camdessus, the
head of the International Monetary Fund, at a Congress for French Christian businessmen. Camdessus explains:

> Surely the Kingdom is a place: these new Heavens and this new earth to which we
> are called to enter one day, a sublime promise; but the Kingdom is in some way ge-
> ographical, the Reign is history, a history in which we are the actors, one which is in
> process and that is close to us since Jesus came into human history. The Reign is
> what happens when God is King and we recognize Him as such, and we make pos-
> sible the extension, spreading of this reign, like a spot of oil, impregnating, renew-
> ing and unifying human realities. "Let Thy Kingdom come."[50]

Note the conception of history at work in Camdessus's speech. God's reign is
a promise, but a promise that is part of history, a history that has a time and a
place in this world. God's reign, moreover, is one that is brought about at least
partly by our own actions; we are also responsible for the extension of that Kingdom. The conception of history in relation to God is the same as liberation theology's. Camdessus continues by addressing the businessmen present directly:

> Our mandate? . . . It is a text of Isaiah which Jesus explained; it says (Luke 4, 16–23):
> "The spirit of the Lord is upon me. He has anointed me in order to announce the
> good news to the Poor, to proclaim liberation to captives and the return of sight to
> the blind, to free the oppressed and proclaim the year of grace granted by the Lord."
> And Jesus had one short response: "Today this message is fulfilled for you that you
> should listen." This today is our today and we are part of this grace of God, we who
> are in charge of the economy (the administrators of a part of it in any case): the al-
> leviation of suffering for our brothers and the procurers of the expansion of their lib-
> erty. It is we who have received the Word. This Word can change everything. We
> know that God is with us in the work of spreading brotherhood.[51]

In his speech, Camdessus makes the International Monetary Fund God's vehi-
cle on earth. He takes central tenets of liberation theology—the focus on the poor,
the Reign of God, and liberation—to develop a theology whose practical political outcome is support for the very same structural adjustment policies denounced by liberation theologians. Hinkelammert draws two crucial consequences: First, "The fact that these two contrary theologies (the theology of the
International Monetary Fund and liberation theology) cannot be distinguished on
the level of a clearly theological discussion stands out. At this level liberation theology does not visibly distinguish itself from the anti-theology presented by the
International Monetary Fund. The conflict seems to be over the application of a
theology shared by both sides."[52] Second, "Imperial theology is in agreement
with the preferential option for the poor and with the economic and social incar-

nation of God's Kingdom. It presents itself as the only realistic path for fulfilling those demands . . . the option for the poor can no longer identify any specification and natural affinity for liberation theology. Now the question is over the realism of the concretization."[53]

In response to this situation, Hinkelammert outlines a critique of the neoliberal market economy's utopianization of the market. The critique takes two steps, one that points out the internal contradictions within capitalism itself and another that expresses that contradiction and its consequences in theological terms. In the first place, Hinkelammert argues that capitalism's understanding of efficiency, measured as it is exclusively according to profitability, is both inefficient and irrational. For Hinkelammert, "the exclusion of a growing number of persons from the economic system, the destruction of the natural bases of life . . . are the nonintentional results of this reduction of rationality to rentability. The market laws of total capitalism destroy society and its natural environment."[54] Capitalism, therefore, is not a rational system. On the contrary, it is irrational in that it is self-destructive. Any system whose laws threaten the economic and ecological basis of human life is irrational; the market cannot be universalized without destroying the human and natural foundation on which it is based. Second, drawing from Paul's "Letter to the Romans," Hinkelammert develops the theological interpretation of his critique: "Paul makes visible that the law . . . leads those who fulfill it or who are obliged to fulfill it to death."[55] Liberation theology can draw from Paul's understanding of the relationship between the law and human life:

> Christian freedom returns, therefore, in the sense pronounced by Paul, as a freedom that is sovereign before the law. The free subjects are free to the degree that they are able to make the law relative with respect to their own needs. . . . Considering market-based law, freedom consists precisely in being able to subordinate and even to break the law, if the needs of the subject demand it.[56]

Hinkelammert places two Gods and two laws against each other. Liberation theology's God is a God of life, and thus its ultimate law lies in what benefits human beings. Such a God never imposes a law that ends in death. Freedom, in fact, is the freedom to break those laws that lead to death. But opposite the God of life lurks capitalism as God. The extension of capitalism's law of profitability requires the increasing poverty of the great majority of humankind; capitalism requires human sacrifices to flourish. For Hinkelammert, sovereignty from the law differentiates liberation theology's preferential option from the poor from imperial theology's. In liberation theology, the life comes first and the law is judged by its contribution to human well-being. In imperial theology—the theology of capitalism—the market law of profitability is the standard by which life is measured. Here the law is never relativized. It stands absolute even before increasing human misery and ecological destruction.

To recapitulate position three: This position's starting point is the recognition that modernity is idolatrous rather than secularized.[57] It thus makes the critique of modernity's idols—capitalism, the market, and socialism—the central task.[58] Critique takes place by unmasking the sacrificial logic behind the idol. For liberation theology, God is a God of life. Idols, on the other hand, require human sacrifices. Idolatry is present when upholding a law is placed above human life. Christian freedom lies in refusing to follow laws that lead to death. Sin, in this case, comes from upholding the law. So, in the case of capitalism, profitability requires laying off workers. Profit takes priority over life. Socialism too suffered from the same logic. Here profitability was pursued by the forced uprooting of entire communities and their reorganization according to laws that were supposed to lead to greater efficiency.[59] Position three's strength lies in recognizing that theology today cannot be limited to a narrowly defined religious sphere: the most dangerous idols, those that affect the greatest number of people, hide behind a secular disguise that must be unmasked.[60]

Note that Hinkelammert's analysis of the co-option of liberation theology's terminology reveals the limited contribution of position one—reasserting core ideas. The heart of position one was the attempt to protect liberation theology's core ideas from the fall of socialism. But today even liberation theology's opponents espouse those ideas. The International Monetary Fund wholeheartedly accepts the preferential option for the poor, liberation, and the construction of God's reign.[61] Liberation theology's basic ideas do not need safeguarding at the level of their reassertion. What they require is redefinition through the incorporation of new social, scientific, and cultural mediations. As Hinkelammert highlights, the problem becomes one of differentiating the same theological concept—be it liberation, the preferential option, or the reign of God—by imbuing it with different political, economic, social, and cultural content. The attempt to revise basic categories moves in this direction but does not go far enough. Hinkelammert's solution, however, is inadequate as well. His argument develops life as the absolute criterion by which society is judged. But liberation theology's opponents would agree with this criterion. The disagreement begins with the problem of what institutions best serve the goal of enabling human life.[62] The real question comes after the critique of idolatry: What do we do instead? What can we propose? In addition, the concept of an idol is the negative counterpart to a positive affirmation. If the idol is the only available option, it is not really an idol but becomes necessary, becomes a god. To show the idol as idol, alternatives are needed. Criteria must be able to distinguish between viable options. A key problem, therefore, lies in the lack of viable options.[63]

## THE MISSING HISTORICAL PROJECT

Missing from all three positions—the reassertion of core ideas, the revision of basic categories, and the critique of idolatry—is a concept once central to liberation theology, the notion of a "historical project." In the next section, I will outline one way this notion can be recovered for use in devising alternatives to globalization. Here, however, I will briefly elucidate the role the historical project played in early liberation theology, since, in my mind, the problems current positions exhibit in moving from critique to the construction of alternatives can be read in relation to this concept's absence. In the first place, the historical project was the means to give content to liberation theology's theological terms. It was through the historical project that liberation theologians thought through their theological terms; this gave them a greater degree of specificity and thus they protected themselves from groups who ostensibly thought alike but in practice espoused different goals. The second function of the historical project, therefore, was one of differentiation between groups that at face value held the same ideals but differed in the understanding of their practical import. The problem of differentiation and co-option that Hinkelammert identifies is not a new problem but one that was understood and resolved through the historical project. Finally, the historical project combated two types of idolatry, the idolatry of society as it stands and the idolatry of future revolutionary plans.

In his classic text *Doing Theology in a Revolutionary Situation*, José Míguez Bonino explains:

> "Historical project" is an expression frequently used in our discussions as a midway term between a utopia, a vision which makes no attempt to connect itself historically to the present, and a program, a technically developed model for the organization of society. A historical project is defined enough to force options in terms of the basic structures of society. It points in a given direction. But frequently its contents are expressed in symbolical and elusive forms rather than in terms of precise technical language. . . . It is in this general sense that we speak of a Latin American socialist project of liberation.[64]

For Bonino, in the early 1970s, the historical project included seven elements.[65] First, it involved a rejection of "developmentalist" attempts to solve Latin American political and economic woes through further integration into the international capitalist system. Latin America must break away and follow a path independent of (but not necessarily isolated from) the "Empires." Second, element one is only viable with a parallel social revolution within Latin American society itself. The great majority of Latin Americans needs to be mobilized politically to remove from power the oligarchic elites that cooperate with foreign interests. Third, while acknowledging the dangers in such a move, Bonino claims that a strong centralized state is required to overcome foreign and local resistance to such a program. Fourth, change needs to occur not just from the top down but from the bottom up. The people themselves must be awakened to their condition of oppression and thus also to the need they have to participate in their own emancipation. This process is termed *conscientization* or *politicization*. Fifth, because a transfer of power among segments of the population is necessary, primary emphasis is given to the political sphere. Changes in all other spheres—whether technical, cultural, social, or economic—are subordinate to the political.[66] Sixth, the historical project involved the search for an authentic Latin American social- ism that met the needs of the continent. Bonino stresses that liberation theology rejects all dogmatism (Marxist or otherwise) in this search. No model (Eastern Europe or Cuban) is a stereotype to be copied. Seventh, development must be un- derstood as wider than mere economic change. In the end, "liberation is the process through which and in which a 'new man' must emerge, a man shaped by solidarity and creativity over against the individualistic, distorted humanity of the present system."[67]

These, therefore, are the elements Bonino sets up as liberation theology's his- torical project. My interest, however, lies not in the specific content of the historical project but in the role it played in liberation theology's self-definition. Despite having fallen from use, the notion of a historical project was central to liberation theology's own understanding of itself. Bonino's debate with Jürgen Moltmann—liberation theology and political theology—serves as one example.[68] As the major European progressive theology of the time, German political theol- ogy was a source for liberation theology. At the same time, however, liberation theology consciously defined itself *against* political theology. Liberation theol- ogy's disagreement with political theology revolves around the relationship be- tween God's reign and politics, and at the center of this dispute lays the notion of a historical project. This was the main dividing issue. Bonino asks: "Do histori- cal happenings, i.e., historical human action in its diverse dimensions—political, cultural, economic—have any value in terms of the Kingdom which God pre- pares and will gloriously establish in the Parousia of the Lord?"[69] He notes that Moltmann and Metz explicate the relationship between politics and God's reign with terms like "anticipation," "sketch," and "analogy." The result is that there is no causal connection between the two. Bonino concludes: "In other words, his- torical action is not really significant for the Kingdom; at most, it may succeed to project provisory images which remind us of it. These images must not be taken too seriously in order to avoid absolutizing them. The historical significance of the expectation of the Kingdom is preeminently to protect us from any too strong commitment to a present *historical project!*"[70] Note how Bonino understands the connection between a historical project and God's reign as much closer than does Moltmann.[71] For Moltmann, God's reign serves a critical function that keeps us from turning any earthly project into an idol. There is thus an absolute distinction between God's reign and a historical project. For Bonino and liberation theology, however, such an absolute distinction pushes theology into the hands of the sta- tus quo: "We believe that European theologians must de-sacralize their concep- tion of 'critical freedom' and recognize the human, ideological contents it carries. When they conceive critical freedom as the form in which God's eschatological Kingdom impinges on the political realm, they are simply opting for *one* partic- ular ideology, that of liberalism."[72] Liberation theology's first point against political theology, therefore, is that there is no standpoint that escapes thinking in terms of historical projects. For the simple reason that theological concepts have political import, every theology is tied to a historical project whether that project is explicitly stated or not. The very attempt to stand above and relativize all human politics ends by supporting one particular historical project, that of the status quo.

Liberation theology also argues that its central theological terms cannot be properly understood independent of a historical project. Referring to Moltmann's *The Crucified God*, Bonino states, "Moltmann . . . names five 'demonic circles of death' under which man suffers: poverty, violence, racial and cultural deprivation, industrial destruction of nature and meaninglessness or Godforsakenness. Consequently, justice, democracy, cultural identity, peace with nature and meaningful life are the concrete contents of historical hope. Quite clearly this brings us to the area of politics."[73] Bonino adds:

> Can we remain satisfied with a general description of the 'demonic circles of death,' without trying to understand them in their unity, their roots, their dynamics, i.e., without giving a coherent socioanalytical account of this manifold oppression? Are we not taking lightly the stark historical reality of the cross when we satisfy ourselves with an impressionistic description of man's alienation and misery? In other words, it seems that, if theology means to take history seriously, it must incorporate—with all the necessary *caveats*—a coherent and all-embracing method of sociopolitical analysis.[74]

It is only by this incorporation that the "failure to give a concrete content to 'identification with the oppressed'" can be avoided.[75] Bonino further insists

> it is indeed possible and necessary to underline a continuum, a direction and a purpose in God's historical action . . . which is conveyed through such expressions and symbols as 'justice,' 'peace,' 'redemption,' in their concrete biblical 'illustrations.' At the same time, *it is equally necessary to stress the fact that such insights cannot be operative except in terms of historical projects* which must incorporate, and indeed always do incorporate, an analytical and ideological human, secular, verifiable dimension.[76] (emphasis added)

The historical project, therefore, is needed to give content to theological terms. Without the historical project, terms such as liberation, the preferential option for the poor, or the reign of God lack concrete content.

Hugo Assmann also places the development of a historical project at the center of liberation theology's self-understanding. For him

> *We must go back to essentials, and stress what distinguishes theological reflection in Latin America from that of the affluent nations.* This, to my mind, lies in the fact that we have assimilated—somewhat confusedly, maybe, but still characteristically and effectively—three levels of approach necessary for historical reflection on faith as

the practice of liberation. If theological reflection is to be historically and practically valid, then it has to operate on these three levels, which are:

1. The level of social, economic and political analysis; the level, that is, of an attempt at rational interpretation of the reality of history—which in itself implies an ethical and political decision in the very selection of the instruments of analysis, since these can never be completely neutral.

2. The level of opting for particular political theories and approaches. These could be "imposed" by the results of the initial work of analysis, but their choice is also determined by an ethical element not derived from the analysis itself: man's capacity for making himself responsible for history.

3. The level of strategy and tactics. The general political theories require planned implementation, and this implies obedience and discipline—to borrow traditional terms—within an effective form of political action.[77] (emphasis added)

For Assmann, therefore, the political dimension of faith "implies a consciousness of *the fact that the real act of faith, as a concrete bodily realization of a praxis placed within the historical process, always includes an option related to historical projects.*"[78] He insists that "the abstract option has to be translated into real action according to the circumstances. There can be no real commitment to liberate one's country on the general level alone."[79] He is well aware of the danger of vacuity in the rhetoric of "liberation." Without a historical project, the very language of liberation loses its specificity and can be taken up by groups with agendas different from that of liberation theology.[80] Indeed, Assmann suggests that the deepest divisions in the Latin American church revolve around fundamental differences in the historical projects espoused.[81]

Gustavo Gutiérrez best systematizes the relationship between the concept of liberation and historical projects. He outlines three levels of liberation in his classic work *A Theology of Liberation*.[82] On a first level, he writes, liberation "expresses the aspirations of oppressed peoples and social classes, emphasizing the conflictual aspect of the economic, social, and political process that puts them at odds with wealthy nations and oppressive classes."[83] On a second level, liberation is applied to an understanding of history. Here "man is seen as assuming conscious responsibility for his own destiny. . . . The gradual conquest of true freedom leads to the creation of a new man and a qualitatively different society."[84] On a third and final level, liberation allows for a different approach to biblical sources. Now "Christ is presented as the one who brings us liberation. Christ the Savior liberates man from sin, which is the ultimate root of all disruption of friendship and of all injustice and oppression."[85] For Gutiérrez, while these levels can be held analytically distinct, they are really part of a single process. Holding them together allows the theologian to avoid "idealist and spiritualist approaches, which are nothing but ways of evading a harsh and demanding reality, and second, shallow analyses and programs of short-term effect, initiated under the pretext of meeting immediate needs."[86] Note, therefore, that the notion of liberation needs to bring together two elements. On the one hand, it must be given enough specificity so that it actually directly addresses, rather than glosses over, real oppression and suffering. On the other hand, however, liberation cannot be just a governmental program of immediate assistance. While liberation is not just political, there is an irreducible political element to the concept.

Later in his argument, Gutiérrez connects the notion of liberation to the idea of a historical project. For Gutiérrez, *"the mediation of the historical project* of the creation of a new man assures that liberation from sin and communion with God in solidarity with all men—manifested in political liberation and enriched by its contributions—does not fall into idealism and evasion"[87] (emphasis added). At the same time, because the historical project is not merely a political program but also a vision of an ultimately just society *"this mediation* [the historical project] keeps us from any confusion of the Kingdom with any one historical stage, from any idolatry toward unavoidably ambiguous human achievement, from any absolutizing of revolution."[88] The historical project is thus intimately linked to the idea of liberation. It is, in fact, what allows the notion of liberation to both address current society and yet not be reduced to a particular political program. It protects us from a dual idolatry—of society as it now stands and idolatry of any future social form.

Bonino, Assmann, and Gutiérrez all make the notion of a historical project a defining point of liberation theology's self-understanding. It is, for Bonino, the centerpiece of his dispute with political theology. For him, theology cannot find a position above a historical project. The historical project is either explicitly developed and theorized or implicitly hidden. In the latter case, the project ends by tacitly supporting the status quo. For Assmann, too, the connection between theology and a historical project differentiates liberation theology from other theologies. Gutiérrez develops these insights in a more systematic fashion. He links the notion of a historical project to the concept of liberation. Without a historical project, liberation either loses its connection to the real world or too quickly identifies itself with a political program. The historical project protects theology from the idolatry of society as it stands and the idolatry of future, short-term, revolutionary plans. Without a historical project, liberation theology's key concepts lose specificity, become vacuous, and are easily taken over by other groups.[89] For all three, the only way to truly understand and begin to realize their religious ideals is to think them through in relation to a particular historical project.

## FROM CRITIQUE TO CONSTRUCTION: AN ALTERNATIVE APPROACH

Let me now briefly outline elements of an alternative approach to opposing the rise of neoliberal market capitalism—one that places the imagination of a new historical project at the forefront—from which liberation theology may draw.[90] This approach starts from an interpretation of liberation theology's contemporary situation that is different from the three positions reviewed and embarks upon a constructive path that can complement and strengthen those positions: First, this approach suggests that liberation theology's current situation is characterized by a theological victory and a political defeat. If imitation is the sincerest form of flattery, then liberation theology's co-option (as identified by Hinkelammert) is a tribute to its impact within theology and beyond; even liberation theology's opponents espouse the preferential option for the poor, liberation, and the Reign of God.[91] At the same time, however, this co-option is made possible by liberation theology's present inability to give its theological terms concrete sociopolitical content beyond the celebration of civil society. Remember, that position one has no answer to liberation theology's co-option; position one, in fact, aids that co-option by drawing a strict distinction between the paradigm and the mediation that gives that paradigm content. Position one separates what early liberation theology—via the historical project—refused to separate. It ends, therefore, by facilitating the emptying and subsequent takeover of liberation theology's basic terminology. Position two revises liberation theology but has yet to construct upon the new foundation. Construction would require the initial elaboration of a new historical project, going beyond the promotion of civil society that is position two's constructive proposal. In this way, position two fails to fully address the increasing vacuity of the language of liberation. Position three also remains inadequate. Hinkelammert's critique of idolatry does not provide an alternative to the International Monetary Fund's understanding of the means by which liberation might be achieved. For this reason, position three cannot give any more content to liberation theology's central terms than positions one or two. Now the key question is not whether liberation theology is valid as theology but how its insights are to be translated into the sociopolitical realm. The vacuity of liberation theology's terminology, therefore, needs to be addressed.

Second, liberation theology can give content to its theological terms in the same way it did in the past—through the notion of a historical project. The problem of co-option and differentiation is not new. As we saw, the belief that theological positions at times must be distinguished through a historical project is found in the movement's foundational works. Today, as before, a key question lies in what historical project is pursued under the rubric of liberation. Remember, for example, Gutiérrez argued that the preferential option for the poor is liberation theology's most important legacy.[92] This may be true, and its co-option points to its evocative power but leaves us empty handed when confronted with other, conflicting, interpretations of the term. What exactly is meant by the preferential option for the poor? What exactly is meant by liberation? Leonardo Boff once warned:

> What sort of liberation are we talking about? Here we must be careful not to fall into the semantic trap of endowing the same word with several very different meanings. The liberation involved here has to do with economic, social, political and ideological structures. It seeks to operate on structures, not simply on persons. It proposes

to change the power relationships existing between social groups by helping to create new structures that will allow for greater participation on the part of those now excluded.[93]

While Boff alludes to the danger inherent in not specifying the concrete meaning of liberation, he also remains too vague. At this level of generality, there is nothing in his statement that the International Monetary Fund could not also espouse. It is, in fact, the abandonment of the notion of a historical project that makes possible the co-option of liberation theology's terminology.[94]

Third, central to the notion of a historical project is the intimate link between thinking about ideals and thinking about institutions, thus requiring attention to both the religious (or secular) ideal and the concretization that might approach that ideal.[95] Concepts such as the preferential option for the poor and liberation hide more than they reveal about the way life chances and social resources may be theoretically approached and institutionally realized. The focus, therefore, needs to fall on the practical political and economic mediations of these ideals and concepts; otherwise, the mechanisms by which such abstract goals are to be achieved are handed on a platter to liberation theology's opponents. An alternative position believes that for liberation theology, political construction is not a secondary moment in the theological task—coming after the clarification of our theological concepts—but is the very means by which those concepts are given a degree of analytical rigor and are clarified and understood.

Fourth, there are two reasons why the notion of a historical project has been dropped, one external to liberation theology, the other internal; the first examined, the second unexamined. The external reason lies in the fact that the worldwide context is dramatically different from the time of liberation theology's birth and development. Liberation theologians accept this fact; the positions reviewed all start from the recognition that today radical structural change is no longer on the agenda. There is also, however, an unacknowledged reason internal to liberation theology itself. Liberation theology theorizes capitalism as an abstractly defined, indivisible, monolithic entity.[96] We need to understand, however, that capitalism operates discursively as well as materially. Here liberation theology needs to be aware of the "performativity of social representations—in other words, the ways in which they are implicated in the worlds they ostensibly represent."[97] The very way that liberation theology theorizes capitalism makes change a virtual impossibility. Take, as one example, the following statements from Pablo Richard: "We don't yet have the power to construct an alternative to the market as a total system, but we do have the strength to construct an alternative to the *spirit* of the system. We live inside the system but can reject the system's spirit, its logic and rationality. We can't live *outside* the system, since globalization integrates everything, but we can live *against* the spirit of the system."[98] The system, of course, is capitalism and its parallel expressions such as the market and globalization.[99] Note that capitalism is presented as total and all encompassing to the point that resistance can only take the form of a shift in attitude; in this conceptualization there is no room for economic change, all avenues are blocked. Capitalism, moreover, has completely taken over the political sphere as well: "For the 'people' *[el pueblo]* (the popular sectors, social movements at the base) political power has become *impossible* (the system does not allow for the orientation of political power in benefit of popular interest), political power has become *irrelevant* (since everything is determined by market logic and it is impossible to govern against that logic)."[100] This understanding of capitalism effectively paralyzes any attempt to think in terms of a historical project. In the face of such a beast, all liberation theology can do is engage in prophetic critique, as in position three, and community building, as in position two. Devising alternatives to such a capitalism is a close-to-impossible task.

Fifth, liberation theology can adopt the notion of "alternative pluralisms," the idea that representative democracies, market economies, and civil societies can take different institutional forms.[101] To do so, liberation theology needs to stress the artificial, contextual, and haphazard nature of political and economic systems. This would allow liberation theology to approach society as partial, fragmentary, and incomplete, in an attempt to open up a space for alternatives (i.e., historical projects) that are excluded *a priori* from a picture of capitalism as a unified system encompassing not just the economic sphere but culture and politics as well.[102] Such an approach has three main traits: First, it claims that the political and economic institutions that compose society do not form a systemic whole. Second, it is contextual and finds its starting point in existing debates about economic and political reform. Third, this thinking envisions a type of change that is neither revolution nor reform but revolutionary reform: the step-by-step change of the formative context of society. This formative context includes, for example, the relations between branches of government, the relation between the state and private enterprise, and rules of inheritance; in short, what could be called the rules of the game. So, for example, liberation theology could draw from the social science literature on flexible specialization regimes to argue for a market economy that saw productive property as a bundle of rights to be vested in governments, intermediate organizations, communities, and firms. Such a system would distribute the benefits of property ownership more democratically by restricting the absolute claim any one group could make on its productive base. The end result is neither capitalism nor socialism, but a democratized market economy.[103] In addition, liberation theology could also propose reforms to strengthen the state, making the state less of a prey to the interests of moneyed elites. One could imagine a democratic regime with rules of mandatory voting, proportional representation, free access to the media for political parties, and public financing of campaigns. This could be coupled with a constitutional design that resolves the impasse between branches of government by appealing, through plebiscites or referenda, to the general populace as well as anticipated elections.[104] These moves would begin to recover specific content for the preferential option for the poor and liberation, terms that remain vacuous as long as one forgets the intimate link between thinking about ideals and thinking about institutions central to devising a historical project.

Sixth, note that the path I outline remains faithful to position one's reassertion of core ideas and position two's revision of liberation theology's basic categories. With position two, I believe that the dichotomy between reform and revolution must be avoided, that capturing state power need not be the obsessive focus of politics, and that the poor can no longer be elevated to the exclusive bearers of liberation. But devising an alternative to globalization in the guise of neoliberal market capitalism requires refusing to accept this position's limitations. In position two, and liberation theology in general, the failure of revolution leads to a call for solidarity and community building that ends by leaving society's political and economic framework untouched. That change is not possible at these levels is a bias that must be overcome. The focus on civil society (and its focus on culture, gender, and ecology) needs to be complemented by a focus on the reconstruction of the market and the state. The critique of idolatry can also be strengthened through the alternative outlined; it is political construction that fashions alternatives to reveal the idol as an idol.

Seventh, my position contributes to, and draws strength from, liberation theology's demotion of Western philosophy and theology as an undeniably influential, yet colonialist, racist, and provincial school of thought usually taken for the history of philosophy and theology per se.[105] Within Western philosophy, Europe positioned itself as the carrier of civilization for the rest of the world.[106] But if this tradition is one flawed tradition among many, then its primary exports today, capitalism and democracy, need not be taken as the end points of social development.[107] Indeed, Latin American elites' desire to emulate political and economic forms received from the First World rests on the assumption that Europe and the United States possess something of universal significance that the rest of the world lacks. If this assumption is dropped, then the critique of Western philosophy and theology, the critique of modernity, can open itself up to a critique of inherited versions of the market economy and of democracy. In this way, liberation theology can strike a balance between the theological critique of modernity and the institutional reconstruction of society: The former must inform the latter, but the latter should be the ultimate goal. As Gutiérrez once wrote: "At stake in the first instance is not doing theology, what really matters is liberation."[108]

## CONCLUSION

Liberation theology has devised three responses to globalization understood, in this chapter, as the rise of neoliberal market capitalism. These responses—reasserting the core ideas, revising central categories, and critiquing idolatry—possess different strengths but share the same weakness. They are all incapable of moving from critique to the construction of alternatives to globalization. To address this situation,

I suggested that the once central notion of a historical project needed to be recovered and placed at the forefront of liberation theology. It is by thinking about ideals in relation to thinking about institutions that liberation theology can develop alternatives to neoliberal capitalism. My final section outlined the elements of a position that can begin to put this approach into practice. Central to this approach is the attempt to theorize political and economic systems as alternative pluralisms. Finally, let me mention two aspects of the general relation between liberation theology and political construction that I do not touch on but that nonetheless need to be acknowledged. First, my attempt to open a space in which to develop localized alternatives to the reigning economic order must also be tied to a transformation of the world-system as a whole.[109] This requires paying attention to the cultural, economic, political, and ecological linkages between the rich and the poor nations and how those linkages hinder, block, and deny attempts by the latter to become masters of their own fate.[110] Finally, in this chapter I stress the indissoluble link between the theological and the political in liberation theology. While I focused on the implications of this link for recovering the notion of a historical project in an attempt to devise alternatives to globalization, I also believe that liberation theology is a spiritual exercise, a call to both social *and* personal conversion that is grounded in a hope for ultimate redemption. I do not want to forget that, to paraphrase Georges Friedmann, in order to prepare for the revolution, we must seek, in addition, to become worthy of it.[111]

## NOTES

1. For an analysis of the various positions taken on globalization see David Goldblatt et al., *Global Transformations: Politics, Economics and Culture* (Stanford, Calif.: Stanford University Press, 1999). This is the most comprehensive book available on globalization thus far.

2. I thus use "globalization" and "neoliberal market capitalism" interchangeably throughout the chapter. In a nutshell, neoliberal capitalism is characterized by the retreat of the state, extensive deregulation at the national level (the flexibilization of labor serves as an example) and the international level (the push for a free flow of financial capital flows serves as an example), as well as the rollback of networks of social protection. Globalization is a process that helps to extend and consolidate the hegemony of this type of capitalism worldwide. See Ramesh Mishra, *Globalization and the Welfare State* (Cheltenham, U.K.: Edward Elgar Publishing Limited, 1999), 8.

3. The chapter also introduces the non-Spanish reading public to recent literature that remains mostly unavailable in English. Unless otherwise specified, all translations are my own.

4. I provide a cursory measure of historical background so the reader can better grasp the shift in liberation theology's context. I draw from Arthur McGovern, *Liberation Theology and Its Critics: Toward an Assessment* (Maryknoll, N.Y.: Orbis Books, 1989), 4–11. McGovern's first chapter is the best quick introduction to the movement's

history until the early 1980s. Another fine book with a longer and more detailed historical survey is Christian Smith, *The Emergence of Liberation Theology: Radical Religion and Social Movement Theory* (Chicago: The University of Chicago Press, 1991). A good overview in Spanish can be found in Enrique Dussel, *Teología de la Liberación: Un Panorama de Su Desarrollo* (Ciudad de Mexico: Potrerillos Editores, 1995).

5. For a good, succinct examination of import substitution (ISI), see Ray Kiely, *Industrialization and Development: A Comparative Analysis* (London: UCL Press Limited, 1998), 83–97. For an evaluation of the current state of development studies, see Ray Kiely, *Sociology and Development: The Impasse and Beyond* (London: UCL Press Limited, 1995); and Richard Peet and Elaine Hartwick, *Theories of Development* (New York: The Guilford Press, 1999).

6. The documents can be found in Joseph Gremillion, ed., *The Gospel of Peace and Justice: Catholic Social Teaching Since Pope John* (Maryknoll, N.Y.: Orbis Books, 1976).

7. As McGovern notes, liberation combined a sociopolitical sense with the biblico-theological sense of God acting in history to save people from all enslavement. McGovern, *Liberation Theology and Its Critics: Toward an Assessment*, 9.

8. One can divide liberation theology into four phases: its gestation (1962–1968), a period of rapid growth (1968–79), its consolidation (1979–1987), and one of revision (1987–present). See João Batista Libanio, "Panorama de la Teología de América Latina en los Ultimos Veinte Años," in *Cambio Social y Pensamiento Cristiano en América Latina*, ed. José Comblin, José González Faus, and Jon Sobrino (Madrid: Editorial Trotta, 1993), 57–78.

9. Two of liberation theology's major congresses were held at the Escorial in Spain, one in 1972 and the other in 1992. The differences in the historical context and in the expositions of the liberation theologians themselves come out in a comparison of both volumes. See *Fe Cristiana y Cambio Social en América Latina* (Salamanca: Ediciones Sígueme, 1973); and José Comblin, José I. González Faus, and Jon Sobrino, eds., *Cambio Social y Pensamiento Cristiano en América Latina* (Madrid: Editorial Trotta, 1993). See also José Comblin, *Called for Freedom: The Changing Context of Liberation Theology*, ed. Phillip Berryman (Maryknoll, N.Y.: Orbis Books, 1998).

10. Michael Löwy, for example, argues that "the main challenge to liberationist Christianity is Rome's neo-conservative offensive in Latin America." Michael Lowy, *The War of Gods: Religion and Politics in Latin America* (New York: Verso, 1996), 131.

11. For one expression of this sentiment, see José Gómez Caffarena, "Diálogos y Debates," in *Cambio Social y Pensamiento Cristiano en América Latina*, ed. José Comblin, José I. González Faus, and Jon Sobrino (Madrid: Editorial Trotta, 1993), 330. For another expression, this time from a philosopher, see Santiago Castro-Gómez, *Crítica de la Razon Latinoamericana* (Barcelona: Puvill Libros, S.A., 1996), 16.

12. Mishra, *Globalization and the Welfare State*, 1–3.

13. See Comblin, *Called for Freedom: The Changing Context of Liberation Theology*, xv–xix, for a more detailed exposition of each one of these points.

14. Cardinal Joseph Ratzinger: "The fall of the European governmental systems based on Marxism turned out to be a kind of twilight of the gods for that theology." Joseph Ratzinger, "Relación Sobre la Situación Actual de la Fe y la Teología," in *Fe y Teología en América Latina* (Santafé de Bogotá, Colombia: CELAM, 1997), 14. Position one is a response to such statements.

15. See, for example, Leonardo Boff, "A Implosão Da Socialismo Autoritário e a Teologia Da Libertação," *Revista Eclesiástica Brasileira* 50, no. 197 (March 1990): 76–92; and Frei Betto, "A Teologia Da Libertação: Ruiu Com o Muro de Berlim?" *Revista Eclesiástica Brasileira* 50, no. 200 (December 1990): 922–29; Frei Betto, "O Socialismo Morreu. Viva o Socialismo!" *Revista Eclesiástica Brasileira* 50, no. 197 (March 1990): 173–76; Frei Betto, "El Fracaso del Socialismo Alemán y los Desafíos de la Izquierda Latinoamericana," *Pasos* 29 (May–June 1990): 1–7.

16. Gustavo Gutiérrez, "Una Teología de la Liberación en el Contexto del Tercer Milenio," in *El Futuro de la Reflexión Teológica en América Latina* (Bogotá, Colombia: CELAM, 1996), 102–03; see also Gustavo Gutiérrez, "La Teología: Una Función Eclesial," 130 (December 1994): xix, 15; and Gustavo Gutiérrez, "Renovar 'la Opción por los Pobres,'" *Revista Latinoamericana de Teología* 36 (September–December 1995): 269–90.

17. Gutiérrez, "Una Teología de la Liberación en el Contexto del Tercer Milenio," 107.

18. Gutiérrez, "Una Teología de la Liberación en el Contexto del Tercer Milenio," 109.

19. Jon Sobrino, "La Teología y el 'Principio Liberación,'" *Revista Latinoamericana de Teología* 35 (May–August 1995): 115.

20. Jon Sobrino, "La Teología y el 'Principio Liberación,'" 116.

21. Jon Sobrino, "La Teología y el 'Principio Liberación,'" 118.

22. See also Jon Sobrino, "¿Qué Queda de la Teología de la Liberación?" *Exodo* 38 (April 1997): 48–53, for a short piece where Sobrino ties the heart of liberation theology to the preferential option for the poor.

23. For another example of position three that makes the "Reign of God" liberation theology's central paradigm, see José María Vigil, "¿Cambio de Paradigma en la Teología de la Liberación?" *Alternativas* 8 (1997): 27–46.

24. Sobrino, "La Teología y el 'Principio Liberación,'" 129.

25. Gutiérrez, "Una Teología de la Liberación en el Contexto del Tercer Milenio," 156.

26. On page 159, note 77, Gutiérrez cites Luiz Razeto's interesting work but does not incorporate it into his analysis. See Luis Razeto, *Economía Popular de Solidaridad* (Santiago: Area pastoral social de la conferencia episcopal de Chile, 1986); and Luis Razeto, *Crítica de la Economía, Mercado Democrático y Crecimiento* (Santiago: Programa de economía del trabajo, 1994), among other works.

27. See Pedro Trigo, "El Futuro de la Teología de la Liberación," in *Cambio Social y Pensamiento Cristiano en América Latina*, ed. José Comblin, José I. González Faus, and Jon Sobrino (Madrid: Editorial Trotta, 1993), 297–317; and Pedro Trigo, "Imaginario Alternativo al Imaginario Vigente y al Revolucionario," *Iter. Revista de Teología (Caracas)* 3 (1992): 61–99.

28. For a scathing critique of this concept by one of liberation theology's founding fathers, see Hugo Assmann, "Apuntes Sobre el Tema del Sujeto," in *Perfiles Teológicos para un Nuevo Milenio*, ed. José Duque (San José: DEI, 1997), 115–46.

29. Trigo, "El Futuro de la Teología de la Liberación," 299–300.

30. Trigo, "El Futuro de la Teología de la Liberación," 300.

31. See also, Víctor Codina, *Creo en el Espíritu Santo. Pneumetología Narrativa* (Santander: Sal Terrae, 1994).

32. Trigo, "El Futuro de la Teología de la Liberación," 300.

33. Trigo, "El Futuro de la Teología de la Liberación," 301.

34. Trigo, "El Futuro de la Teología de la Liberación," 300.

35. Trigo, "El Futuro de la Teología de la Liberación," 310.

36. Trigo, "El Futuro de la Teología de la Liberación," 312.

37. Here, Trigo is reminiscent of Michel Foucault. See what Foucault has to say about overcoming the sovereign view of power in Michel Foucault, *Discipline and Punish: The Birth of the Prison*, trans. Alan Sheridan (New York: Vintage-Random House, 1979); Michel Foucault, *An Introduction* (New York: Random House, 1980); Michel Foucault, *The History of Sexuality*, trans. Robert Hurley, vol. 1 (New York: Pantheon, 1978); and Michel Foucault, *Power/Knowledge: Selected Writings and Other Interviews 1972–1977*, ed. Colin Gordon, trans. Colin Gordon et al. (New York: Pantheon, 1980).

38. Trigo, "El Futuro de la Teología de la Liberación," 314.

39. So Trigo writes: "In the same way that bankers . . . feel no temptation to become politicians because they know that the political dimension of their economic power is so decisive that it can place politicians at their service, so too the political power of the people resides in the political dimension of its social organizations. If these organizations are numerous, self-created, unified within themselves and coordinated between themselves, then the people's political clout is much greater than it would be as a political party and even as government." See Trigo, "El Futuro de la Teología de la Liberación," 315.

40. Trigo, "El Futuro de la Teología de la Liberación," 316.

41. See Trigo, "El Futuro de la Teología de la Liberación," 316, for an implicit critique of liberation theology as potentially elitist.

42. Juan Carlos Scannone has noted that liberation theology is currently shifting toward what was called the "Argentine School" of popular pastoral practice that privileges the use of historical-cultural analysis as mediation over socioeconomic categories. Scannone's work draws heavily from Trigo and serves as another example of the move toward privileging civil society and popular culture as the preferred venues for liberation theology. See Juan Carlos Scannone, S.J., "El Comunitarismo Como Alternativa Viable," in *El Futuro de la Reflexión Teológica en América Latina* (Colombia: CELAM, 1996), 195–242. On the shift away from state power toward civil society, see also Pablo Richard, "Caos o Esperanza. Fundamentos y Alternativas para el Siglo XXI," *Diakonia* 74 (June 1995): 59–67. Pablo Richard provides another example of option two. See Pablo Richard, "Teología de la Solidaridad en el Contexto Actual de Economía Neoliberal de Mercado," in *El Huracán de la Globalización*, ed. Franz Hinkelammert (San José, Costa Rica: DEI, 1999), 223–38. For another example of this trend that includes essays by liberation theologians and sympathetic commentators, see G. De Schrijver, ed., *Liberation Theologies on Shifting Grounds: A Clash of Socio-Economic and Cultural Paradigms* (Leuven, Belgium: Leuven University Press, 1998). I would also place the ecologically oriented work of Leonardo Boff in category two. See Leonardo Boff, *Cry of the Earth, Cry of the Poor*, trans. Phillip Berryman (Maryknoll, N.Y.: Orbis Books, 1997); and Leonardo Boff, *Ecology and Liberation: A New Paradigm* (Maryknoll, N.Y.: Orbis Books, 1995). Finally, for an essay that relates liberation theology to anarchism as a possible mediation, see Rui Manuel Gracio das Neves, "Neoliberalismo, Teología de la Liberación y Nuevos Paradigmas," *Alternativas* 9 (1998): 57–96.

43. Trigo, "El Futuro de la Teología de la Liberación," 310.

44. Scannone, S.J., "El Comunitarismo Como Alternativa Viable," 210.

45. On this, see R. N. Gwynne and Cristobal Kay, *Latin America Transformed: Globalization and Modernity* (London: Arnold, 1999).

46. Trigo, "El Futuro de la Teología de la Liberación," 316.

47. For a critique of the focus on civil society in political science, see Ash Amin, "Beyond Associative Democracy," *New Political Economy* 1, no. 3 (1996): 309–33.

48. See Terry Eagleton, chap. 1, in *The Illusions of Postmodernity* (Oxford: Blackwell Publishers, 1996), for this argument in reference to the North American and European literary and academic left.

49. For the English version, see Franz Hinkelammert, "Liberation Theology in the Economic and Social Context of Latin America: Economy and Theology, or the Irrationality of the Rationalized," in *Liberation Theologies, Postmodernity, and the Americas*, ed. David Batstone et al. (New York: Routledge, 1997), 25–52. For the Spanish version, see Franz Hinkelammert, *Cultura de la Esperanza y Sociedad Sin Exclusión* (San José, Costa Rica: DEI, 1995), 355–87. For another example of this position, see Hugo Assmann, *La Idolatría del Mercado* (San José, Costa Rica: DEI, 1997); and Jung Mo Sung, "Economía y Teología: Reflexiones Sobre Mercado, Globalización y Reino de Dios," *Alternativas* 9 (1998): 97–118; Jung Mo Sung, *Economía: Tema Ausente en la Teología de la Liberación* (San José, Costa Rica: DEI, 1994); Jung Mo Sung, *Neoliberalismo y Pobreza* (San José, Costa Rica: DEI, 1993); and Jung Mo Sung, *La Idolatría del Capital y la Muerte de los Pobres* (San José, Costa Rica: DEI, 1991).

50. Hinkelammert, "Liberation Theology," 39.

51. Hinkelammert, "Liberation Theology," 40.

52. Hinkelammert, "Liberation Theology," 44.

53. Hinkelammert, "Liberation Theology," 44–45.

54. Hinkelammert, "Liberation Theology," 45.

55. Hinkelammert, "Liberation Theology," 46–47.

56. Hinkelammert, "Liberation Theology," 47.

57. See Sung, *Economía: Tema Ausente en la Teología de la Liberación,* for an excellent study that sees the acceptance of the secularization thesis by some segments of liberation theology as the root of its economic impasse.

58. For a collection of essays that exemplifies this position, see Pablo Richard et al., *The Idols of Death and the God of Life* (Maryknoll, N.Y.: Orbis Books, 1983).

59. For an examination of the idolatry behind *both* capitalism and existing socialism, see Franz Hinkelammert, *Crítica a la Razón Utópica* (San José, Costa Rica: DEI, 1990).

60. This claim is best presented in Franz Hinkelammert, "La Crítica de la Religión en Nombre del Cristianismo: Dietrich Bonhoeffer," in *Teología Alemana y Teología Latinoamericana de la Liberación: Un Esfuerzo de Diálogo* (San José, Costa Rica: DEI, 1990), 45–66.

61. On this co-option, see also Helio Gallardo, "La Teología de la Liberación Como Pensamiento Latinoamericano," *Pasos* 56 (November–December 1994): 12–22. "New liberationists," seeking to construct a new liberation theology, serve as another example of this phenomenon. See Humberto Belli and Ronald Nash, *Beyond Liberation Theology* (Grand Rapids, Mich.: Baker Book House, 1992).

62. Here I agree with Michael Novak when he writes that "the option for the poor *is* the correct option. Everything depends, however, upon the next institutional step." Michael Novak, *Freedom with Justice: Catholic Social Thought and Liberal Institutions* (San Francisco: Harper and Row, 1984), 192; italics in original.

63. Richard Peet, arguing against modernization theories of development, makes a similar point: "Modernization can be countered only through alternatives that are more convincing and persuasive, alternatives written from the positions of excluded groups, or al-

ternatives based in criticisms of the very concept of development." See Peet and Hartwick, *Theories of Development*, 90.

64. José Míguez Bonino, *Doing Theology in a Revolutionary Situation*, ed. William H. Lazareth, Confrontation Books (Philadelphia: Fortress Press, 1975), 38–39.

65. This draws from Bonino, *Doing Theology in a Revolutionary Situation*, 39–40. For discussions of liberation theology's historical project, see John Pottenger, *The Political Theory of Liberation Theology: Toward a Reconvergence of Social Values and Social Science* (Albany, N.Y.: State University of New York Press, Albany, 1989), 119–21; and Smith, *The Emergence of Liberation Theology: Radical Religion and Social Movement Theory*, 45–50.

66. Note the differences with Trigo's redefinition of liberation theology.

67. Bonino, *Doing Theology in a Revolutionary Situation*, 40.

68. Among Moltmann's many works, see Jürgen Moltmann, *Theology of Hope: On the Ground and the Implications of a Christian Eschatology*, trans. James W. Leitch (New York: Harper Torchbooks/Library-Harper and Row, 1967); Jürgen Moltmann, *The Crucified God: The Cross of Christ as the Foundation and Criticism of Christian Theology*, trans. R. A. Wilson and John Bowden (New York: Harper and Row, 1974); and Jürgen Moltmann, *The Church in the Power of the Spirit: A Contribution to Messianic Ecclesiology* (New York: Harper and Row, 1977). For Bonino on Moltmann, see Bonino, *Doing Theology in a Revolutionary Situation*, 137–53. For Moltmann's response to Bonino, see Jurgen Moltmann, "An Open Letter to José Míguez Bonino," in *Liberation Theology: A Documentary History*, ed. Alfred Hennelly (Maryknoll, N.Y.: Orbis Books, 1990), 195–204.

69. Bonino, *Doing Theology in a Revolutionary Situation*, 139.

70. Bonino, *Doing Theology in a Revolutionary Situation*, 140.

71. Of course, these differences are also related to the different social contexts from which these theologies emerge. Moltmann draws from Karl Barth's Barmen Declaration and seeks to safeguard the Christian message from its political abuse. For Bonino, however, that safeguarding easily slides into a spurious neutrality that ends by upholding the status quo. Whether liberation theology's assessment of political theology is correct, however, is not the point of this discussion. I want to show that the "historical project" was central to how liberation theology understood itself as different from political theology.

72. Bonino, *Doing Theology in a Revolutionary Situation*, 149.

73. Bonino, *Doing Theology in a Revolutionary Situation*, 146.

74. Bonino, *Doing Theology in a Revolutionary Situation*, 147.

75. Bonino, *Doing Theology in a Revolutionary Situation*, 148.

76. Bonino, *Doing Theology in a Revolutionary Situation*, 151.

77. Hugo Assmann, *Teología Desde la Praxis de la Liberación* (Salamanca: Ediciones Sígueme, 1973), 104–05; Hugo Assmann, *Theology for a Nomad Church*, ed. Paul Burns (Maryknoll, N.Y.: Orbis Books, 1975), 111–12.

78. Assmann, *Teología Desde la Praxis de la Liberación*, 168. The whole second half of Assmann's foundational text was not included in the English translation. It is this second half that includes the bulk of Assmann's reflection on "historical projects."

79. Assmann, *Teología Desde la Praxis de la Liberación*, 124; Assmann, *Theology for a Nomad Church*, 131.

80. Assmann, *Teología Desde la Praxis de la Liberación*, 111–13; Assmann, *Theology for a Nomad Church*, 117–19.

81. Assmann, *Teología Desde la Praxis de la Liberación*, 166.

82. Gustavo Gutiérrez, *A Theology of Liberation: History, Politics and Salvation*, trans. Caridad Inda and John Eagleson (Maryknoll, N.Y.: Orbis Books, 1985).

83. Gustavo Gutiérrez, *A Theology of Liberation*, 36.

84. Gustavo Gutiérrez, *A Theology of Liberation*, 36–37.

85. Gustavo Gutiérrez, *A Theology of Liberation*, 37.

86. Gustavo Gutiérrez, *A Theology of Liberation*, 37.

87. Gutiérrez, *A Theology of Liberation*, 238. I have revised the translation of this text. The original translation mistakenly translates what by now should be clear is an important technical term of early liberation theology—*proyecto histórico* or historical project—for historical task. "Historical task" fails to convey the fact that Gutiérrez is using a specific term shared by the most influential liberation theologians of that time.

88. Gutiérrez, *A Theology of Liberation*, 238.

89. Gutiérrez does not hesitate to give content to the historical project: "Only the overcoming of a society divided in classes, only a political power at the service of the great majorities, only the elimination of private appropriation of wealth generated by human labor can give us the bases for a more just society. It is for this reason that the elaboration of the historical project of a new society takes in Latin América the route of socialism. Construction of a socialism that does not ignore the deficiencies of many of its actual historical realizations, a socialism that seeks to escape preconceived schemes and which creatively seeks its own paths." Gustavo Gutiérrez, *Praxis de Liberación y Fe Cristiana* (Madrid: Zero, 1974), 33.

90. For more on this alternative approach see my article, "Liberation Theology and Democracy: Toward a New Historical Project," *Journal of Hispanic/Latino Theology* 7, no. 4 (May 2000): 50–67.

91. It is obvious, however, that in the hands of the IMF these terms do not mean the same thing. José Comblin exemplifies this phenomenon through liberation theology's uneasy coexistence with Vatican authority. In 1984 the Vatican's "Instructions on Certain Aspects of the Theology of Liberation" denounced liberation theology in no uncertain terms. Today, instead, such documents as *Libertatis Nuntius* and *Libertatis Conscientia* take up the notions of liberation and the preferential option for the poor. This move can be seen as a tribute to liberation theology's impact, its themes being incorporated into official teaching. Comblin, however, is skeptical: "The words are there, but always in a context that avoids all possibility of conflict: this is a poor and a liberation with which all social classes can identify themselves. No one feels denounced. In this way liberation theology's themes acquire a level of generality, abstraction and also of insignificance so that they become valid for all continents, for all peoples." José Comblin, "La Iglesia Latinoamericana Desde Puebla a Santo Domingo," in *Cambio Social y Pensamiento Cristiano en América Latina*, ed. José Comblin, José I. González Faus, and Jon Sobrino (Madrid: Editorial Trotta, 1993), 51.

92. Gutiérrez, "La Teología: Una Función Eclesial," 15; and Gutiérrez, "Una Teología de la Liberación en el Contexto del Tercer Milenio," 109.

93. Leonardo Boff, *Jesus Christ Liberator: A Critical Christology for Our Time* (Maryknoll, N.Y.: Orbis Books, 1981), 275.

94. Some commentators in the early 1990s pointed out that liberation theology had shifted from its prior political and economic focus to more traditional theological topics such as spirituality and prayer. For a critique of this trend, see Marsha Hewitt, "Liberation

Theology and the Emancipation of Religion," in *The Scottish Journal of Religious Studies* XIII.1 (spring 1992): 21–38.

95. John Dewey knew this: "As for ideals, all agree that we want the good life. . . . But as long as we limit ourselves to generalities, the phrases that express ideals may be transferred from conservative to radical or vice versa, and nobody will be the wiser. For, without analysis, they do not descend into the actual scene nor concern themselves with the generative conditions of realization of ideals." John Dewey, *Individualism Old and New* (New York: Milton, Balch & Company, 1930), 147. For more on the connection between thinking about ideals and thinking about institutions, see Roberto Mangabeira Unger, *Democracy Realized: The Progressive Alternative* (New York: Verso, 1998), 16; Roberto Mangabeira Unger, *What Should Legal Analysis Become?* (New York: Verso, 1996) 4; and Roberto Mangabeira Unger, *False Necessity: Anti-Necessitarian Social Theory in the Service of Radical Democrary*, *Politics: A Work in Constructive Social Theory* (Cambridge: Cambridge University Press, 1987), 10.

96. This is due to liberation theology's reliance on the Marxist strand of dependency theory and world-system theory, as well as liberation theology's tendency to "undertheorize" capitalism. For more on liberation theology and dependency theory, see Sung, *Economía: Tema Ausente en la Teología de la Liberación*, 34–48. For the problems with undertheorizing capitalism, see J. K. Gibson-Graham, *The End of Capitalism (as We Knew It): A Feminist Critique of Political Economy* (Cambridge, U.K.: Blackwell Publishers, 1996), 39.

97. Gibson-Graham, *The End of Capitalism (as We Knew It)*, ix.

98. Pablo Richard, "Teología de la Solidaridad en el Contexto Actual de Economía Neoliberal de Mercado," 228. Italics in original.

99. As with capitalism, liberation theology often portrays globalization as an unstoppable force penetrating every corner of the globe. As such, liberation theology embraces the picture of globalization provided by its most extreme proponents, the only difference is that it sees globalization as a negative rather than a positive force. Embracing such a view of globalization, however, makes it very difficult to find alternatives to it, since the very way globalization is defined rules out the possibility of resistance. As I pointed out at the outset of this chapter, however, globalization remains a fiercely contested concept in social science literature. See Goldblatt et al. For an analysis of how "globalization" functions discursively, see Roger Lee and Jane Wills, ed., sec 2 of *Geographies of Economies* (London: Arnold, 1997). See also Gibson-Graham, "Querying Globalization," in *The End of Capitalism (as We Knew It)*. For an examination of the effects of globalization on the welfare state in Sweden, Germany, and Japan, see Mishra, *Globalization and the Welfare State*.

100. Pablo Richard, "Teología de la Solidaridad en el Contexto Actual de Economía Neoliberal de Mercado," 233. Italics in original.

101. I take the notion of "alternative pluralisms" from Roberto Unger. See Unger, *Democracy Realized*, 27.

102. For examples of this way of thinking about the economy, see Michael Piore and Charles Sabel, *The Second Industrial Divide: Possibilities for Prosperity* (New York: Basic, 1984) and Charles Sabel and Jonathan Zeitlin, "Stories, Strategies, Structures: Rethinking Historical Alternatives to Mass Production," in *World of Possibilities: Flexibility and Mass Production in Western Industrialization*, ed. Charles Sabel and Jonathan Zeitlin (Cambridge: Cambridge University Press, 1997). For an example in politics, see Ernesto

Laclau and Chantal Mouffe, *Hegemony and Socialist Strategy: Towards a Radical Democratic Politics* (New York: Verso, 1985). For work that highlights the diversity of forms "capitalism" takes in different contexts, see Herbert Kitschelt et al., eds., *Continuity and Change in Contemporary Capitalism* (Cambridge: Cambridge University Press, 1999); and Colin Crouch and Wolfgang Streeck, eds., *Political Economy of Modern Capitalism: Mapping Convergence and Diversity* (London: Sage Publications, 1997).

103. The notions of "alternative pluralisms," "revolutionary reform," and "formative context" are taken from Roberto Unger, as well as the examples of revolutionary reform provided. See Unger, *Democracy Realized*, 95–105; Unger, *What Should Legal Analysis Become?* 12–13; Unger, *False Necessity: Anti-Necessitarian Social Theory in the Service of Radical Democrary*, 480–506; see also Fred Block, *PostIndustiral Possibilities: A Critique of Economic Discourse* (Berkeley: University of California Press, 1990), 191–94. For another attempt to rework and escape the socialism/capitalism dichotomy, see Geoffrey Hodgson, *Economics and Utopia: Why the Learning Economy Is Not the End of History* (London: Routledge, 1999). Hirst and Zeitlin define flexible specialization as the "manufacture of a wide and changing array of customized products using flexible, general-purpose machinery and skilled, adaptable workers." Flexible specialization includes small-scale production units that blur division between supervision and execution, an embedded view of the economy (success depends on presence of associational networks including firms, local governments and communities—so that small-scale firms can tap large resources). Currently, this type of production takes place in India, Brazil, and Malaysia, as well as parts of the developed world; the most successful economic districts today follow this pattern. Their article is the best short introduction to this approach to economics. See Paul Hirst and Jonathan Zeitlin, "Flexible Specialization Versus Post-Fordism: Theory, Evidence, and Policy Implications," in *Pathways to Industrialization and Regional Development*, ed. Michael Storper and Allen Scott (New York: Routledge, 1992), 70–115. For more on flexible specialization, see Sabel and Zeitlin, and Piore and Sabel. For the political and cultural background required for flexible specialization as well as its role in the affluence of northern Italy, see Robert Putnam, *Making Democracy Work: Civic Traditions in Modern Italy* (Princeton, N.J.: Princeton University Press, 1993).

104. See Unger, *Democracy Realized*, and for a summary, see pages 264–66; also Unger, *What Should Legal Analysis Become?* 15–17, 163–69; and Unger, *False Necessity: Anti-Necessitarian Social Theory in the Service of Radical Democrary*, 444–76. Political science and political economy literature stress the importance of a "hard" state for economic development. See Alice Amsden, *Asia's Next Giant: South Korea and Late Industrialization* (New York: Oxford University Press, 1989); Stephen Haggard, *Pathways from the Periphery: The Politics of Growth in the Newly Industrializing Economies* (Ithaca, N.Y.: Cornell University Press, 1990); Robert Wade, *Governing the Market: Economic Theory and the Role of Government in East Asian Industrialization* (Princeton, N.J.: Princeton University Press, 1990). Hard states, however, have often been achieved through authoritarianism. What is most interesting about the reforms briefly outlined is that they may soften the tension between the radical changes often needed for development and the incrementalism that is part of democracy. This is the challenge that a "democratic developmental state" must meet. See Adrian Leftwich, "Forms of the Democratic Developmental State: Democratic Practices and Developmental Capacity," in *The Democratic Developmental State: Politics and Institutional Design*, ed. Mark Robinson and Gordon White (Oxford: Oxford University Press, 1998), 52–83.

105. For this argument see Enrique Dussel, *Etica de la Liberación en la Edad de la Globalización y de la Exclusión* (Madrid: Editorial Trotta, 1998); and Dussel, *The Underside of Modernity*.

106. See, for example, Immanuel Kant, "What is Enlightenment?" in *The Philosophy of Kant: Moral and Political Writings*, ed. Carl Friedrich (New York: The Modern Library, 1949), 132–39; Georg Wilhelm Friedrich Hegel, preface to *The Philosophy of History*, by Charles Hegel, translation of preface by J. Sibree, with an introduction by E. J. Friedrich (New York: Dover, 1956); and Jürgen Habermas, *The Philosophical Discourse of Modernity: Twelve Lectures*, trans. Frederick Lawrence, Studies in Contemporary German Social Thought (Cambridge, Mass.: MIT Press, 1987), 17. Again, Dussel provides the best critique of this hubris.

107. See Francis Fukuyama, "The End of History?" *The National Interest* (summer 1989): 3–18; and Francis Fukuyama, *The End of History and the Last Man* (New York: Free Press, 1992).

108. Gustavo Gutiérrez, *Teología Desde el Reverso de la Historia* (Lima, Peru: Ed. CEP, 1977) 393.

109. Note my use of world-system over world system. I agree with Dussel's analysis of the origin and dating of the contemporary world-system, which sees 1492 as its inaugural event, over Andre Gunder Frank's. Dussel's position is closest to James Blaut's. For Blaut, see James Blaut, *1492: The Debate on Colonialism, Eurocentrism and History* (Trenton, N.J.: Africa World Press, 1992). For the argument over world system versus world-system between Frank, Immanuel Wallerstein, and others, see Andre Gunder Frank and Barry Gills, eds., *The World System: Five Hundred Years or Five Thousand?* (New York: Routledge, 1993).

110. This must be done, however, without theorizing capitalism as a monolithic entity encompassing the whole globe. This is a flaw in current versions of world-system and world system theory.

111. Georges Friedmann, *La Puissance de la Sagesse* (Paris, 1970), 359. Cited in Pierre Hadot, *Philosophy as a Way of Life* (Cambridge, U.K.: Blackwell Publishers, 1995), 81, and other essays in the collection.

# 12

## An Alternative to Globalization: Theses for the Development of an Intercultural Philosophy

*Raúl Fornet-Betancourt*
*(Translated by Mario Sáenz)*

These theses that follow set forth for discussion some proposals for a project in intercultural philosophy. Hence, I will briefly define at the outset the meaning of intercultural philosophy. It is neither a new philosophical discipline nor a new formulation of what is known as the philosophy of culture. Also, it is not an expression of comparative philosophy. Intercultural philosophy is instead a work project that seeks to provoke a paradigm change in the doing of philosophy. It does so by breaking the barriers created by the monocultural structures of traditional philosophies or, stated in a more positive way, by cultivating a philosophical attitude that starts from the recognition of the plurality of philosophies with their respective cultural matrices and their consequent ways of argumentation and grounding. Intercultural philosophy arises, then, from a type of thinking that, aware of its own cultural limitations, not only tolerates other forms of thinking but also attains solidarity with them. And precisely because it recognizes those other forms of thinking as "worlds" in their own right does it recognize that only through those other universes can it open itself up to the universal. Intercultural philosophy seeks to be, in short, a philosophy that is practiced from the standpoint of *mutual cultural assistance.*[1]

Intercultural philosophy regards cultural diversity as a form of human wealth, and it defends the right of peoples to have and cultivate their own cultures. From that perspective, and faced with the worldwide phenomenon that imposes itself under the name of globalization, the first thing that must be questioned is the *justice* of the *right* to that imposition. It is thus legitimate to ask, With what justice does one impose globalization? This question is all the more urgent and legitimate to ask insofar as the phenomenon of globalization confronts us today with a process of crushing consequences that transform our conditions of life. It is directed by a neoliberal economic policy that believes it possesses the exclusive key to the future of humanity. In essence, globalization is actually the result of an uncontrolled expansion of political and economic neoliberalism, with the express purpose of imposing homogeneity and monotony on the planet according to the requirements of the capitalist market.[2]

That is why, in intercultural analysis, globalization implies an ideology or, if one prefers another expression, a philosophy of history that consists in supposing that the history of humanity has only *one* future, namely, the future foreseen and projected by neoliberalism. From the neoliberal perspective, history, as a constant effort to search for diverse alternatives that would do justice to cultural differences and to the complex diversity of irreducible life worlds, has ended, since there is no longer any alternative to the "reality" that the civilizing project of neoliberalism configures. Hence, any attempt to resist and oppose the "realist" dynamics of neoliberal globalization appears as a stubborn and anachronistic act, characteristic of unregenerate romantics who, lacking in historical sense, do not accept *la force des chôses* and condemn themselves to remain outside the historical process.

Calling attention to the ideology and philosophy of history underlying the neoliberal discourse on globalization, intercultural philosophy asks with what justice the system that today defines globalization is itself "globalized," and it questions fundamentally the ethical and cultural legitimacy of globalization. It raises these questions because it perceives that the great majority of humanity is not the agent of processes of globalization, but rather an object who suffers the effects of that phenomenon. In short, humanity does not globalize itself, but rather it is becoming globalized by the totalitarian process of a civilizing model. Thus, globalization is not growth in universalization or universality. On the contrary, it represents a reductive process that, in the name of the deceitful promise of building one world, instead levels differences and homogenizes the planet, at least on its surface.

Without entering into a discussion here on the meaning and reach of the distinctions between "surface" and "depth," or the "external" and the "internal," we still want to point out that by making the surface of the planet uniform, neoliberal globalization takes hold of the contextualization of the world; that is, it arrogates for itself the power to configure the forms *[contornos]* of culture. As contexts become uniform and part of a structural contextuality perfectly identifiable in any region of the planet, human cultures lose their materiality. More exactly, cultures lose their own "territory," where they would test and exercise their own capacity to influence efficaciously the modeling of their own space and time based on their own values and goals. With neoliberal globalization, cultures lose territorial sovereignty. Cultures find themselves compelled to live, or survive, under conditions of spatial and temporal occupation by the patterns of a civilizing model that cuts cultures off from their own territory.

At this level, the reductionist dynamics of globalization also implies a process of marginalization and exclusion. For cultures are excluded from those instances in which the economic, political, and social future of humanity is really decided, since their force for material and social influence (i.e., their capacity to organize social life) is neutralized. Cultures lose weight and importance as forces for shaping and transforming concrete historical reality. They are not eliminated, but they are relegated to a second plane and, frequently, to a sterile survival in "cultural reservations"; in this way, their connection with the course of history is completely severed, and their right to intervene with their own voice in the processes in which humanity crystallizes its future is trampled.

Intercultural philosophy takes a decisive and radical option for cultural differences. As such, it must be understood as a contribution to the reorganization of the relations between cultures and peoples and as an alternative to neoliberal globalization. Its option for cultures is thus the taking of a position against the process of homogenization and exclusion that imposes itself on them today. The nucleus of this alternative is rooted in the idea of "interculturality" as the guiding thread for developing a *praxis* that consistently abides by the ruling principle of the rights of human beings to have their own cultures. In this way, intercultural praxis both foments and cultivates the plurality of world visions and mutual respect among them and tries to be an adequate instrument for the concrete realization of a plurality of real worlds. We propose intercultural theory and practice, then, as an alternative vision. It allows for the reorganization of the world order by insisting on the just communication among cultures as different cosmovisions and by stressing that it is of the utmost importance to leave spaces and times open so that the various visions of the world may become real worlds.

The alternative proposed by intercultural philosophy implies, therefore, a new comprehension of the universal, for it has to do with a universality that presupposes the liberation that realizes all the cultural universes. For that reason, it neither imposes itself through the empire of some center, nor is it achieved at the high cost of the reduction and leveling of difference. Instead, it grows from below as a web of free communication and of solidarity.

From this perspective, the alternative of *interculturality* proposed here may be summarized in one imperative: We must renew the ideal of universality as a praxis of solidarity among cultures.

The proposal to oppose globalization with an alternative model of just and free intercultural relations is complemented by intercultural philosophy's description of a plan to reconfigure the world in such a way that the actual course of human history is decentered from the core that today pretends to totalize it. That is, it seeks to liberate the world and history from the ruling dictates of the prevailing civilizing model. If globalization produces uniformity and presents only one future as possible, intercultural philosophy asserts the polivalence of history. It wants to show that as long as there are cultures, humanity can realize several possible futures; furthermore, the greater or lesser historical universalization of any of those possible futures is something that must be decided by a dialogue among cultures.

The liberation of the world and of history from today's centering on the neoliberal project of globalization implies, obviously, the revindication of the right of cultures to configure their contexts—especially their economic context—from within themselves. On this point, intercultural thought insists on not dissociating the economic sphere from culture. Rather, it takes the position that the economy is a specific function of the cultural order. That is why every culture has a right to practice the type of economy that its own matrix finds most appropriate for it.

In order to avoid any possible misunderstanding, it should be pointed out, in a brief excursus, that intercultural philosophy does not defend any ontologization of cultures. That is to say, it does not view cultures as sacred entities, carriers of untouchable and decidedly good metaphysical values. Rather, intercultural philosophy considers human cultures to be ambivalent processes that reflect contradictions of all sorts among its own members who, by themselves, ought to critically discern those contradictions.

Cultures are not, then, homogeneous blocks of rigid coherence of meaning. On the contrary, they require continuous hermeneutic work because of their historical ambivalence. Their members must appropriate cultures, including those that we call our own and that are given to us as our traditions of origin; it is in those processes of appropriation in which the quality, vitality, and fate of a culture are really decided. The human being is not, therefore, a mere object of his or her culture. True, the culture of origin conditions and situates the human being; however, this being is, at the same time, the instance before which his or her respective culture must be legitimated. The human being lives in his or her culture and has a right to it, although this is also a right to create or possibly transform culture and not merely mechanically reproduce it, for culture does not cancel freedom. In this way, cultures make and remake themselves in a background of indeterminacy or human freedom, which remains in its concrete creations a historical possibility of innovation, transformation, and correction.

One can see then that intercultural philosophy has a historical vision of cultures. It does not sacralize cultures because it really understands them, not as ends in themselves, but as conditions for the realization of its members. Cultures, in short, are not monuments to an untouchable artistic patrimony but are, rather, historical configurations in the service of the full realization of the human.

However, intercultural philosophy is opposed to the tendency to make of culture an affair of the "inner life." Thus, if it is true that cultures should not be ontologized, it is still true that they should not become objects of "psychological privatization" *[intimización]*. Cultures must be public; that is, they must have at their disposal recognizable and identifiable spaces as *their* very own spaces; these would be spaces that would embody a culture's values and ends. From this it follows, incidentally, that intercultural philosophy rejects the traditional distinction between civilization and culture. Does one not rob cultures from "publicity"

when, on the basis of distinction between culture and civilization, one ends up excluding from the authority and scope of cultural influence whole sectors that are
determinant in the shaping of life, reality, and history, and instead, one allows for
an expansion (at a planetary level!) of a civilizing project of known regional origin? And is not what is being spread with the resounding name of "planetary civilization" *only one* version of *one* cultural variant of humanity?

Faced with the challenge of neoliberal globalization and the concomitant reinforcement of the planetary imposition of that "civilization" we just called into
question, intercultural philosophy articulates an alternative plan. It is—we re-
peat in order to stress that our focus is neither a political strategy nor a juridical
proposal—an ethical option. Intercultural philosophy denounces neoliberal
globalization as a new crusade—a crusade carried out in the name of the market
and for the global establishment of the kingdom of the market. We are confronted by a new form of totalitarian intolerance. Intercultural philosophy responds to it based on an ethics of respect, tolerance, and solidarity.

Focusing now on the direct consequences that the intercultural position has
for the doing of philosophy and retaking the central idea presented in the first
thesis, it may be pointed out that intercultural philosophy proposes a program for
transforming philosophy at the levels of both theoretical articulations and historical reconstructions. Concretely, it posits the necessity of pluralizing the
birthplaces and principles of philosophy and of pluralizing and diversifying its
methods and forms of articulation. But it posits, furthermore, the necessity of
broadening philosophical traditions and sources, as well as the criteria that now
determine the acceptance or nonacceptance of authors and canons that we regard
as "classical."

The intercultural transformation of philosophy posits, therefore, as its program
a reconstruction of the past and, at the same time, a configuration of a present in
which philosophy recognizes itself as such without having to place itself in a
monocultural conceptual system. Instead, it is aware that it arises from, and articulates itself within, the communication among different traditions. It recognizes, then, that it is not monological, but polyphonic.

Human cultures always reflect processes of interaction and exchange, since
they are realities that are configured through historical processes; in fact, cultures are in themselves open historical processes. They do not represent metaphysically pure stable realities, but rather they are *made*; that is, their preferred
self-referential traditions take shape—without entering now into the question of
the conflicts inherent to this process—through commerce with other cultures. In
each culture there are, then, moments of intercultural exchange. In what each
culture calls its own *[lo propio],* there are traces of that commerce with the other
and, because of that, culture carries in its own territory the sting of the intercultural. Intercultural experience is not, therefore, a possibility that is only given to
the outside of the frontiers of one's own culture. It is also an internal experience
or, better said, it is a frontier that is lived at the very interior of each culture.

It seems to us that the intercultural perspective can be verified in any concrete cultural universe. In spite of everything, we think that the world we call the Iberoamerican cultural world is especially representative of this phenomenon. For there are in fact very few cultural universes in which one can confirm the constitutive presence of so many and so varied cultural matrices as in that world.

We will start, then, by proposing as a special challenge the task of taking consistent advantage of the wealth of cultural matrices and traditions that constitute the Iberoamerican world, in order to elaborate from it a model of intercultural philosophy that reflects the weave of our diversity through a looking glass of many prisms. It would be a question, on the one hand, of reorganizing with intercultural sensibility the lines of our philosophy, as a result of the encounter of five great cultural configurations: the Christian-Occidental, the Islamic, the Jewish, the Amerindian, and the Afro-American.

But it would also be a matter of showing, on the other hand, how, through the braid of philosophical cultures that characterize "Iberoamerican philosophy," this philosophy has at its disposal a capacity to see and realize the world interculturally, that is, "pluri-visionally" *[plurivisionalmente]*. This places it in the position to trace an alternative plan to the neoliberal globalization of our times. But we should caution that we are not thinking of resurrecting old models, such as the Arielism of Rodó or the "cosmic race" theory of Vasconcelos, to mention only two examples; rather, we are referring to the creation of a movement for organizing economically, politically, socially, and culturally the ecumenic union of peoples and cultures, which in order to affirm themselves or realize their identity do not need to negate the other—be this "other" a culture or a part of nature. For, in its cultural matrix, there is already inscribed a universalist vocation of welcoming the other, who today resounds with renewed vigor in, for example, the demand by the Zapatistas to create a society in which there is a place for everybody or in the initiative of the international forum of humanity against neoliberalism.

We believe that this concrete universality grows from below. Precisely because it grows from the particularities that attain solidarity with each other in the common goal of making life possible for everybody, in a movement that universalizes *[mundializa]* tolerance and coexistence, can it be today the guiding aim of an Iberoamerican intercultural philosophy in the face of globalization. For in this way one could oppose, against the logic of exclusion that rules the project globalized by neoliberalism, a strong counterweight that promotes instead the spirit of a culture that opens a place for the stranger and calls us to an inclusive universalism, which grows without dominating or reducing everything to sameness. This universalism becomes universal *[mundializado]* through warmth, hospitality, and sympathy, that is, through the *mundialización* of a universe in which all cultures know themselves and are respected as subjects and in which, on that account, cultures can transform themselves mutually without fear of colonialism.

## NOTES

1. Cf. Raúl Fornet-Betancourt, *Filosofía intercultural* (Mexico, 1994); Raúl Fornet-Betancourt, *Kulturen der Philosophie. Dokumentation des I. Internationalen Kongresses für interkulturelle Philosophie* (Aachen, Germany: Augustinus Verlag, 1996); and Raimon Panikkar, "Sobre el diálogo intercultural" (Salamanca, Spain, 1988); and "La mística del diálogo," *Jahrbuch für kontextuelle Theologien* 1 (1993): 19–37.

2. Cf. Franz J. Hinkelammert, *Cultura de la esperanza y sociedad sin exclusión* (San José, Costa Rica: 1995).

# Index

ACLA. *See* Free Trade Zone of the
Americas
Afro-Americans: Anglo-American
intellectualism and, 80; Latin
Americanism and, 78–79; Latinidad
and, 79, 98; and religion in Latin
America, 91–92
Agamben, Giorgio, 52
Aguirre, Isidora, 181n27
AIDS, deregulation of drugs for, 49
Albó, Xavier, 97, 98
Albrow, Martin, 42
Alemán, José Arnoldo, 173
alterity. *See* other/otherness
Alvarez, Sonia, 192, 195
Americas Initiative, 68–69
Amerindians: Anglo-American
intellectualism and, 80; Latin
Americanism and, 78–79, 80;
Latinidad and, 79. *See also* Indians;
Native Americans
Amin, Samir, 42
Ángel, Albalucía, 181n27
antiglobalization protests, 8
apartheid, 138–39, 150

Apel, Karl-Otto, 44, 50
Appadurai, Arjun, 42
Aquinas, Thomas, 124
Araújo, Helena, 181n27
Arciniegas, Germán, 135
Area de Libre Comercio de las
Americas. *See* Free Trade Zone of
the Americas
area studies, 78
Arendt, Hannah, 158–59, 160
Aristotle, 8
Assmann, Hugo, 213–14, 215
Associated Press (AP), 67
Avelar, Idelber, 105–6, 112–13, 115,
117, 118

Bacon, Francis, 27
Barber, Benjamin R., 42
Barnet, Richard J., 42
Barrios, Domitilia, 172
Barros, Pía, 181n27
Baudrillard, Jean, 36
Beck, Ulrich, 36
Bell, Daniel, 47
Benjamin, Walter, 52

237

195–97; and national culture, 25; present state of, 36–37
culture: concept of, 36, 94; globalization and, 102–3, 230–35; link to nation of, 29–30, 94; national, 25, 29–33, 35–36; taxonomic function of, 29–33

D'Amato-Kennedy Act, 64
debt, foreign, 61, 63, 68
Decade for the Advancement of Women. *See* International Decade of Women (1975–1985)
decentralization: globalization and, 33–37; postmodernism and 33–37
*Declaration des droits de l'homme et du citoyen*, 157
Declaration of Independence, 157
Deleuze, Gilles, 44, 46, 107
Deloria, Vine, Jr., 80, 92–93
democracy: academic studies on, 193–95; cosmopolitan order and, 154; Latin American women and, 173, 191, 194; liberation theology and, 218; market influence in, 195–96; national development and, 155; and neoliberalism, 141–46; OAS policies on, 69; radical versus middle class, 8; theories of governance and, 56; transition to, 164–65; transnationalization threat to, 64, 194
demographics, current trends in, 46–47
dependency theory, 46
Derrida, Jacques, 44, 90, 91
Descartes, René, 5, 124, 149
development: economic versus political, 185; feminist ethics of, 185; and globalization, 140, 154–55; Latin American feminism and, 175
Dhareshwar, Vivek, 104
difference, ix: colonialism and, 78; cultural, 232; equality and, 138, 149; market exploitation of, 196
Dirty War, 146, 147, 172, 174

domination: colonialism as, 4; and globalization, 126–27; of masses, 3; of nature, 27; transnational, 57; by transnational finance oligarchy, 62, 63
Dusseck, Micheline, 181n27
Dussel, Enrique, 4, 5, 44, 45–46, 52, 80, 104

efficiency, in governance, 56
Eloy Martínez, Tomás, 115, 117, 118
Eltit, Diamela, 108
embargo, Cuban, 141
empowerment, through globalization, 128
"end of history," 6, 142, 145–46
Engels, Frederick, 5
engineering, 148, 151
environmental issues, 34–35
equality, political: negation by neoliberal state of, 10–11; political development and, 185
ethics: comparative philosophy and, 50; global feminist, 186; global hermeneutics and, 51; and globalization, 50–52; issue-oriented, 50; world or planetary, 50
ethnoracial pentagon, 89
Etxezarreta, Miren, 61
Eurocentrism: and colonialism, ix; ethical issues about, 50; in globalization theories, 42
Europe: and identity, 137; and recent globalization, 136–37; two aspects of, 135–36
European Union, transnationalization in, 67–68
everyday life, social construction through, 205–6
evil, 159

Faria, José Eduardo, 194
Femenías, María Luisa, 194–95
feminism: and critique of globalization, 187–90; and discursive voice, 107;

world trade. *See* global market
World Trade Organization, 29, 60, 63, 189
world-systems theory, 1
writing: and identity, 114–19

Zapatista movement, xi, 8, 86, 161–63, 235
Zea, Leopoldo, 11, 45
Zedillo, Ernesto, 161, 162
Žižek, Slavoj, 90

# About the Contributors

**Linda Martín Alcoff** is a professor of philosophy, political science, and women's studies at Syracuse University. Her books include *Feminist Epistemologies*, coedited with Elizabeth Potter (1992); *Real Knowing: New Versions of the Coherence Theory of Knowledge* (1996); *Epistemology: The Big Questions* (1998); and *Thinking From the Underside of History: Enrique Dussel's Philosophy of Liberation,* co-edited with Eduardo Mendieta (2000).

**Debra A. Castillo** is a Stephen H. Weiss Presidential Fellow and professor of romance studies and comparative literature at Cornell University. She specializes in the contemporary narrative from the Spanish-speaking world, women's studies, and cultural theory. She is an author of several books, including *The Translated World: A Postmodern Tour of Libraries in Literature* (1984), *Talking Back: Strategies for a Latin American Feminist Literary Criticism* (1992), and *Easy Women: Sex and Gender in Modern Mexican Fiction* (1998). She is also a translator of Federico Campbell's *Tijuana: Stories on the Border* (1994) and a coeditor of various volumes of essays. Her most recent book (cowritten with María Socorro Tabuenca Córdoba) is *Border Shorts: Theory in Practice* (Minnesota, forthcoming).

**Santiago Castro-Gómez** is an assistant professor in the faculty of social sciences and a research fellow at the Institute of Social and Cultural Studies, both at Javeriana University. He has published the following books: *Crítica de la razón latinoamericana* (1996); *Teorías sin disciplina,* coedited with Eduardo Mendieta (1998); *Pensar (en)los intersticios,* co-edited with O. Guardiola and C. Millán

(1999); and *La reestructuración de las ciencias sociales en América Latina*, editor (2000).

**Rafael Cervantes Martínez** holds a doctorate in economic sciences. He is the director of the Marxism-Leninism Collective and holds the chair of social sciences at the Technical-Military Institute José Martí of Havana, Cuba. His publications include the edited book *Teoría sociopolítica. Selección de temas*, Vol. II (Editorial Féliz Varela, Cuba), and "Historia Universal y Globalización Capitalista" (with Felipe Gil, Roberto Regalado, and Rubén Zardoya).

**Jorge J. E. Gracia** is a Samuel P. Capen Chair and SUNY distinguished professor of philosophy at the State University of New York at Buffalo. He is the author of ten books—*How Can We Know What God Means? The Interpretation of Revelation* (2001); *Hispanic/Latino Identity: A Philosophical Perspective* (2000); *Metaphysics and Its Task: The Search for the Categorial Foundations of Knowledge* (1999); *Texts: Ontological Status, Identity, Author, Audience* (1996); *A Theory of Textuality: The Logic and Epistemology* (1995); *Philosophy and Its History: Issues in Philosophical Historiography* (1992); *Individuality: An Essay on the Foundations of Metaphysics* (1988); *Introduction to the Problem of Individuation in the Early Middle Ages* (1984, 1986); *The Metaphysics of Good and Evil According to Suarez* (1989); and *Suarez on Individuation* (1982)—and around 150–200 articles. He is the editor of more than a dozen books, including *Latin American Philosophy in the Twentieth Century* (1986); *Philosophical Analysis in Latin America* (1984); *Philosophy and Literature in Latin America* (1989); and *Filosofía e identidad cultural en América Latina* (1983). He has been president of the Society for Medieval and Renaissance Philosophy, Society for Iberian and Latin American Thought, International Federation of Latin American and Caribbean Studies, Metaphysical Society of America, and American Catholic Philosophical Association. He was the first chair of the American Philosophical Association Committee for Hispanics in Philosophy and has been a member of the Executive Committee of the same association. He sits on the boards of more than twelve philosophy journals and edits an interdisciplinary series on Iberian and Latin American culture and thought.

**Raúl Fornet-Betancourt,** born in Cuba, has doctorates in philosophy from the universities of Salamanca (Spain) and Aachen (Germany). He also has a postdoctoral degree *(Habilitation)* from the University of Bremen, where he is now a professor of philosophy. He is also honorary professor of the University of Aachen and director of the Department of Latin American Studies at the Institute of Missiology of Aachen. He is the editor-in-chief of *Concordia: Revista Internacional de Filosofía*. He has more than two hundred publications, including *Introducción a Sartre* (1989), *Estudios de Filosofía Latinoamericana* (1992), *Filosofía Intercultural* (1994), *José Martí* (1998) and *Interculturalidad y Globalización* (2000).

**Felipe Gil Chamizo** is a philosopher, political theorist, and diplomat. He works for the Department of Foreign Relations of the Central Committee of the Communist Party of Cuba. His publications include "Historia Universal y Globalización Capitalista" (with Rafael Cervantes, Roberto Regalado, and Rubén Zardoya).

**María Pía Lara-Zavala** is a professor of philosophy at the Universidad Autónoma Metropolitana (Mexico City). She has published *Democracy as an Identity Project* (1992) and *Moral Textures* (1998). She recently edited the book *Rethinking Evil* (2001). She has just completed her book *Globalizing Justice* (forthcoming) and is currently working on a book tentatively called *Narrating Evil: A Postmetaphysical Theory of Reflective Judgement*.

**María Mercedes Jaramillo,** born in Colombia, has a Ph.D. from Syracuse University and is a professor at Fitchburg State College in the humanities department. She has published several articles about Colombian theater, Colombian women writers, and Colombian literature. In 1992, La Universidad de Antioquia published: *El Nuevo Teatro Colombiano: Política y Cultura*; she is a coauthor of *¿Y Las Mujeres? Ensayos sobre Literatura Colombiana* (1991); also, she is a coeditor of *Voces en Escena: Antología de Dramaturgas Latinoamericanas* (1991); *Antología Crítica del Teatro breve Hispanoamericano* (1997); *Literatura y Diferencia: Escritoras Colombianas del siglo XX* (1995); *Las Desobedientes: Mujeres de Nuestra América* (1995); and *Literatura y Cultura Colombiana en el Siglo XX* (2000).

**Eduardo Mendieta** teaches philosophy at SUNY-Stony Brook. He is the editor and translator of Enrique Dussel's *The Underside of Modernity* (1996), and coeditor of *Thinking from the Underside of History: Enrique Dussel's Philosophy of Liberation* (2000) and *Latin America and Postmodernity* (2001). He is the author of *The Adventures of Transcendental Philosophy* (2002).

**Walter D. Mignolo** is a William H. Wannamaker Professor and a director of the Center for Global Studies and the Humanities at Duke University. Among his most recent publications are *The Darker Side of the Renaissance: Literacy, Territoriality and Colonization* (1995); and *Local Histories/Global Designs* (2000). He is coeditor with Elizabeth Hill Boone of *Writing Without Words. Alternative Literacies in Mesoamerica and the Andes* (1994). He recently edited, with an introduction, *Geopolitíca del Conocimiento: El Eurocentrismo y la filosofía de la liberación en el debate intelectual contemporáneo* (2001). He is also the founder of *Dispositio/n. American Journal of Comparative and Theoretical Studies* and cofounder and coeditor of *Nepantla: Views from South*.

**Iván Petrella** is an assistant professor of religious studies at the University of Miami, Florida. His article "Liberation Theology and Democracy: Toward a New Historical Project" appeared in the *Journal of Hispanic/Latino Theology*, vol. 7, no. 4 (May 2000). A native of Argentina, in his spare time he roams Miami Beach or Buenos Aires in search of pickup soccer games.

**Roberto Regalado Álvarez** is a journalist. He is also the director of the Group of Analysis of the Americas of the Department of Foreign Relations of the Central Committee of the Communist Party of Cuba. His publications include "Historia Universal y Globalización Capitalista" (with Rafael Cervantes, Felipe Gil, and Rubén Zardoya), *"El Manifiesto comunista y la transnacionalización de la dominación política,"* and numerous journalistic pieces on contemporary social issues.

**Mario Sáenz** is a professor of philosophy and director of the Integral Honors Program at Le Moyne College. He is the author of *The Identity of Liberation in Latin American Thought: Latin American Historicism and the Phenomenology of Leopoldo Zea* (1999) and essays on Latin American and Continental philosophy, including "Cartesian Autobiography/Post-Cartesian Testimonials" (1999) and "Dussel on Marx: Living Labor and the Materiality of Life" (2000).

**Ofelia Schutte** is a professor of women's studies and philosophy at the University of South Florida. Her areas of specialization are feminist theory, Latin American social thought, and continental philosophy. She has written extensively on the construction of identity and difference from a perspective integrating European continental, Latin American, and feminist issues. She is the author of *Cultural Identity and Social Liberation in Latin American Thought* (1993), *Beyond Nihilism: Nietzsche without Masks* (1984), and numerous papers in her areas of research and teaching. She is currently engaged in research on postcolonial and transnational feminisms.

**Rubén Zardoya Loureda,** doctor in philosophical sciences, is dean of the faculty of philosophy and history at the University of Havana, interim director of the School of Social Workers of Cojímar, Cuba, and associate director of the journal *Contracorriente*. His publications include *La filosofía burguesa posclásica* (published by Félix Varela, Cuba); "Los grados de libertad entre la economía y la política *(Contracorriente);* "Gramsci y el capitalismo contemporáneo"; "Historia Universal y Globalización Capitalista" (with Rafael Cervantes, Felipe Gil, and Roberto Regalado); "El fetichismo de la reflexión filosófica vulgar" *(Debates Americanos);* "Globalisierung und Staat" (ISW); and numerous essays on social theory and the phenomenon of globalization.

**Leopoldo Zea** is professor emeritus of the National Autonomous University of Mexico. He is the founder of Mexico's *Centro Coordinador y Difusor de Estudios Latinoamericanos* and the director of *Cuadernos Americanos*. His numerous publications include books such as *Latin America and the World*; *The Latin American Mind*; *En torno a una filosofía Americana*; *América como conciencia*; *Dependencia y liberación de la cultura americana*; *La filosofía en México*; *Introducción a la filosofía: La conciencia del hombre en la filosofía*; *La filosofía Americana como filosofía sin más*; *¿Por qué América Latina?*; *La filosofía como compromiso*; *Filosofía de la historia americana*; *El positivismo en México: Nacimiento, apogeo y decadencia*; *Simón Bolívar: Integración en la Libertad*; *Fin de siglo XX ¿Centuria perdida?*; *Discurso desde la marginación y la barbarie*; and many others translated into English, French, German, Portuguese, Italian, and Russian. He has also written hundreds of articles in scholarly journals, and editorials for newspapers and magazines.